DATE DUE		

Pagan

Ananda Temple, Pagan

Pagan

THE ORIGINS OF MODERN BURMA

Michael Aung-Thwin

UNIVERSITY OF HAWAII PRESS

HONOLULU

Library of Congress Cataloging-in-Publication Data

Aung-Thwin, Michael.
  Pagan: the origins of modern Burma.

Bibliography: p.
  Includes index.
    1. Burma—History—To 1824.   2.   Pagan (Burma)—History.
I.   Title.
DS529.2.A86   1985   959.1'02   85–14862
ISBN 0–8248–0960–2

To Maria, Maitrii, and Amita

Contents

Maps

Figures

Tables

A Note on Romanization

Except for certain commonly used names and terms such as Kyaukse, Narapatisithu, and Narathihapade, Burmese words follow what is called "standard transliteration" in John Okell, *A Guide to the Romanization of Burmese*. "Standard phonetic transcription" without diacritics, however, is used for names and terms that appear in the post-Pagan period, such as Alaunghpaya and Bodawhpaya. Where inconsistencies in spelling exist in the inscriptions themselves, I have not attempted to correct them, for that in itself may be significant to scholars of language. Pali words follow A. P. Buddhadatta's *Concise Pali-English Dictionary*, unless they too are spelled differently in the inscriptions, in which case the latter is given. Sanskrit words follow those found in A. L. Basham's index in *The Wonder That Was India* (New York, 1959).

Acknowledgments

There are certain people who have sparked my imagination at critical points in my life who are never forgotten. If one were to thank only those who were responsible directly for helping me publish this book, those who have inspired me intellectually who perhaps deserve that recognition even more would never be recognized. And although in a scholarly work most people may not wish to see a list of high school basketball coaches as part of the Acknowledgments, there is one person at Kodaikanal School in south India whom I wish to thank. One boring morning in seventh or eighth grade, Mr. George Fisher, off the top of his head, got onto the subject of continental drift theories. Although there were occasions thereafter at Kodai when I was intellectually stimulated, I do not remember attaining the height of excitement I reached then. Several years later at a small liberal arts college, Doane, in Crete, Nebraska, I was again stimulated intellectually, this time in a sustained manner and in the discipline of history, by Professor Kenneth Rossman, whose field was actually an aspect of the American Revolution. It was he and the four years under his stern but extremely caring discipline that made me choose history as a career. During my first year as a graduate student at the University of Illinois, another person, this time in Southeast Asian anthropology, the well-known F. K. Lehman, inspired me to take the direction I was to take, namely, the history of the country of my origins, Burma. At the University of Michigan where I received my doctorate, several professors were instrumental in helping me attain my goals: John Whitmore, my advisor, probably the most patient man I have ever met, who in addition to putting up with us read each of our papers at least twice; Pete (Alton) Becker, who always found something positive in my ideas, even if it took years thereafter for me to discover what he really meant; Tom Trautmann, who actually scared me with his absolutely unmuddled mind and was a model of clarity that I am still attempting to emulate; Norman Owen, who fortunately forced me to consider quantification as a legitimate part of historical methodology, though at the time I resented it; and at the University of London where I spent an academic year of research, John Okell, without whose selfless attitude about giving his time and sharing his superior knowledge of Burmese, I would not have been able to learn to read Old Burmese so quickly. Lastly I would like to thank my friends and colleagues: those who kept me accountable, such as Vic Lieberman; those who criticized the manuscript, such as U Bokay of Pagan and David Wyatt of Cornell; those who carefully and patiently advised me on the technical aspects of the manuscript, as Damaris Kirchhofer, editor at the University of Hawaii Press, did; and those many scholars of Southeast Asia, whose company alone meant intellectual excitement that invariably found its way into this book.

In addition to these individuals who were critical to my intellectual development, I wish to thank the Center for South and Southeast Asian Studies, the University of Michigan, which provided me with part of the funds that allowed me that essential year in London, and especially the JDR 3rd Fund, which supported my research and travel at the same time. The Social Science Research Council/American Council for Learned Societies supported me with over a year and a half of postdoctoral research while the latter provided me with additional funds to turn my dissertation into a book. The National Endowment for the Humanities' Translations Program provided me with a generous one-year grant to translate a volume of Old Burmese inscriptions, a study that was very valuable for this book. To all three organizations, I wish to extend my most sincere thanks.

For a small liberal arts institution concerned primarily with teaching, Elmira College in the past five years has been very supportive of research and writing, particularly by providing its faculty with the necessary funds to attend professional meetings, unlimited use of computer time and supplies, and by encouraging members of the library staff to aid us in any way possible to obtain research materials not available here. To the institution as well as to individuals—such as Jan Kather who gave her time and talents to certain items needing photographic work, Ingrid Lindeqvist who somehow found and from somewhere managed to borrow obscure books and articles related to my work, and all the accommodating staff at the computer center—I give my thanks. Lastly, I wish to thank my mother for, well, virtually everything, as well as my immediate family for putting up with me throughout the ordeal.

INTRODUCTION
Pagan's Place in Burmese and Southeast Asian Studies

THE PERIOD between the eighth and thirteenth centuries A.D. in Southeast Asian history was a tremendous watershed. It was the time when the Theravāda Buddhism of Mainland Southeast Asia, still very strong today, and the pre-Islamic religion of Island Southeast Asia were firmly implanted; when the critical features of the region's subsequent polities had their fermentation; when the fundamental structures of Southeast Asia's economic institutions were being established; when the principles undergirding Southeast Asia's legal structure were being formed; and when the distinctive character of its social organization began to take root. This was, in other words, the time when Southeast Asia's classical states—Śrī Vijaya, Pagan, Angkor, Sukhodaya, Đai Việt, and somewhat later, Majapahit—to which Southeast Asia today owes many of its institutions, blossomed.[1] Research on any one of these states would be a significant contribution to the whole of premodern Southeast Asian history and culture, and especially to the particular society that it spawned. This study focuses on the twelfth- and thirteenth-century Kingdom of Pagan to which Burma owes its heritage.

Theoretical, Methodological, and Organizational Concerns

Such a critical and challenging period in Burmese[2] history should have attracted more students, for it is, after all, the formative period of Burma, the counterpart of Mauryan India, Heian Japan, and Anuradhapuran Śrī Laṅka. One might even argue that without a study of the Pagan period, one's understanding of Burmese society subsequently, though not unimportant, is incomplete. Although

Pagan has certainly fascinated more people, when compared to the colonial and modern periods of Burmese history, few have actually made serious commitments to its study. The Old Burmese language, the relative paucity of data on dramatic political events, and the difficulty in interpreting such data continue to be hindrances.

As a result of this disciplinary ambivalence, one of the problems that precolonial Burmese history has had to face is the lack of awareness and interest shown by early Burma historians for the social sciences and the advances they have made in Southeast Asian studies, particularly in the United States during the 1960s and 1970s. This has circumscribed the study of early Burmese history and society both methodologically and empirically. Until Victor Lieberman's book on the Toungoo dynasty (and to a lesser extent, Frank Trager and William Koenig's work on Burmese *sittans*)[3] the historiography of premodern Burma had adopted, unwittingly perhaps, the view that history was no more than a series of important events derived from an organized assortment of facts. Cast in the nineteenth-century mold of von Ranke, Burma's premodern historians had approached Burmese history with the primary goal of recording facts, unconcerned for the most part with issues raised in other disciplines, particularly in anthropology. These problems were compounded by the irony that while Burmese historians with the language skills have been weak in current theoretical issues, Western historians of Burma endowed with a wealth of theory have been weaker in the indigenous language. Many of the latter therefore chose to study the short, colonial period in Burmese history instead, from approximately 1886 to 1948, where English language sources are readily available as primary data, further exacerbating the problem of "autonomous history" raised by John Smail many years ago.[4]

Far from an indictment of our pioneers who were influenced by the priorities of their own generation, it is more an assessment of the degree to which certain academic trends in the West have affected (rather not affected) Burmese history as a discipline. Certain issues were simply never raised, certain questions never asked. To which type of economic system, among those described by economic historians such as Karl Polanyi,[5] did the premodern Burmese economy belong? Was Burma's early political system more similar to a Wittfogelian "bureaucratic" model or to the "charismatic" type, offered as an alternative by Edmund Leach?[6] Perhaps it resembled neither completely, possessing a distinctly Southeast Asian form with features of both. Yet, without the comparison to these and other models, it belongs—at least academically—nowhere. In the context of South and Southeast Asia itself, how differently organized was Burmese society from the Indian "caste" system, sanctioned by Hindu values, as opposed to the (for example) Singhalese model, which had combined Buddhism with caste? Did Buddhism in Southeast Asia in the absence of true castes create a pattern altogether different from both? Lastly, in the context of European feudalism, how should Burmese—indeed, Southeast Asian—society in the premodern period be portrayed: as a phenomenon of type or one of time? as an exception in the world context or the rule?—both issues in feudal studies. In order to broaden Burmese history by raising these issues and questions, we need not necessarily answer any of them directly. By simply being aware of such theoretical concerns in the process of research and analysis of Burmese history and society, the study invariably would be placed in a larger context.

Such a study rests not so much on recovering the chronology of events or of individual accomplishments but on reconstructing institutions and their development. As Paul Wheatley so well stated in his 1982 Presidential Address to the Association for Asian Studies, when one attempts to resurrect the origins of the state anywhere "there is no question of recovering anything like a continuous sequence of individual events. . . ." We have no choice "but to deal with developmental *patterns,* with *types* of actions, with *forms* of social, political, and economic action, in short with generalized *institutional evolution.*" To do this, the Geertzian method of recovering the past—concerned "not with individual thoughts and actions but with formal developmental trends, not with incidents of the moment but with secular rhythms of sociocultural change"—is ideal and precisely how I intend to reconstruct the Kingdom of Pagan, the classical Burmese state.[7] The history of the Pagan kingdom is thus more than simply the account of a dynasty and its leaders. It attempts to describe a whole society, its strengths and weaknesses, its organizing principles, its raison d'être, and the legacy it left to its successors. The story recreates the evolutionary path of a world-class civilization, one that was certainly comparable in significance and sophistication to other Asian and non-Asian civilizations of the time.

This study attempts, therefore, to reconstruct mainly from primary, indigenous sources an institutional history of the Kingdom of Pagan: that eleventh-, twelfth-, and thirteenth-century society from which the modern Burmese state originates. The book seeks to describe and analyze the most important conceptual and structural components of Pagan society—those principles that guided and influenced the "Classical Burmese State"—and attempts to show their effects on certain important events during that period as well as on the broad patterns in later Burmese history.

The organization of the work deliberately separates the conceptual, the structural, and some of the important events into Parts I, II, and III. Although in doing this, human society is admittedly compartmentalized into realms—of ideas and of things material, of things economic and things political, of things social and things legal, and of things permanent as well as things transforming—it is done only for purposes of clarity and organization. It need not imply a theoretical preference, either for the dissection of a society that was very much a unity or for distinguishing synchronic from diachronic historical methodologies, both essential to this study. To paraphrase the great social historian Marc Bloch, it is tolerable to carve up the creature of flesh and blood into phantoms *homo oeconomicus, philosophicus, juridicus* only if we refuse to be deceived by it.[8] In a word, the study describes the relationship between the conceptual and the structural and the effects of that relationship on the Pagan dynasty as well as on Burmese dynasties yet to come.

In addition to the historical framework presented in chapter 1, Part I consists of what I think were the most significant components in the belief system of the Kingdom of Pagan. Entitled "Components of the Indigenous Conceptual System," it refers to, in chapter 2, religious beliefs defined broadly and in chapter 3 to political ideology. The former is concerned mainly with an analysis and description of ideas and attitudes, extracted from contemporary Pagan sources, that became a system of beliefs—an ideology—whose ultimate aims were the desire for and acquisition of merit defined within the context of Buddhism. Chapter 3, on the other hand, focuses on those perceptions that governed leadership, more specifically Burmese kingship, also found within the context of Buddhism. The reader should be aware that one often found a good degree of variance in both categories of beliefs with canonical Buddhism and the "correct" (Indic) forms of political thought, both of which were invariably reconstituted to suit Pagan's needs. Indeed, it is this adaptation of Indic forms, "drained of their original significance," as O. W. Wolters has written,[9] that should attract the reader's attention most; for not only does it address a critical issue in Southeast Asian history and culture raised by the Social Science Research Council on indigenous conceptual systems but more accurately represents the beliefs of the Pagan people. Chapter 2 thus deals with Burmese-Buddhist cosmogony, including Hindu, Brahmanic, and Mahayanist elements present in it; Burmese supernaturalism; the society's attitudes toward concerns such as time; and, most importantly, with the overriding desire for salvation through merit. Chapter 3 shows how these different beliefs supported and influenced the numerous ways in which power in general was perceived and the king in particular was and wanted to be perceived: as a human, a deity, and a spirit.

In Part II, the bulk of the work, I deal with the institutional context, consisting of two broad categories—the organization of material and of human resources. Though separated artificially, I tend to incline toward the view that society was holistic. That, however, need not imply the absence of conflict or structural contradictions within a society. Indeed, as the reader will notice, these structural contradictions and ideological paradoxes were what gave Pagan (and Burmese) society its dynamism as well as its completeness. Because Southeast Asian history and society have made little sense without a knowledge of whole societies over long periods of time, historians of early precolonial Southeast Asia have been compelled to deal with whole kingdoms over centuries, even if the discipline of history in recent years has encouraged the study of narrower subjects over shorter periods of time. This has made it necessary to draw from other disciplines, anthropology and religion in particular, whose influence is obvious in this work. Partly because of this, and mainly because the evidence has dictated it, the Kingdom of Pagan is depicted as a holistic entity, its integrative and centripetal forces persisting, giving subsequent periods of Burmese history a relatively similar ideological and institutional framework in which to operate.

Another point that needs to be clarified is the distinction between the "real" and the "ideal," still made an issue by some, even if current cognition theory no longer recognizes it. In Burmese society, these two categories are not so far apart as one might envisage. What the society states the king should or should not do, how the monks should or should not behave, how people should or should not worship, in fact determine, or at least influence, the course of historical events. Of course, if one insisted on documentation that would explicitly and unequivocally show "real" motives, no such case can be made. It is difficult enough to determine "real" motives in oneself—disguised and obscured as they are by one's subconscious—that those of individuals living centuries ago would be virtually impossible to know. The only scholarly alternative, it seems to me, is to consider the statements of individuals at face value, and instead of ascribing to them "motives" that are highly conjectural in any case, deal with the behavioral consequences of those statements. This is not to deny the presence of economic or political motivation in (say) religious activity—indeed, I imply this with regard to royal behavior in *sāsana* reform—but only to suggest that what were declared as religious had observable economic and political consequences. Admittedly, the use of primarily religious donations as evidence has invariably influenced my perspective: the society being described is seen through religious lenses. But this is something over which the Old Burma historian has little control—stone inscriptions of religious dedications survived while palm-leaf manuscripts of an administrative and more secular genre did not. I have had to read between the lines, interpret, and put into perspective and context the picture as I believe the data command. But at least three things can be determined: what the people of Pagan *said* their motives were; the *behavior* stemming from those statements; and the results of both, reflected in institutions.

The result of all this is Part II's "Institutional Context," that framework in which the ideologies and beliefs described in Part I operated. Chapter 4 reconstructs the organization of people; chapter 5, the land and revenue system; chapter 6, law and justice; chapter 7, the political structure.

The final section, Part III, attempts to show the relationships between beliefs and institutions and how both affected events. Although most scholars of Southeast Asia are in general agreement concerning the debt owed to Indian and Chinese intellectual influences in the development of Southeast Asia's "classical" civilizations, the well-worn debate has centered around the extent to which state formation owed these influences on the one hand or indigenous ones on the other. Certainly Hindu-Buddhist and Sinic conceptions of the universe, the state, and of kingship have been adopted in the process of Southeast Asian state formation, but how that was done and the degree to which they had been altered remain issues that still need to be studied. Most of us accept the premise, although not without qualification, that ideology (foreign or indigenous) acted as a major force in historical and institutional change, characteristic of the French school to which George Coedès belonged. The more important concern to me is determining how, precisely, ideology affected events and institutions, a subject still ambiguous or incompletely thought out. At the time Coedès and his students were writing about Southeast Asia, and to a large extent even today, the institutions of "classical" or early precolonial Southeast Asia had not been adequately reconstructed. Thus clear relationships between concrete, material aspects of state formation—such as economic and demographic growth; administrative development; military expansion; and, until recently, the emergence of the city, thought to be critical to state formation—and the more intangible but equally important ingredients such as political and religious ideology, could not have been demonstrated in any case. Only Paul Wheatley, in his usual magisterial way (in *Nāgara and Commandery*),[10] has addressed many of the issues that linked ideologies involved in state formation —albeit in "pre-classical" Southeast Asia—with the development of the city. It is true that earlier, some scholars like Bernard Groslier with ingenious use of aerial photography did attempt to clarify the relationship between the construction of Angkor's temples—which were certainly "ideological"—and the presence of hydraulic works that surrounded them. Here at least was a clue that an explicit and sensitive relationship existed between the glorification of the state, king, and religion (in temple construction) and agricultural production. But there it ended: few pursued this ground-breaking thrust any further, particularly in the way Burton Stein and George Spencer did with south Indian temples and their economic function.[11] Neither did many pursue the path suggested years ago by Merle Ricklefs in his article on land and law in Angkor, directly pertinent to the kinds of relationships being discussed here.[12]

To add to these ambiguities over Southeast Asian state formation and organization, the explanations given for the process of state disintegration were equally vague. Again the answers failed to establish a more precise link between political and economic weakness with ideology. In this case, "revolutionary" ideas found in Theravāda Buddhism were said to have been responsible for destroying the elitist and royal religious cults.[13] Thus it was argued that Southeast Asia's classical states emerged because of "certain" Sinic and Indian ideologies and declined because of "certain" Theravāda Buddhist ideas. Not that ideas were uninvolved, but how they inspired certain behavior, how that behavior was related to material and social institutions, and how that relationship influenced events were questions left unanswered.

Part III of this book attempts to show that relationship: between ideology and behavior, between behavior and institutions, and between institutions and events pertinent to the formation as well as the decline of the Kingdom of Pagan. Chapter 8 therefore describes the relationship between the desire for salvation and the economy, chapter 9 explains the decline of the Kingdom of Pagan by linking that relationship to the immediate events in the thirteenth century, while the concluding chapter explores the legacy of Pagan in Burmese and Southeast Asian history.

The Sources

The most important category of primary data used in this study consists of stone epigraphs, the inscriptions that recorded the pious deeds of Pagan's merit-seeking donors. Most are in Old Burmese, a few are in Pali, and over a hundred important ones in Mon have been found and published. More than five hundred of the Old Burmese inscriptions are original; that is, they were inscribed contemporaneously to the event they describe and therefore are by far the most reliable. Another group of original Old Burmese stone inscriptions exists but are, however, inscribed subsequent, though not too distant in time, to the events they describe. They too are extremely valuable and certainly to be considered primary data. A third category of Burmese inscriptions consists of good stone copies of originals, inscribed centuries after the originals were made. In certain cases where their originals still exist, the reliability of these copies can be determined. But when these copies only summarize the contents of the originals, they retain neither the original terms nor the original orthography and are therefore far less useful. Despite these problems, they do represent on occasion the only chronological and biographical data that we possess. As such they have been more important to historians interested in narrative rather than institutional history. On the whole in any case, the number of originals "far surpasses that of copies; and in the copies themselves, it is only a comparatively small percentage . . . that has been wrongly dated."[14]

There are mainly three published but untranslated versions of Old Burmese inscriptions that I have used for this study: Pe Maung

Tin and G. H. Luce's edition and compilation of *Selections from the Inscriptions of Pagan,* published in 1928; U E. Maung's edition of *Pagan Kyauksa Let Ywei Sin* [Selected Pagan inscriptions], published in 1958; and the Archaeological Survey's *She Haung Myanma Kyauksa Mya* [Ancient Burmese inscriptions] in two volumes, published in 1972 and 1982. They overlap to some degree, but all three are necessary. The first one is a selection of what Luce and Pe Maung Tin considered original inscriptions. The second includes several inscriptions omitted by the first and in some cases provides a different reading. The third, the latest, is an attempt to systematically reread and rearrange chronologically all Old Burmese inscriptions in a series of volumes, by a tedious but accurate process of hand-copying and mimeographing, without some of the printers' mistakes contained in the first two. More important, inscriptions that were discovered since the other two were published are included in this one. When the reading of a word makes a significant difference in interpretation and the three works do not agree—only rarely does this occur—I resort to the *Inscriptions of Burma,* also compiled by Luce and Pe Maung Tin, as the ultimate authority, for it provides the closest reproductions of the stones themselves.[15] In addition to these major sources, I have used a variety of other less valuable editions and compilations of inscriptions, described, with the others, in the Bibliography.

Most of the Mon inscriptions and the few in Pali are mainly of a political genre, and their value lies in issues concerned with legitimacy. The Burmese epigraphs also fulfill several additional functions: for Pagan society, they were public, legal notices that confirmed the *bona fides* of religious donations. They also had the religious function of announcing to the public the relative amount of piety each donor had. For historians today, they are sources of a statistical nature similar to title deeds recorded in local government offices in the United States, usually devoid of the types of biases we might find in documents with political bias, such as later chronicles, whose authors explicitly claim their intent as "using history for purposes of state and religion."[16] Yet, as mentioned above, the scholar compelled to use the inscriptions invariably adopts a religious perspective, and although religion may well reflect the paramount concern of Pagan's men and women, for an institutional history, one wishes that sources of a different character, which we know were kept on palm-leaf manuscripts, had survived also.

In addition to these functions, the inscriptions had certain social and political implications that, at first glance, are not so obvious. One of the consequences of Buddhism in Burma was the education of the young in monastic schools, thereby creating a literate public. Learning in general and the written word in particular received a tremendous amount of veneration, especially since the Burmese script was perceived to have been the Buddha's, in which the Buddhist scriptures were written. (Even today, one would not think of putting one's foot—a degrading gesture—on a book.) The written word, beyond what it had to say, itself commanded respect. A literate public, furthermore, meant that stone inscriptions, whether announcements of individual piety or legitimizing genealogy of kings, would not go unnoticed, not only during the lifetime of the donors but more or less permanently since they were written on durable material. The records of piety became models of ideal behavior to be publicly honored, tantamount to today's naming of a library, museum, or an a institute after a donor, while legitimizing statements of royalty on stone would come to be accepted as part of public, common knowledge, affirming society's assumptions about itself and therefore extremely difficult to change or refute.

At the same time, the general attitude toward learning and literacy was also shared by, indeed expected of, society's leaders, who became accustomed to making decisions in writing and were not thereby ordinarily obliged to reconstitute their past decisions solely from memory. The general influence of literacy on governmental functions eventually resulted in written archives, which became a critical part of government and governance. Lists of dues from fiefs, accounts, registers of population, their occupations and locations, those who owed service, those exempt, titles and descriptions of landed estates—all were part of precolonial Burma's administration. Even if archives were often destroyed between the rise and fall of dynasties, duplicates of central records were usually stored in provincial, township, village, or monastic repositories; and each new regime, if it wished to rule long and effectively and to have access to government's traditional sources of revenue, made an effort to secure and reproduce these lost records. If incomplete, such information was solicited from surviving members of officialdom by retaining and encouraging high-ranking functionaries of the previous court to serve in their old positions, in order to determine exactly how the past administration was run. This commissioning of past members of court to compile treatises on subjects such as court punctilio included stipulating the interior design of each room in the palace, the color to be worn by various members of the royal family, the number of white umbrellas assigned to each prince of varying rank, and the proper terms to be used on different occasions at court. By behaving in ways that were considered "correct," the image so important to new dynasties was thereby enhanced. Any new leader, foreign or indigenous, thus had the potential where-withal not only to recapture the legitimacy of the past in terms of its public image but to recover the use of past administrative structures and revenues, for there were always written records and literate people available.

If, with the rise of each new dynasty, the king and court were being compelled by practical needs to resurrect rather than shed the past and were more often than not disinclined to behave differently in form or substance from their predecessors in any case, little change could have occurred at the top, the only segment of Burmese society that could effectively lead in the transformation of the entire system. Even if there were an inclination to change, rules and precedents preserved in village and monastic depositories, as well as on nonperishable stone displayed conspicuously in well-frequented places such as temples, would continually remind a literate public that cherished and lawful ways were being tampered with. The inscriptions themselves, not to mention their content, were thus agents of governmental and cultural continuity.

Although the inscriptions constitute the bulk of my source material, other primary though not necessarily contemporary data have been used, mainly as supplements, and as an aid to understanding otherwise obscure institutions. They generally fall into four categories in order of importance to this study: *dhammathat* or law codes; *thamaing* and *sittan* or histories of localities and administrative records, respectively; chronicles of a later age; and, lastly, a miscellaneous category of "literature" that throws light on a subject. *Dhammathat* refers in fact to the *Wagaru Dhammathat,* a thirteenth-century civil code, and the *Dhammavilāsa Dhammathat,* a possible twelfth-century code. (Their value is assessed more fully in a later chapter.) *Thamaing* and *sittan* refer largely to *Zambudipa Okhsaung Kyan,* in all likelihood a fifteenth- or sixteenth-century administrative record with limited information on the Pagan and considerably more on the post-Pagan periods of Burmese history. As for the chronicles, three are pertinent: the *Hmannan* (a section of which commonly is known as *The Glass Palace Chronicle*), an early nineteenth-century compilation but clearly based on earlier data; the *Mahayazawindaw Gyi* of U Kala, an eighteenth-century work, also clearly based on earlier sources, some now lost to us; and the *Jatatawbon (Zatabon)*, a sixteenth-century (?) part-narrative, part-statistical account, also with obvious access to earlier sources now lost.

The use of chronicles, even if only in supplemental form, can be problematic because in addition to being a record of events, their authors were also concerned with legitimizing the dynasty under which they lived. To do this effectively, they used certain literary devices—such as prophecies, omens, manipulation of language classifiers—to provide supernatural and other types of sanctions to events and persons.[17] They are not, however, useless as a result, for the biases themselves often reveal Burmese criteria for determining certain issues important to the society: issues such as conceptions of authority, order and disorder, morality and justice. Moreover, the chronicles provide us with the only available narrative account of Burmese history—events, dates, rulers—unavailable elsewhere for the most part. Third, the chronicle tradition in Burma is a cumulative one—in fact, a tradition continued by many Western historians like Phayre, Harvey, and Hall—and as such contemporaneity is less serious a problem than one might think. Lastly, there is considerable factual/empirical information in the chronicles, which with care, can be utilized.

As for Burmese literature, although many of the inscriptions certainly qualify as literature (for example, Aloncañsū's prayer on the Rhuykū [Shwegu Gyi] Pagoda), more strictly defined, it has not survived before the fifteenth century, since all of it must have been written on perishable material. In any case, the contribution of this genre of source material is minor to our study and need not become an issue of any significance.

In short, the primary Burmese source materials present certain difficulties, most notably their inaccessibility, the language in which they are written, and the obscurity of their social, political, and cultural context but not their availability, as often claimed. It is this context, particularly of the "classical age" in Burmese history that the present study will attempt to reconstruct.

PART I

Components of the Indigenous Conceptual System

1

The Historical Framework

THROUGHOUT Mainland and Island Southeast Asia, and in parts of southern China, there appears to have existed a broad culture more or less equivalent to the traditional archaeological typology of Neolithic and Chalcolithic. Because the culture is so widespread throughout Southeast Asia and because Southeast Asian scholars needed a term that would not have to succumb to the chronological or other theoretical parameters of stone and metal cultures found elsewhere, in recent years this culture has come to be known as the Hoabinhian, named after the locality in Vietnam, Hoa Binh, where significant evidence of it was apparently first unearthed. In certain areas, it is datable to approximately 10,000 B.C. or even earlier.[1] Since the 1930s, archaeological excavations in Burma, though infrequent and spotty, have yielded enough information to suggest the presence of what is called an Early Hoabinhian culture—roughly equivalent to the Paleolithic—that lasted until approximately 4000 B.C. This early stage was followed by what is known as the Late Hoabinhian and contemporaneous metal manufacturing age between 4000 and 2000 B.C., after which a fully metal manufacturing period appeared, between 2000 and 1000 B.C. Between 1000 and 200 B.C. is a blank, followed by some of the first urban sites to be found in Burma. The origins of urbanization in Burma have become somewhat clearer only in the last decade or two. In this endeavor, epigraphy and archaeology have led the search, but a better understanding of later Burmese narrative accounts (even if concerned largely with legitimation) and painstaking analysis of Chinese and Arabic sources have also been significant.[2] The picture is clearer from 200 B.C. onward, enabling us to divide Burmese history proper into five major periods.

From 200 B.C. to approximately the early ninth century A.D. is the Pyu period, named after the Tibeto-Burman speaking Pyu people, thought to have been the dominant culture in Burma at the time. It is what I have called the formative period in Burmese history. This is followed by the classical age of Burma's history, the Pagan period, the efflorescence of the previous age, lasting politically at least until the end of the thirteenth century A.D. and the focus of this study. A period of political disorder seems to have characterized the next two centuries, known as the Ava period, which, however, was a time of intellectual ferment as well. A unified age once more emerged under the strong Toungoo dynasty, which lasted until the first half of the eighteenth century and was replaced by the Konbaung dynasty of the mid-eighteenth and nineteenth centuries, in turn terminated by the British in the last quarter of the nineteenth century.

The Hoabinhian Culture in Burma

The Early Hoabinhian culture can be found in Burma in sites scattered on or near the banks of the Irrawaddy River throughout the central plains of Burma known as the dry zone. Some sites are also found farther to the east in the Shan Hills, where in fact the evidence for it has been most dramatic. Although the study of Burma's Early Hoabinhian culture is in its infancy, it nevertheless offers evidence of broader Southeast Asian features of this time: cord-marked, kiln-fired, and wheel-turned pottery; polished and rough stone adzes, axes, choppers, and scrapers; and in the Padhalin Caves in the Shan States, wall paintings of the sun, a fish, cattle giving birth, elephants, deer, wild boar, and palm prints.

Subsequently, a bronze culture appeared, largely upon the remains of, as well as coterminously with, the Early Hoabinhian. Many of the bronze implements uncovered, for example, appear to have been copies of their stone counterparts. It is, again, another period of Burmese prehistory with very little data available but enough to suggest the presence of an indigenous bronze casting "industry" with an affinity to other Hoabinhian sites in Southeast Asia. Between the end of the Bronze Age in Burma (say, 1000 B.C.) and the earliest urbanized site so far discovered (approximately 200 B.C.) is a data gap, undoubtedly reflective of work still to be done.

The Urbanized Polities and the Pyus

From 200 B.C. until the first nine centuries A.D. is the Pyu period, though one might prefer to call it (as I do) the period of early urbanized polities. Who exactly the Pyu people were is still an open question, but it was a period and culture that we can identify distinctly. Because of the priority given by the Archaeological Survey of Burma to two better known cities of this period, Śrī Kṣetra and Beikthano, it was at first thought that civilization moved south to north, for these two cities are found south of the dry zone, considered the "cultural core" of Burma. Subsequently in the late 1960s, the Archaeological Survey began to find other urbanized sites belonging to this same culture in the dry zone itself, particularly Hanlaṅ (Halin), north of Pagan. But then in the 1970s, Winka, far in the south, located near Thaton (Sadhum) in coastal Burma, was discovered. In the late 1970s and early 1980s, several more "Pyu" sites, notably Binnaka and Mongmai, were unearthed, once more, in the heart of the dry zone and close to some of Burma's earliest irrigation works, near Kyaukse, the economic mainstay of all (except one) subsequent Burmese dynasties (see Map 1).

The archaeological remains of this pre-Pagan urbanized culture show that it is uniform to a significant degree. Mongmai, Hanlaṅ, Binnaka, in the central dry zone, and Śrī Kṣetra, Beikthano, and Winka, south of it, were related in several ways. They apparently used the same Tibeto-Burman language (Pyu) and wrote in Devanagari, Kadamba, and the Pallava script of Andhra. They created virtually identical artifacts, making (and buying) clay water vessels with rouletted patterns and long spouts, used carnelian and onyx beads, and imported (?) Red Polished Ware (thought by some to be Roman and by others to be Indian). Their belief system included Sarvāstivādin Buddhism (an early branch of the Hīnayāna whose doctrines were similar to those of the later Theravāda and who wrote their texts in Sanskrit), elements of Hinduism, and a rather widespread Southeast Asian practice of urn burial.

More important, some of their material and ideological culture show continuity with the Pagan period. Their ideology of salvation, for example, was closely related to the doctrine of the future Buddha

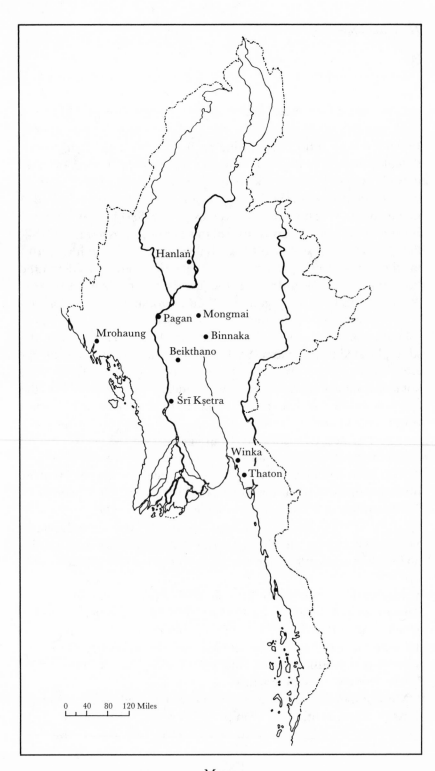

MAP I
Urbanized Sites

(Metteyya) and the Four Buddhas of this *kappa* (the present cosmic age), as it was to the Burmans at Pagan, while their religious edifices set a standard for the smaller temples of Pagan. Certain features of their secular buildings and the ideology that went with them also became standard. Their fortified cities were arranged according to patterns that persisted into the nineteenth century: the number of gates (twelve); the central location of their palaces; and the high-walled cities constructed of relatively uniform bricks with their temples forming a protective ring around them. The predominant livelihood of these people appears to have been largely but not exclusively agrarian (numismatists point to a Pyu coinage system with a uniform set of symbols struck on both sides, specimens of which are found as far east as present-day Saigon).[3] The juxtapositioning of several hinterland cities with several coastal or near coastal cities also suggests a dual economic and political relationship among certain pairs of them, not unlike several ancient civilizations (such as Harappā and Mohenjo-Daro) where the inland city controlled the agricultural resources and the coastal one the commercial ones—a pattern to be followed by subsequent Burmese kingdoms. The Pyu political culture, lastly, seemed to have been structured around a dynasty composed of several royal families, whom the chronicles mention, in part confirmed by a short list of names in a Pyu inscription found at Śrī Kṣetra.

The picture of this pre-Pagan, urbanized culture, though certainly incomplete, has nevertheless become clearer since the mid-1960s and has several implications for Burmese history and prehistory. First, urbanized culture in Burma did not "move" in any particularly significant direction prior to the founding of Pagan but had been present in the core area for a millennium, from which later political, economic, and social institutions apparently developed. Preliminary dating of some of the remains show, in central Burma at least, a first millennium (200 B.C.?) occupation with a probable Hoabinhian or early Neolithic base. Therefore, previous conclusions about Beikthano's status as the earliest Pyu city (first century B.C.–second century A.D.) may have to be revised. Not only would the revised chronology be significant, but the location of these sites may place, for the first time, the origins of urbanization in Burma in the dry zone itself—the nucleus of subsequent centers of Burmese culture and for long an important part of Burmese origin myths. In fact, most of these urbanized sites remained as cultural and often

political centers to give a total picture of dry-zone political para-
mountcy during the next millennium. Second, it is now clear that
this Pyu culture was far more extensive than heretofore imagined
(from dry-zone Hanlan to coastal Winka), thereby linking central
Burma not only to the Isthmus of Kra but to the international commercial network that stretched from the Mediterranean world to
China. Third, because the choice of digging at these sites was dictated not by archaeological surveys but first by a search in the chronicles for records of ancient cities (written well before archaeology
became an academic discipline), the case for the antiquity of some of
the chronicles' data as well as the cumulative tradition of Burmese
historical writing deserves serious reconsideration. Lastly, the new
evidence suggests that the development of Pagan in the central
plains of Burma from a small fortified city to a sophisticated and
bustling metropolis to become, in fact, the political and cultural capital of eleventh- , twelfth- , and thirteenth-century Burma, was not
at all sudden or dramatic—as we had thought—but rather a gradual
growth from the socioeconomic and cultural foundations established
by these urbanized sites of the first nine centuries A.D.

The Rise of Pagan

By A.D. 638 at the latest, the Pyus had become the dominant power
in the Irrawaddy River basin, with their capital at Śrī Kṣetra. By the
early eighth century, that city had apparently been destroyed and
another Pyu city, Hanlan, had replaced it. For the next century, the
center of political gravity remained there. Then in A.D. 832 and 835,
the powerful kingdom of Nanchao that dominated western Yunnan
for at least two centuries—peopled by Tibeto-Burman speakers
(Lolo) said to be akin to Burmese—raided and sacked Hanlan, the
last major center of the Pyus in central Burma, as well as Mi-ch'ên,
a Mon center in Lower Burma. And it was probably this political
and demographic vacuum that the Burmans exploited. Where the
Burmans came from and to what extent they might have migrated
from Yunnan with the Nanchao troops (as some scholars suggest), is
an issue still to be resolved. It is true that the Burmese chronicles
attribute the founding of Pagan to Pyuminhti (Pyusawhti) and the
names of his descendants follow the typical Nanchao nomenclature
—that is, parts (usually the last) of the father's name were used as

the first (or middle) part of his son's. Moreover, the date given for the founding of Pagan by the chronicles, A.D. 849, is reasonably close to the destruction of the last Pyu city in 832. It is uncertain what happened to the Pyus thereafter—some were taken as prisoners by Nanchao according to the *Man-Shu,* a Chinese account of Yunnan around the eighth and ninth centuries—but it is also clear that some of the Pyu sites such as Binnaka were not abandoned, showing continuous occupation, with Pagan, Ava, and even Konbaung artifacts uncovered there.[4] Pyu inscriptions have also been found after this date (one in the thirteenth century).

In any case, in or about 849, a fortified city located at a strategic point on the Irrawaddy was built on what may have been remains of an earlier Pyu village, and certainly according to earlier Pyu designs. It was to become known later as Pagan (or Pukam, Pukaṁ, Pokām, Pukām), whose meaning is still unclear, and in Pali as Arimaddanapūra, "the city [that is a] crusher of enemies." The earliest mention of Pagan occurs in Cham and Mon inscriptions in A.D. 1050 and 1093, respectively, while a Chinese source, the *Chu-fan-chih* of Chao Ju-kua, reported that envoys from the "P'u-kan kingdom" visited the Sung capital in A.D. 1004.[5] With the founding and subsequent growth of this new city and its dynasty, a millennium of cultural and political development centered in the plains of the dry zone began once more.

The next two centuries saw expansion by the Burmans of Pagan in several directions as central Burma reasserted its hegemony. It was a period of development, a period concerned with unification and centralization of resources, both material and intellectual. Labor was imported from adjacent territories, while certain ideologies dealing with legitimation of authority and society were evolving based on foundations already established by the Pyus as well as on prevailing thought in the Asian world.

Each of the Pagan kings in this period insured the perpetuation of the civilization in his own way, according to the needs of his own generation. The earliest king about whom we have inscriptional information but know little else is the tenth-century monarch Caw Rahan (Sawyahan), grandfather of the well-known Aniruddha, who probably attained the throne around A.D. 956—not by legitimate succession it seems but by some form of usurpation. He was followed by Kloṅ Phlū Maṅ (Kyaunghpyu Min) about 1001. Again, the legitimating legends that surrounded this king suggest that he

too was not in line for the throne but was a person with obvious ability who worked his way up at court and attained the kingship
through military talent and the consolidation of his fief in the nearby
district and town of Nyaung-U. He had three sons who battled for
the throne, which was won by Aniruddha, one of the great unifiers
of Burma. With the accession of the latter in 1044, more contemporary sources become available, placing Pagan's history on firmer
ground.

FIGURE I

List of Kings

Names	Jatatawbon Yazawin	Provisional
Caw Rahan (Sawyahan)	A.D. 956–1001	—
Kloṅ Phlū Maṅ (Kyaunghpyu)	1001–1021	—
Aniruddha (Anawrahta)	1044–1077	
Co Lu (Sawlu)	1077–1084	
Kalancacsā (Kyanzittha)	1084–1111	
Aloṅcañsū (Alaungsithu)	1111–1167	1113–1169/70
Narasū (Kalakya)	1167–1170	1169/70–1170
Narasiṅkha (Naratheinkha)	1170–1173	1170–1174
Narapatisithu	1173–1210	
Nātoṅmyā (Nadaungmya)	1210–1234	
Klacwā (Kyazwa)	1234–1249	
Uccanā (Uzana)	1249–1254	
Narathihapade	1254–1287	
Klawcwā (Kyawzwa)	1287–1300	

Aniruddha consolidated his position at court and improved his
administration by building up his defenses north of the capital, as
well as by repairing and creating new irrigation works in the rich,
perennially watered plain of Kyaukse. He then exploited the fertile
plains of Maṅbū (Minbu), southwest of Pagan. To maintain this system effectively and efficiently, he needed laborers. And to make
Pagan more than a military kingdom, he found it necessary to incor-
porate the manifestations of culture into the state he was building:
translated into human terms, that meant importing artisans, priests,
scribes, and scholars.

In 1057, Aniruddha moved downriver and gained hegemony over
the Mon capital of Thaton, from where he brought back much of
Pagan's skilled artisan and scholarly population who were so important to the growing kingdom. This was one of the primary means by
which state development was enhanced in early Southeast Asia—the
importation of scarce labor into the capital to insure the productivity

of the abundant and fertile land, to build the monuments so necessary for legitimacy, and as well to augment the supply of manpower
for the armed forces. Although for most Pagan kings labor scarcity
was a constant problem in the struggle for survival, Aniruddha with
this expedition at least temporarily solved it, and along with it the
need for "culture." Leaving most of the Irrawaddy River Valley and
the Lower Burma port cities relatively secure with garrisons and
appointed governors, he returned to Pagan where, in the next year,
he built one of his many pagodas to commemorate the victory, whose
inscription survives.[6]

Another critical development in this early period was Aniruddha's
relationship with the *sangha,* the Buddhist church. Without fully
realizing the implications of his actions, he increased patronage to
the *sangha,* which by now had become the standard beneficiary of
conquered wealth. The flow of wealth to the church initially enhanced the economic and cultural development of the kingdom, but
it also created a situation that would become a problem for his successors.

The challenges of the subsequent generation were the demands
for form, order, and some sort of accommodation to the "chaos"
created by the diverse cultural influences introduced into Pagan by
Aniruddha's conquests. Since no single cultural influence was as yet
completely dominant, there had to be an amalgam. King Kalancacsā (Kyanzittha, 1084–1111) rose to meet these needs. One word best
describes the demands of his age as well as the age itself—syncretism. It was an age characterized by Burman military rule, Pyu
traditions, Mon culture, and Theravādin spirit. To say that Pagan
was, at this time, an ethnic Burman civilization is to speak only of
the ruling class; to call it Mon ignores the political and military realities; to call it Pyu overestimates the longevity of that tradition; to call
it Theravādin oversimplifies the religious milieu. All these elements
made up eleventh- and early twelfth-century Pagan.

Kalancacsā was the person around whom this amalgam could
unite. He cemented the fissures of decentralization by appeasing all
cultures and groups. He patronized Mon scholars and artisans; their
language became the lingua franca of the court and, in effect, the
Mons emerged as the intellectual elite. He satisfied the Burmans by
maintaining their rule. He provided a sense of continuity to the
older traditions of the society by linking his genealogy to the real and
mythical ancestors of Śrī Kṣetra, the symbol of the Pyu golden past.

Lastly, he supported and favored Theravāda Buddhism while toler-
ating other religious groups. Art and architecture, religion, language and literature, ethnic plurality—in effect the whole society
during Kalancacsā's reign—reflected assimilation and syncretism.
By the end of the eleventh century the same cultural influences
imbibed by the Pyus—Brahmanism, Hinduism, Buddhism, and
local beliefs concerned with the supernatural—had been synthe-
sized, a process that was continued into the twelfth century.

This age of syncretism, however, eventually yielded to a new one,
itself a response to syncretism. Because the culture under Kalancacsā was invariably a mixture there was a need after his reign for some
sort of permanent, definable, and distinct tradition—not temporary
assimilation, cosmopolitanism, or amalgamation. Syncretism by its
very nature had created intellectual and structural uncertainty. King
Aloṅcañsū (Alaungsithu, 1113–1169/70) filled precisely that vacuum, by beginning the process that institutionalized what was to
become the Burmese Theravāda Buddhist tradition.

What Aniruddha and Kalancacsā had struggled for—unification
of human and intellectual forces—Aloṅcañsū took for granted.
Theravāda Buddhism, the constant, no longer required royal manipulation of folk and other beliefs to be supreme. As a result, in
Aloṅcañsū's reign few if any conscious innovations in the field of
political ideology are to be found, at least those that had to accom-
modate Buddhism with the various folk beliefs prevalent in the culture. Kalancacsā had already accomplished that. It was not Aloṅcañsū's task to seek the components that might comprise a tradition;
his was to establish cultural permanency by standardizing more tangible elements such as the administrative and economic systems.

Once this tradition was defined, culture was standardized, and, in
general, the society was stabilized, new conditions emerged that dictated the needs of the following generation. Wealth and prosperity,
efficiency of administration, stability of political, social, and economic conditions had put pressure on the fixed relationship between
productive land and population. Although population had probably
increased among the artisans, a result of prosperous conditions in
the construction sector and general stability, because of the relationship between hereditary status and occupation the need for labor in
crown services, particularly in the agricultural and military sectors,
could not be met fully by the growth of the artisan and other non-
crown classes. In the generation that followed Aloṅcañsū, therefore,

expansion and conquest became a solution to some of these problems.

King Narapati Cañsū (Narapatisithu, 1173–1210), known for his expansion and conquest, proceeded to increase the agricultural base of the kingdom with new and, as a result, uncommitted labor from conquered areas, securing the needed wealth for a growing royalty and officialdom. Indeed, of the four centuries that the Pagan dynasty ruled, the height of its political and administrative development was the hundred years between the end of the twelfth century and first half of the thirteenth, especially during the reigns of kings Narapatisithu and Nātoṅmyā (Nadaungmya, 1210–1234). It was a period in which the kingdom expanded physically to an extent never to be surpassed during its life; when military organization and success reached their zenith; when monumental architecture achieved a qualitative (and quantitative) standard that subsequent dynasties attempted to emulate but did not succeed in doing; when the government defined and established its ideologies of legitimacy and the society its criteria for being; and it was a time when the court finally developed the complex organization that was to be a model for later dynasties. It was also a period during which the agricultural economy reached its Upper Burma potential; when the *saṅgha* enjoyed one of its most wealthy periods; and one in which customary (civil) and criminal law were codified to become the basis of jurisprudence for subsequent ages.

More specifically, the Irrawaddy River Valley from Bhamo on the China border to the Tenassarim Peninsula had been unified, ruled by a king of an established hereditary royal family, and supported by an officialdom whose power was based mainly on "the royal compassion." The state was (1) founded upon an economy of redistribution embedded in institutions not necessarily economic in nature; (2) administered by a semibureaucratic structure, with a relatively centralized taxation system and an imperial army; (3) dependent upon a populace legally placed into crown, non-crown, and exempt categories; (4) whose people were educated and "pacified" by a large, ubiquitous, and at least horizontally united Buddhist church the head of which was appointed by the king with its members the paramount beneficiaries of the dominant belief system, kammatic Buddhism; and (5) stabilized by a uniform judicial system based on codified law written in the vernacular, Burmese.

By the late twelfth and early thirteenth centuries then, because

Pagan had leaders with vision as well as necessary human and economic resources, it could and did establish a sound administrative, political, and economic system—in effect a permanent tradition the essence of which was to persist to the nineteenth century. It is this Pagan, built by Narapatisithu and some of his predecessors and inherited by Nātoṅmyā and his successors, that is the primary focus of study.

The imperial milieu of Narapatisithu's reign, however, in turn created new conditions for the following generations, which became accustomed to power, affluence, and an elegant culture. Narapatisithu's successors—Nātoṅmyā (1210–1234) and Klacwā (Kyazwa, 1235–1249), as well as those who followed them—simply reaped the benefits of his efforts without strenuous effort or much sacrifice on their part at state building. And largely because of the stable and bountiful conditions that were passed down, kings like Narathihapade, who lived in the last half of the thirteenth century (1254–1287), faced more acutely a problem that had become an invariable part of the society, one that most Pagan monarchs since Aniruddha had to contend with, though on a smaller scale: namely, the devolution of wealth in the form of taxable land and corvéeable labor to the religious sector. It was a problem that plagued Burmese society for the next millennium.

Briefly stated, the process (discussed more thoroughly in the Conclusion) occurred in the following manner. The merit-path to salvation—the spending of one's material resources on religious things to insure a better rebirth—dominated religious belief. The ultimate material result of this belief was the construction on a tremendous scale of temples and monasteries, permanently endowed with productive but tax-exempt land and labor. Because most workers were paid in cash, in kind, or in rights to good land, perpetually scarce labor was attracted to the capital, invariably increasing the amount of cultivated land or its productivity (hence, state revenues), while enlarging the pool of people liable to per capita taxation not only at that particular point in time but for subsequent generations, for tax liability was normally hereditary.

Cultivable land in Pagan at first was plentiful, and productive acreage increased during the first three centuries in proportion to the state's demographic growth. And since the state held or took the best (irrigated) lands and had revenue rights to virtually all others, except for those given in perpetuity to the *saṅgha,* it was easier and more profitable for newcomers to cultivate partially or fully developed state-owned land for a share of the produce than to clear and settle on virgin land by themselves.

As more temples were built and more revenues generated, the state grew in strength and grandeur, attracting more people from external sources while general prosperity stimulated natural population growth domestically. Moreover, the expansion of state coffers increased the size of its administrative, political, and especially military apparatus. With it, as in the mid-eleventh century, neighboring centers of population were conquered and large numbers of people were brought back to be resettled around the capital. Again, such increases in population, especially of military specialists, skilled artisans, and monk/scholars, greatly enhanced the growth of the political, material, and intellectual/religious institutions of the state, bestowing upon the state even greater legitimation than conquest by itself could have done. Because Buddhism and its structure had become institutionalized as essential to political, social, economic— indeed total—legitimation of the state, royal patronage and support of the religion and *sangha* in moral as well as material ways could continue indefinitely. The more one donated to the religion—the bigger the temple built, the larger the land and labor endowments one made—the more legitimate the king and his state became. The scale increased as others in the society followed the royal example. Initially then, there was a direct (and circular) relationship between spending on religion, increased agricultural production, proportional demographic expansion, and state development.

But after two hundred years of spending on what were in effect perpetually tax-free endowments, the state began to feel the strain of the cumulative effects of wealth flowing to the religious sector, without being able to retrieve significant portions of it. By then also, Pagan had probably reached a population commensurate with its natural productive capacity, which meant that cultivable land and labor to work it, were in equilibrium. Moreover, with the growth and development by then of other regional polities, the competition for labor outside the nucleus grew more intense; labor was no longer as easily obtainable as it once had been. There thus came a time when the expenditures of each new reign were at the outset too heavily committed to the church.

To regain some of this wealth in a socially acceptable and legal manner, Buddhist kings used what scripture called *sāsana* reform or purification of the Order. In effect, this reform enabled the government (more precisely the king), to regain its influence over the *sangha* in matters of the latter's behavior vis-à-vis temporal matters such as wealth and power. Cultivable land and corvéeable labor belonging to the *sangha* could be legally confiscated, and per capita tax on heretofore exempt categories could once again be imposed. The process also restored the king's image and position as defender of the faith. The success of purification, a sign of effective leadership, could determine the longevity of the dynasty, while unsuccessful purification perpetuated the uncontrolled growth of the *sangha*.

In the late thirteenth century, as the Buddhist church grew rich and its temples and monasteries were gorged with wealth, no strong leaders emerged to successfully purify it. At the same time the state could not simply take back this wealth illegally without compromising the belief system on which its own survival rested, nor would it simply destroy the *sangha* militarily. With the revenues on which royal power rested seriously drained, the invariable factionalism at court eventually led to civil war, finally destroying the unity and centralizing capabilities of the state, while it became a tempting object of plunder for enemy as well as tributary states.[7] The Kingdom of Pagan declined because the factors that had nurtured it in the first place became, *in time,* forces that contradicted and destroyed it. To put it differently, because Pagan society was unable (and unwilling) to change once constructive forces when they became destructive ones—creating an "inexorable dialectic"—the political power of the dynasty collapsed. Ultimately the Kingdom of Pagan declined not as a result of Mongol invasions or the egalitarian ideologies of Theravāda Buddhism (as it is conventionally argued) but because internally generated forces first rendered the state incapable of resisting the Mongols and other centrifugal forces, which in essence merely provided the coup de grace to an institutional fait accompli. Yet this pattern of development and decay did not end with the Pagan dynasty; it recurred at least three more times in Burmese history, until the last dynasty, weakened for fundamentally the same institutional reasons, was conquered by another waiting neighbor: the British.[8]

With one exception—the circumstances of which were anomalous —the centers of Burmese politics and culture from at least the ninth century have lain in the dry, central plains of Burma, dependent upon surrounding oases of intensively irrigated tracts of land.

Inland and agrarian, with trade playing a minor role in the acquisition of wealth, rainfall barely wetting the soil, and with the swamps of Lower Burma not yet drained and filled to be a factor in the economy, the wealth (hence power) of the first Burmese state relied on essentially two ingredients: cultivable land and labor. It was here in this demanding and limiting material environment that Burma had its origins as a state, and it was here that it ended its monarchical career. The room to deviate from this physical environment was meager, and the inclination to do so—once the Kingdom of Pagan had been fully formed by the middle of the thirteenth century—was not there; had it been there, a major transformation of thought concerning the nature and purpose of man and his role in the universe would have been evident in the sources. Nevertheless, the most was made out of this environment, and it is with the results of these efforts of the eleventh, twelfth, and thirteenth centuries—the institutions that evolved, the beliefs and thoughts that shaped and formed Burmese society, and their relationship to the events of the time—that we are primarily concerned.

2

Beliefs About Man and His World

THE CONCEPTUAL WORLD of Pagan's men and women revolved around two systems. Their formal world was based on Indic religious beliefs that included elements of Brahmanism and Hinduism, Mahāyāna and Theravāda Buddhism, and Buddhist cosmogony in general. Their informal world was that of Burmese supernaturalism, permeating mainly the terrestrial realms but also parts of the celestial. In some cases, the formal and informal worlds were inextricably intertwined, whereas in others they were patently contradictory. But whatever may have been the particular belief or doctrine, whatever the religion, whatever sect or school may have contributed to the mental environment in Pagan, it was the expressed desire for merit that dominated attitudes about man and his role in this world—a desire found at all levels of Burmese life. Merit was linked to birth, position, wealth, power, authority, legitimacy, and one's raison d'être. It was, in short, the most compelling motivating factor for behavior.

According to Burmese-Buddhist cosmogony, the universe is divided into three levels: Kamma Bhavi, the material world, where the laws of *kamma (karma)* apply; Rūpa Bhavi, a corporeal world but one where *kamma* ceases to play a role; and Arūpa Bhavi, an incorporeal world of formlessness. The inhabitants of the latter, which is also known as Brahma Loka, have attained a more exalted state than those of Deva Loka, who reside in Rūpa Bhavi. In Kamma Bhavi there are eleven divisions, seven happy and four unhappy states. The lowest of the former is Manussa, the world of man. Above this level begins the six inferior celestial regions, called "the six levels of the abode of the *nats*" *(nat prañ chok thap)*, *nats* being spirits and supernatural beings.

The first of these, Catummahārājika, the land of the Four Great

Kings (the Four Lokapālas), is followed in ascending order by Tāvatiṁsa, where the Thirty-Three Lords reside; Yāmabon, land of Yāma, the old King of the Dead; Tusita, often visited by the Buddha and inhabited by Metteyya, the future Buddha; Nemmanarati, the land of Mara, whose past merits were so good that even all his subsequent evil deeds could not bring him lower; and lastly, Vasavatti, where Pāramitā (the "perfect" deity) resides.[1]

At the center of the earth is Mount Myinmo (Meru), above which is Tāvatiṁsa, ruled by Sakka (or Indra), who "heads the [thirty-three] *Nat* Kings,"[2] and around which lay the Four Great Islands (Mahādipa). Of them, the southern one, Jambudīpa, is the most important.[3] Sakka of Tāvatiṁsa is placed above all Brahmas, even though the world of *devas* (celestial *nats* or deities) is technically inferior to the world of Brahmas.[4] The celestial *nats* often quit their places in Deva Loka and interfere with the chief events that take place among men. They are also constantly attentive in ministering to all the wants of the future Buddha, Metteyya, in Tusita Pura.[5] The *nats* in Deva Loka have not yet attained *nibbāna,* that perpetual, tranquil nothingness, but theirs is a place of pleasures and enjoyments, allotted to those who in former existences had done some meritorious work.[6] It is an abode everyone aspired to reach. When kings died, the inscriptions and chronicles declared that they had departed to *nat rwā* (Deva Loka), and when ordinary persons prayed for a boon, it was to be reborn a *nat* in Tāvatiṁsa. Parts of this formal Indic world were familiar to the average person; parts of it were rarely mentioned. Those relevant here include Catummahārājika, Tāvatiṁsa, and Tusita, which were well-known entities to the people of Pagan. Tāvatiṁsa and Tusita were apparently part of daily conversation, as were Jambudīpa and Mount Myinmo.

But there also existed an informal (largely non-Buddhist) world in relation to which everyone knew how to behave: the everyday, present fearsome world of nature in which man must get along. Nature was not considered incompatible with man, for spirit guardians of nature could be propitiated if man desired to live in harmony (even if uneasy) with them. Natural order would prevail as long as proper rituals were followed. This applied equally to government, the workings of which were indiscriminately associated with floods, fire, famine, and other natural phenomena; if proper rituals and procedures were observed there, too, political order would follow. Nature was harsh, but it was not man's enemy. Man's enemy was himself. As Buddhism taught it, his greed, lust, and hate were the real obstacles to *nibbāna*. And Buddhism did not simply leave it there; it provided (as did Burmese supernaturalism) explicit rituals one could perform to attain this eternal world of peace. The behavior of the average Burmese was in large measure determined by such attitudes and beliefs concerning nature and the world.

Elements of the Pagan Belief System

Supernaturalism

Nature was filled with spirits called *nat*s, which, however, referred to a variety of supernatural beings. Their propitiation comprised a large segment of social—and at another level—political life.[7] Aside from celestial *deva*s (also called *nat*s), there were essentially two kinds of terrestrial spirits: humans who had died and spirits who inhabit rivers, lakes, trees, and virtually all of nature. The former could be, though not exclusively, mythical and "biological" ancestors who had become guardians of the family and, by extension, of households, villages, towns, cities, and the kingdom. They could also be humans who had died "green deaths"—people killed violently whose spirits hover near the vicinity of their deaths—and were usually malevolent unless properly propitiated. The second kind, the spirits of nature, were associated with inexplicable natural calamities such as drought, floods, and earthquakes. If their hegemony over specific geographic areas such as lakes, rivers, or forests was not respected and was transgressed without the proper rituals, natural disasters would ensue. Both kinds of spirits were similar in that they were essentially guardians, filling a position in a world that humans could not.

Thus, nature did not act without cause; human ignorance and carelessness aroused the spirits of nature to wreak havoc on society. Nature was not inexplicable, without order, or unreasonable: it was more often human folly that brought down the wrath of its guardians, the *nat*s, in some natural form. One could live with nature in the same manner one could live with government—by propitiation.

The general role of nature spirits in Burma is fairly well known. What needs further analysis is the role of human spirits, to which the ancestral component in supernaturalism was linked. Although Burma does not appear to have practiced the forms of ancestor worship found in China or Vietnam, ancestors, as spirits of humans who had died, were very much a part of Burmese supernaturalism. In fact, the guardian spirit of each Mon household, *einhsaung nat,* may have had some former relationship to ancestral propitiation, for among other features, exogamous rules applied to those who possessed the same household *nat.*[8] Certainly they were intermediaries between the living and the dead, potent forces with which the living had to contend.[9] Ancestor or not, the spirit of the violently killed would hover in the vicinity of the place of death to protect the spot from human as well as supernatural forces. If a person was buried alive under the foundations of new or significant buildings such as palaces and forts, his spirit would remain in and protect the area.

It is not clear whether the people of Pagan used this as a means of protection, but the Mon king Manuha and his sister Queen Ma Paw, brought back from Thaton after Aniruddha's conquest, were said to have been buried alive in his temple, the Nanpaya, which still stands today.[10] An inscription from A.D. 1212, written when the boundary pillars of a *sīmā* (ordination hall) were being erected, notes that there was a person "who gave up his life [*asak lhwat pi sū*]" in the ceremony.[11] But under Buddhism and Buddhist kingship, such practices would not have been tolerated officially, and the terminology that may have been used originally for these victims (*sak siy,* literally "life dead") may have continued in use for those who now testified to the sanctity of an edifice as living witnesses who heard and saw these acts.[12] In fact, most references to *sak siy* in Pagan inscriptions involved live witnesses even if the term may have been once used for sacrificial victims.[13] In other words, what may have once been sacrificial victims, who as spirits "heard" and "saw" an important act, were, in the context of a Buddhist society, live witnesses who legally rather than supernaturally "testified." Nevertheless, the desire to preserve the order of the natural world in such rituals, despite Buddhism's teachings, was so strong that even by the sixteenth century, King Bayinnaung had to issue edicts prohibiting such practices, which he conceded had occurred twice in his reign.[14]

Although the belief in a human spirit is not necessarily contrary to Buddhist doctrine, belief in the existence of a soul is. It is at the crux of individuality and ego, the cause for ignorance, which is the cause of suffering, which is life. Yet Burmese supernaturalism allows for the presence of a human soul, which appears in the form of and is symbolized by a butterfly *(lip phrā).* At death, people are individually judged under the Tree of Forgetfulness by Nga Thein, their judge.[15] Here everything that has ever happened to them in the past is forgotten; they re-enter the living world as souls of new-born persons. Thus in the strict Buddhist scheme of things, nothing should be further from its doctrine of *kamma* and rebirth than such a "judgment day." Understandably then, Burmese supernaturalism in un-amalgamated form rarely appears in Buddhist donations of Pagan. The absence of individual souls, however, would have been a concept difficult to accept, and parts of it made their way into the prayers of Buddhist devotees. One woman, for example, prayed that she, as a specific individual, might be reborn as a man in her next life because the "status of wife is inferior" and at the same time asked that she ascend to Tāvatiṁsa, "where she (will become) the consort of Sakka surrounded by 100 attendants."[16] In both her requests, belief in an individual soul is clearly implied. The *Glass Palace Chronicle* glossed over the difference between the belief in souls and Buddhism's doctrinal denial of it (and in general between Buddhism and Burmese supernaturalism) by stating that "looking to the future," the Buddha is worshipped, while "looking to the present, (one worshippeth . . . spirit(s)."[17]

Hinduism and Brahmanism

Hindu and Brahmanic influences also shaped aspects of Pagan's belief system.[18] The deities Viṣṇu and Śiva had figured prominently ever since the first and second century A.D. in Beikthano Myo.[19] By the Pagan period, a Vaiṣṇava temple called the Nānādēsi Viṇṇagar Ālvār ("Viṣṇu temple of those coming from various countries") had been built by the Tamil merchant community in Mraṅ Pagan, just south of the capital. But it had absorbed Theravāda Buddhist priorities, as shown by its inscription:

> I have no regard for merit, none for a heap of wealth, none at all for the enjoyment of lust. Whatever is to happen, let it happen, O God! in accordance with previous action! This alone is to be prayed for and highly valued by me.[20]

"Whatever is to happen" depended on merit, but praying to a god implied divine interference with the course of *kamma*. Even though the concept of *bhakti* epitomized by Viṣṇu—which emphasized the compassion and grace of personal deities in the Indian conceptual system—had by this time in history softened the harsh Law of Kamma, in Pagan, Theravādin influence had preserved the emphasis on "previous action" to the extent that even those deities like Viṣṇu who were propitiated for their ability to affect the course of *kamma* seemed to have been peripheral to it. Although in most respects Viṣṇu was considered a personal savior, this strict interpretation of kammic law virtually ignored that characteristic. Another temple, the Nat-Hlaung-Gyaung, was built for Viṣṇu within the walls of Pagan, as Luce put it, "a 'few minutes' walk from the old palace," while Laksmī, his consort, was known in Burma as Kyāk Srī. In the same temple have been found an image of Sūrya, the Sun God, and some of the Vedic gods, along with their *vāhana* (vehicles), including Brahmā on his Haṁsā, Śiva on his Nandin, and Viṣṇu on Garuda.[21]

In the eleventh century, King Aniruddha erected the Shwesandaw temple for the merchant and artisan classes he had brought back from Thaton after attacking that Lower Burma city. Hair relics of the Buddha *(sandaw)* were ostensibly enshrined in the temple, whose orthodox style, similar to the Shwezigon Pagoda and other cylindrical stupas, was thought to represent pure Theravāda Buddhism.[22] Since the patron deity of traders and merchants, Gaṇeśa, was known also as Mahāpinne in Burma, the temple came to be called the Mahāpinne Pagoda.[23] Even though Gaṇeśa to the Hindus was a son of Śiva, to the Burmese Buddhists he was simply another *nat,* one of the *deva*s who inhabit the heavens. A year after the conquest of Thaton, in A.D. 1058, Aniruddha dedicated a statue of Gavaṁpati, patron saint of Mon artisans and craftsmen, who may have been derived from Gaṇeśa.[24] One found in Pagan not only a mixture of beliefs but also the kinds of associations made in India between deities, such as that between Tārā and Durgā (the former, the *śakti* or consort of Avalokiteśvara and the latter, of Śiva) as shown by frescoes on certain eleventh-century temples. With the patronage of Buddhism by the monarchy, Hindu-style temples like the Nanpaya may have begun to house Buddhist icons.[25] As a champion of Buddhism and defender of the faith on the one hand and as the ruler of various ethnic and cultural groups on the other, the king had to allow some such amalgam.

For the most part, Brahmans and their rituals fulfilled the political needs of royalty, not the daily needs of commoners. In the eleventh century, King Kalancacsā constructed an edifice "in the honor of Nārāyana . . . ," an obscure Brahmanic god who came to be identified later with Viṣṇu,[26] whose ceremony included

> Digging . . . the holes for the pillars of the 2 sides, the *yas* pillars, the *atas* pillars (of) the *siṅghāsin,* the pillars of the four pavilions, and the pillars of the ablution pavilion, and the *juṅ dal* pillars, and all the *atas* pillars on the front. At sunset, *godhuli* (being) *lagna,* the *saṅkrān* Brahmans who carried litters, beat the foremost drum.[27]

Because King Kalancacsā had referred to himself numerous times as an avatar of Viṣṇu, the edifice built for Nārāyana clearly represented the king's palace, dominated by the *siṅghāsin,* the Lion Throne of Burmese kings. Moreover, because *darbha,* the sacrificial grass mentioned in the inscription—and used in Brahmanic rites such as the *Indra-abhiṣeka* (the major coronation of the king)—established "a kind of mystic bond between an item of the sacrificial procedure and some aspect of cosmic phenomena," King Kalancacsā was attempting to represent heaven on earth, not only with his palace, modeled upon Nārāyana's celestial abode, but with his role as king, the earthly counterpart of Viṣṇu.[28] This will be discussed more fully in the following chapter.

Mahāyāna Buddhism

The presence of Mahāyāna Buddhism in Burma has been known for a long time. Most notable in this regard are the works of Nihar-Ranjan Ray, published in the 1930s. More recently, Gordon Luce's *Old Burma–Early Pagán* has added a wealth of detail to the topic.[29] It appears from these works that Mahāyāna Buddhism in Pagan did not simply play a counterculture role but was very much a part of elite, in fact royal, beliefs as well. The temple built by King Kalancacsā's queen Abeyadana is exemplary in this respect. On its interior walls are painted figures of Avalokiteśvara and Tārā. (Their images as well as those of Lokanātha and Mañjuśrī, two Mahayanist deities, have also been found elsewhere in Burma.) To the Mahayanists, Avalokiteśvara was the ideal *bodhisattva (bodhisatta).* He personified compassion, a human need that softened the impersonal Law of Kamma. In the history of Buddhism, according to Edward Conze, Avalokiteśvara came to possess qualities that made him almost equal to the Buddha, having miraculous powers to help in all kinds of dangers and difficulties. Subsequently, he came even to resemble Brahmā and exhibited a variety of cosmic functions and characteristics, such as holding the world in his hands and making the sun and moon appear from his eyes and the winds from his mouth. In the final stages of his development, Conze notes, Avalokiteśvara became a magician, and adopted many of Śiva's characteristics.[30]

Avalokiteśvara's development within the Mahāyāna sect from a personal deity to a magician corresponded with the pattern of growth and development of Tantricism (the mystical aspect) in Buddhism itself.[31] In addition to the Abeyadana temple, built in the eleventh century and thought to be in honor of Avalokiteśvara, as well as the presence of Sarvāstivādin and Sanskritic culture in the Old Burmese dating system before the rise of the Pagan kingdom, evidence of Tantric influence continued through the Pagan period into the late thirteenth century.[32] In temples such as the Payathonzu and the Nandamañña, clear evidence of Tantric Mahayanist features such as the Five Dhyāni Buddhas, Jambhala, and Hayagrīva —the latter of the Vajrayāna pantheon—were also found.[33] Evidence moreover of the Samaṇakuṭṭakas, another Tantric sect whose practices include the eating of beef and the drinking of liquor among other canonically forbidden things, appears in thirteenth-century inscriptions around Maṅnansū (Minnanthu), southeast of the capital, which describe such a sect of unorthodox monks.[34] Some of these monks—referred to in later literature as the Aris—seemed to have enjoyed considerable wealth and perhaps power out of proportion to their number. Although most Theravādins, particularly those under the fifteenth-century, reform-minded King Dhammaceti and those trained in the "pure" Mahāvihāra tradition of Śrī Laṅka, regarded some of these sects as heretics, their presence in Burma until today is well known.[35] They are neither dominant nor persecuted.

Concepts of Messianism and Omniscience

To the Theravādin and Sarvāstivādin, Metteyya was the equivalent of the Mayahanist's future Buddha Amitabha, who resides in the Western Paradise. Most devotees desired to be reborn as humans at the time when Metteyya will descend to the earth to preach the *dhammacakka,* the ultimate sermon. Only because of Metteyya's clarity and ability to preach will humans be able to acquire the under-

standing that extinguishes all ignorance—and ultimately life itself.
In Pagan, the wisdom to which one aspired was often called *sabbrañ-
ñutaññaṇaprāñya* or "infinite wisdom of omniscience."[36] For the
Theravādin, omniscience as wisdom was a goal humans could attain
by meditation or by listening to Metteyya, but to the Mahayanist,
this all-knowing knowledge was called *prajñāpāramitā,* an attribute of
the Buddha only. Originally, Metteyya's messianic role had been
accepted by the Theravādins without much enthusiasm and, according to Edward Conze, had never held a great place among them. But
"for the Sarvāstivādins (who we observed were present among the
Pyu at Śrī Kṣetra) and the followers of the Great Vehicle [Mahā-
yāna], the ideology assumed . . . increasing importance."[37] The
devotees believed that after the current Buddha, Śākyamuni, the life
of men would become depraved and his *dhamma (dharma)* would be
completely forgotten. Once that era has passed, however, Metteyya,
residing in the Heaven of the Satisfied Gods (Tusita), will appear on
earth, which will then be in a particularly fruitful and exuberant
state. Everywhere there will be trees and flowers, pure lakes, and
jewel heaps. All men will be moral and decent, prosperous and joy-
ous. The population will be dense, and the fields will yield sevenfold.
"Those people who at present do meritorious deeds, make images of
the Buddha, build stupas, offer gifts, will be reborn as men in the
time of Maitreya, and will obtain Nirvana through the influence of
his teaching."[38] Accordingly, in Pagan one found a preoccupation
with the messianism of Metteyya, typically illustrated by Prince
Rājakumār, who in A.D. 1112 closed his inscription with a curse:
"After me, should anyone, whether my son, grandson, my relative,
or other persons, oppress the *kywan* [bondsmen] I have dedicated
. . . may they not behold the Buddha Arimittiyā."[39] Other examples
are provided by those who concluded their donations with prayers
that asked for "the boon of saint-hood when Buddha-Master Mittyā
becomes Buddha" and, most often, by those who "wish to be born
as human when Ariyamettañ Purā Loṅ becomes a human."[40]

In the history of Buddhism, the idea of omniscience *(sabbaññu)* had
become important with Mahādeva and the Mahāyāna school of the
Mahāsaṅghikas, a "branch" of the Mahāyāna. According to Conze,
there are two ways to take the idea of omniscience: first, as the goal
for which to strive; that is, the final *nibbāna* of Buddhahood is omniscience. Second, omniscience is an essential attribute of a Buddha.
The first ideal is implied in the concept of the *bodhisattva* and the second is claimed by the Mahayanist to describe the Buddha—He was

omniscient in the strictest sense of the word.[41] The ideal of omniscience in general cannot be attributed to the Buddha, insofar as he was a human being (as the Theravādins believed), or even to his "glorified body" or *dhammakāya*. However, it would be linked essentially to the Buddha as a pure spiritual principle, that is, with the *dhammakāya* or *dhamma* body of the Buddha. In some Pali scriptures, argued Conze, the Buddha expressly disclaims any other kind of omniscience.[42]

The first interpretation of omniscience came to be the one typically used and found in the prayers of Pagan devotees. In 1140, King Aloncañsū donated a temple, saying, "I wish to attain Buddhahood which is called omniscience, which means being saved from the eternity of *saṁsāra* [the cycle of rebirths] . . . ."[43] He later built a magnificent temple that he called Sabbaññu, "The Omniscient." In 1179, after having provided numerous goods and services, a donor prayed:

> As for the benefit of this, the work of merit that I have done, (may) all the *sangha* from the Mahāther downward; all officers and men from my master the great king downward; my mother, my father, my teachers, my uncle the *san krī* who has given me happiness, my wife's parents, grandparents, relatives . . . all: all the (creatures) born in Kāma-Bhavi, Rūpa-Bhavi, and Arūpa-Bhavi, all the creatures born in . . . Li, Visiya, and Anā ages; having escaped (from) this . . . may all attain the peace of *nibbāna*, (may they all) reach (it). I wish for the boon of omniscient Buddhahood.[44]

Similarly, a minister of the court in 1190, in return for his dedication, asked that "Buddhahood, which is called *sabbaññu*" as well as "the end of all the miseries of *saṁsāra* . . ." be granted him.[45] In 1207, Nātoṅmyā, "being desirous of the boon of omniscient Buddhahood, made a (large gift) . . . with unusually decorative jewels throughout."[46] In 1223, a donor expressed omniscience in this manner: "I too desire the reward of omniscient Buddhahood, with all-knowing knowledge and all-seeing sight [*sabbaññutaññana*]."[47]

Time and Salvation in the Burmese-Buddhist World

Time, to people steeped in the precise, mathematical Sanskrit tradition, was calculable to the second. The whole cosmos existed not only in a physically represented space (endless mountain ranges called *cakkavāḷa*) but in a precisely formulated network of time. A person's birth, a king's accession, the erection of a temple were calculated to the precise moment in the universe deduced by the position of the constellations. It is rare when we do not find at the beginning of each donative inscription the precise year, month, day, hour, and position of the stars the moment the *alhū* (religious offering) was made. For those practices and events considered to be important, there was a meticulous regard for keeping accurate time. Dates had to be precise, for one's horoscope—so significant to one's whole earthly existence—was entirely dependent upon the accurate recording of the exact moment of birth. This concern for mathematical accuracy showed itself in Burmese preoccupation with and proclivities toward written records, an essential component of administrative efficiency—and ultimately for the writing of history and codification of law. Nature and time were orderly in the extreme, calculable, rather inflexible, and not to be transformed or conquered but the reverse: they existed to establish the context and limitations by which humans lived. In the Buddhist view, humans lived in cycles—of birth, death, and rebirth—from the smallest to the largest (*mahākappa*s, the time between the origin and destruction of a world system, which continues ad infinitum). Given such a system, it would be pointless to "capture" or "conquer" time even in concept. Rather, one must escape it in *nibbāna* or extinction.

Since Buddhists hold that life is suffering and time in this world prolongs that suffering, the ultimate wish is to be free from the cycle of rebirths (*saṁsāra*). Suffering is caused by ignorance, and the path out of it is intuitive knowledge, ideally achieved by meditation. At the same time, the Law of Kamma implies that people are born unequal; some are endowed with an intellect superior to that of others, with more leisure time than others, or with more discipline than others. Monks have a better chance for salvation because of their discipline and devotion to learning, their way of living, and their superior intellect than do laypersons; men better than women; humans, of course, better than animals. In order to be reborn a *deva*, a monk, or, if a woman, a man, one must abide by at least the basic precepts of Buddhist morality. To be reborn a *deva*, in a state higher than that of a human, or to be reborn a human when Metteyya, the future savior, descends to earth to preach the ultimate sermon—virtually insuring "knowledge" (and *nibbāna*)—one must accumulate an extremely large amount of merit while human. (The Burmese normally equate the building of a temple with outstanding rebirth status.) The accumulation of merit *(kutho),* then, is a preliminary and easier path to a better rebirth, after which, by the orthodox manner (that is, intuitive knowledge), *nibbāna* is attained.

Although merit is technically a preliminary way to achieve salvation, devotees in Pagan viewed it as a direct means to *nibbāna,* making in effect a distinction between kammatic Buddhism (merit-path to salvation) and nibbanic Buddhism (knowledge-path to salvation).[48] The recognition of this distinction was explicitly attributed to the Buddha himself, who stated that the "giving of alms, though good in itself, cannot introduce a being in the path that leads to the deliverance. The Law alone can afford such a benefit." On the other hand, He admitted that "the bestowing of alms could . . . procure an admittance into the seats of *Nats* . . . [while] a perfect compliance with the ordinances of the Law, opened the way to the seats of Brahmas."[49] Queen Phwā Jaw (Pwazaw) of Pagan, realizing that good works and merit would only secure a place in the abode of the *nats,* merely a stepping-stone toward attaining *nibbāna* and not an end in itself, stated in an inscription in A.D. 1271:

> When I become human, I wish to have happiness, luxury and wealth, better than the average person; when I become *nat,* I wish to have the appearance and radiance of excellence and dominion (and) I wish to have long life, to be free from illness, have a good appearance, melodic of voice, good figure, to be loved and respected by all men and gods. I wish to have, in terms of animate things, such things as elephants and horses. I wish to be great in *phun* [glory], dominion, (have a large) retinue, reputation; whenever I am born, I wish to be fully equipped with *danā* [gift-giving], precepts, faith, wisdom, nobility, which are virtues, and not know a bit of misery. At the end, having enjoyed bliss as man and *nat,* I wish the state of arahantship which is noble, having internalized the doctrine of release and the tranquil and serene peace of *nibbāna.* Thus I donate these lands, gardens, *kywan* [bondsmen], cows, and properties. All of these endowed properties are bona fide, none will have cause for argument later.[50]

But she was an exception; for most Pagan Buddhists, merit itself was the desired goal. Kammatic Buddhism became an *alternative* instead of a preliminary path to salvation. As one member of the royal family stated in 1241, "Because (we) wanted to be freed from the misery of *saṁsāra*, and wanted *nibbāna* immediately [literally 'on the spot'], (we) erected a *kū* [temple]."[51] The *method* to achieve salvation, that is, acquiring merit, was now equated with salvation itself, typically illustrated by the words of another devotee: "May I attain *nibbāna* for these my good works and may all my relatives, friends, and those who uphold and support this good deed receive merit with me as a result of my act."[52] Yet another, more self-centered, declared that "the five miseries of existence are old age, death, living with someone you do not like, being parted from someone you *do* like, not getting what you want," and wishing to be freed from these miseries; in 1266 this devotee built a monastery and endowed it with lands, people, and money.[53] Some requested that "if (born a) *nat*, may he live in the 6 heavens as a *nat*, may he arrive at the peace of *nibbāna* . . . with the status which is advanced knowledge, longed for by good people. . . ."[54] More important, if good deeds in this life could neutralize bad *kamma* accumulated over one's many past lives, the Law of Kamma was, in effect, no longer inevitable, and bettering one's economic status might even overcome an immutable law. The content and number of religious endowments in Pagan expressing these ideals demonstrate the extent of the belief and practice of kammatic Buddhism.

Even though Buddhists in Pagan as elsewhere believed in reincarnation, like most people, they feared death. It was not called "death," however, but euphemized as "impermanence," for death was not the end of all things, it merely showed that life was fleeting. All things go through cycles of birth and decay, are doomed for destruction, and are ever-changing, according to the Law of Impermanence. Even the religion (in five thousand years) and the *saṅgha* (periodically) are subject to this law and are destined to decay and destruction. The responsibility for the survival of the religion for the years prophesied, therefore, fell on devotees and the Buddhist king. If the *saṅgha* (the visual and physical representation of the religion's status) and the temples and monasteries (the concrete evidence of its survival) were patronized properly, then perhaps the religion might survive; it might even, as one devotee hoped, "remain permanent."[55] But it was also a personal fear of death that prompted many devotees to give all they had to the religion. As the wife of a minister in 1242 declared: "After our master Maṅ Kaṅkasū passed away . . . the wife of our master Maṅ, the daughter of Ñoṅ Ram Krī (was) seized with the fear of the Law of Impermanence, and being full of respect for her own husband . . . who had ascended to the village of the gods . . . ," dedicated property to the *saṅgha*.[56] Another devotee, having "suddenly realized that her ancestors had to depart this life without taking any of their possessions with them, and that she would have to do the same in her turn and leave behind . . . (everything) . . . thus resolved to give away her personal property . . . (to) . . . charity."[57]

The presence of temples and monasteries filled with monks signified that the religion was surviving and flourishing, even though people did die. And to insure that the religion would last for at least five thousand years—which by human standards meant permanently—endowments and other gifts to the *saṅgha* were made in perpetuity. By supporting the monks who were the custodians of the religion, devotees assured its survival indefinitely. Material donations and the messianism of Metteyya were thus a means to counteract the inevitability of religious destruction implied by the Law of Impermanence.

The Accumulation of Merit

It was possible to accumulate merit by performing good deeds for others or by making endowments and gifts to the *saṅgha,* clearly the best source of merit. The monk and *saṅgha,* to use Melford Spiro's phrase, were "fields-of-merit" from which laypersons could draw. From simply feeding monks and providing them with the basic amenities of life to building temples and monasteries for them (by far the greatest act of merit), individuals obtained merit. However, because socioeconomic differences existed between people—and the quantity of merit received was equivalent to the quality of the gift rendered—the merit-path to salvation insured that the rich would gain better and more merit than the poor. Yet if harmony were to be preserved in the community between those who were wealthy and those who were not, merit had to be transferable and shared with those less fortunate. In 1081, a donor gave fields, cows, and Shan laborers to a monastery and hoped that "the benefit of this offering I have given—the present king, future kings, (my) mother and father, (my) sons and all creatures, may they benefit equally with me."[58] Another donor stated: "I do not wish to have a stingy heart which does not wish to give away property that one has. I do not covet many riches. All my wealth, which is visible or stored away, I . . . will dedicate . . . (to the religion). . . ."[59]

Merit, moreover, could be transferred not only to living persons but to those already dead, not unlike the sale of indulgences for those in purgatory in Medieval Europe. Wishing that her good store of merit be transferred to her deceased relatives, a donor prayed that "the benefit of my work of merit, may it be gained by my husband who has passed away, my dear mother, and my father . . .,"[60] while the son of a headman dedicated gifts to the Three Gems (Buddha, *Dhamma, Sangha*) on behalf of his deceased wife.[61]

More important was the relationship between merit sharing and political and social status. One's social standing in the hierarchy depended upon not how much wealth one accumulated, but how much one gave away (to charity). Similarly, spiritual status was commensurate with the degree to which one shared one's merit. Because the king possessed the most material wealth, with which the grandest temples and monasteries could be built, he also had the most merit to share, making him, in effect, a savior. The desire to appease the suffering of all creatures, and the need for compassion and grace characteristic of the Mahayanist *bodhisattva,* which the Theravādins had discounted for the most part, could now be fulfilled by the Theravāda Buddhist king. His great accumulation of merit, achieved by a massive temple construction program, would provide ample merit for the entire kingdom. King Kalancacsā accordingly built reservoirs (tanks), pagodas, and Buddha statues, so that, he claimed, "all beings might escape out of *saṁsāra.* . . ."[62] Even if for the Theravādin only one's own *kamma* and behavior determined release from *saṁsāra*—not, as the Mahayanist believed, the will and grace of the *bodhisatta*[63]—still merit replaced grace to a large extent in Pagan's religious thought, and the merit-making and merit-sharing king came to embody the savior, whose largesse allowed ordinary folk to be reborn as humans at the time of Metteyya's descent.

Phun: **The Manifestation of Merit**

The "proof" of possessing merit was the presence of *phun,* or glory, similar to *mana* in Polynesia and *sekten* in Java. Although usually only monks were called *phungrī (pongyi),* "(one with) great glory," other powerful men, particularly kings, had *phun* as well. While royal *phun* was normally expressed in courage, dynamic leadership, military skill, physical and (though never stated explicitly) sexual prowess, *phun* in a monk was shown by self-denial, asceticism, and piety—the renunciation of precisely those characteristics that gave the king his *phun*. The ideal man in classical Burma was the dynamic king, yet it was the king who bowed down *(kodaw)* to the monk, not vice versa. Although the king and monk—"world conqueror and world renouncer" to use Stanley Tambiah's very apt phrase—both possessed *phun*, it is never confused. Burmese history on occasion has seen cases of monks becoming kings and kings monks, but it occurred only after one or the other role was relinquished. That is to say, there was no such thing in Burmese history as a priest-king. Even when Dhammaceti, an ex-monk who became king in the fifteenth century, ascended the throne he had shed his saffron robe. When a king entered the monastic order, it was either temporary (something that every Buddhist male does at least once), as a political exile, or permanently; he would not ordinarily become king again.

The possession of *phun* among laymen could be demonstrated— indeed, *had* to be demonstrated—by acts of power, piety, and largesse. Kings therefore built the largest, most expensive temples—a statement of their spiritual status to be sure but also of their political rank. It was also demonstrated through the building of secular works that benefited the kingdom—tanks, irrigation sluices—while largesse for secular clients was expressed by the giving of fiefs to princes, ministers, and servants. The argument was, as in many other aspects of Burmese society, circular: one built the largest temple because one was spiritually superior, and one was spiritually superior because one built the largest temple.

Intrinsically, merit is the same whatever its source, but in relation to its manifestations (power, authority, prestige), it differed when applied to the monk as opposed to the layperson. In the monk, the power was spiritual, the prestige religious, and the authority sacred. The monk had attained the state where secular power, authority, and prestige no longer mattered to him; he was above them. Precisely for that reason, he possessed great merit without a conspicuous display of it. For the laity, it was different. They improved their store of merit through good deeds and gifts to the *sangha*. But donating flowers or oil lamps to a temple simply did not provide one with adequate merit to be reborn a *nat* in one of the higher heavens; one needed to build a temple or monastery. The amount one gave to the religion was equivalent to the amount of merit one received, making those with the most wealth also the most meritorious. When applied to the laity at least, merit, wealth, and power thus became conceptually interchangeable.

The association of merit and *phun* with rank and birth, with power and money, and ultimately with *nibbāna* did indeed "teach" that hierarchy was preordained and that salvation could be better attained by those who were higher in rank and power than by those who were not. It implied that the established order itself could not be transformed; one changed only oneself. Yet, social concepts defining status and prestige demanded that merit be shared. Indeed, social harmony depended on the sharing of both wealth and merit. Wealth was to be spent on merit making and not to be hoarded, and all merit received (like wealth) was to be shared with one's fellow Buddhists. Hoarding wealth was certainly not better than spending it, even on nonreligious things; not only would spending on secular luxuries hinder attaining a better rebirth, it would invite royal confiscation, for conspicuous display of wealth publicly challenged royal status. It was rational therefore that wealth be spent, and spent on religious things.[64] In fact, to use Edmund Leach's phrase, though meant for a different setting, "one gave as much as one could afford rather than as little as one could haggle for."[65]

A person of modest means who performed an act of merit normally named his or her relatives and friends as co-beneficiaries; but a person of royal stature named "all creatures" as co-beneficiaries. Thus even though Theravāda doctrine states that everyone is individually responsible for his or her own salvation, in the context of a harmonious community, salvation was the business of the elite. Since the king was potentially the greatest holder and sharer of merit among the laity, the salvation of the kingdom rested on his actions. At the same time, destined to become a *nat* or *deva* in his next life, the king was in effect a Theravāda *bodhisatta* or *purā loṅ* ("embryo Buddha"), hence the titles *aloṅpurā* and *aloṅcañsū* taken by Burmese kings.

Because merit sharing was more than an abstraction—it meant the redistribution of money, land, and labor (ultimately power)— kammatic Buddhism or the merit-path to salvation made powerful men into kings, kings into *bodhisattas*, villages into capitals, capitals into kingdoms, and kingdoms into the abode of the gods. And it is to these more strictly "political" ideologies that we turn in the next chapter.

3

Political Ideology: Conceptions of Kingship

THREE ESSENTIAL COMPONENTS shaped Burmese conceptions of kingship: the *devarājika,* the *dhammarājika,* and the *kammarājika*—the divine, human, and superhuman attributes of kingship.[1] By aiding the public's desire for salvation and upward spiritual mobility as a *bodhisatta;* for ruling earthly Tāvatimsa—known as Jambudīpa, paradise on earth—as Sakka; and for guarding the supernatural dimensions of the society as a *nat*—for these roles the king acquired a divine image. For administering the state efficiently and morally in the tradition of Aśoka and Mahāsammata, both exemplary humans, he acquired the image of a *dhammarāja.* For successfully conquering the familiar world as a *cakkavattī,* a "universal monarch," he enjoyed the image of superhuman. Yet, because he achieved all this by the merits derived from his past actions, he was, above all, a *kammarāja.*

The *Bodhisatta* or *Purā Loṅ*

Theravāda Buddhist doctrine teaches that each person is ultimately responsible for his or her own salvation. In Pagan, however, where reciprocity and redistribution were expressions of and methods to implement concerns for social harmony, this responsibility fell to the elite, who, with the ability to accrue more merit, were compelled by society (and by scriptural example) to share with those less fortunate. And since among lay people kings possessed the most bountiful store of and potential to acquire merit, their duty to enhance the merit accumulation (and hence salvation) of their subjects became part of the society's expectations of legitimate rulers. In effect, the king's role resembled that of the compassionate Mahayanist *bodhisattva,* a personal savior who filled the void left by the Theravādin *pacceka buddha* who sought salvation only for himself. Indeed, King

Kalancacsā explicitly claimed in one of his inscriptions that he was the "bodhisatva [sic], who shall verily become a Buddha that saves (and) redeems all beings. . . ."[2] Others also implied a role as savior, even if they clothed it in a Theravādin context, as did King Aloṅcañsū in his twelfth-century prayer:

> . . . I would make my body a bridge athwart
> The river of Samāra, and all folk
> Would speed across thereby until they reach
> The Blessed City. I myself would cross
> And drag the drowning over. Ay, myself
> Tamed, I would tame the wilful; comforted,
> Comfort the timid; wakened, wake the asleep;
> Cooled, cool the burning; freed, set free the bound.[3]

The perceptions kings held of their role as savior were often shared by others as well, such as the wife of a high-ranking minister who recalled Aloṅcañsū as the "*bodhisatta* Cañsū Maṅ" ("King Cañsū, the *Bodhisatta*").[4] Sometimes the Burmese word *aloṅ*, which meant "incipient," "embryo," "immanent," and was often attached to *purā* (Buddha), indicating future Buddhahood, would be substituted for the term *bodhisatta*.

It was the concept of reincarnation, or more precisely the belief in avatars, that enabled such a transformation of deity into human, even if on a temporary basis, as shown in King Kalancacsā's genealogy.[5] During the dispensation of the Buddha Kassapa, his inscription noted, Kalancacsā was a wealthy man living in Benares, after which he was reborn into the royal family of Patna, to which Aśoka is linked. In his next existence, he was Rāma, king of Oudh. During Śākyamuni's dispensation, he was the sage Bisnū, and subsequently with the aid of (the indigenous) Gavaṁpati and other deities, he built the city of Śrī Kṣetra. At his death, he departed to Brahma Loka, where other *deva*s convinced him to return to earth as human in the person of King Kalancacsā to rule Pagan, which was to be a great kingdom that would uphold the Buddha's religion. Royal claims to Buddhahood in Burma were thus not necessarily contrary to Buddhist thought, since they were, after all, based on the Law of Kamma: past good behavior eventually led to present royal status. But royal status, once within the context of Burmese political culture, led in turn to future divine status: when the king died, he was said to have departed to *nat rwā,* or Deva Loka.

Sakka

The concept of avatarship allowed a great deal of flexibility: the Burmese king was also a manifestation of Sakka (or Thagyā, from the Sanskrit Sakrā) the Burmese-Buddhist equivalent of Indra, *devānaṁ indo,* lord of Tāvatiṁsa and its thirty-two other *deva*s. Sakka's palace and chariot are both called Vejayanta, his elephant is named Erāvāna, his special weapon is the *vajirāvudha,* and his special drum the *ālambara.* He meets often with his councillors, the Four Lokapālas, creating a paradigm of four points around a center. He is most zealous in the discharge of his duties to the *sāsana* (the religion, i.e., Buddhism) and is characterized as the most devout of the *deva*s of the Buddha. When the latter cut off his hair and threw it in the air, it was Sakka who caught it and enshrined it in his Cūḷāmani Cetiya. When the ponds of Jetavana were dry and the Buddha wished to bathe, Sakka immediately caused the rain to fall and the ponds were filled. Sakka is guardian of the moral law in the world, has twenty-five million handmaidens and five hundred dove-footed nymphs known for their beauty.[6]

Like Sakka, the Burmese kings wielded what was called Sakka's weapon, the *areindama* lance (properly the *cakkavattī*'s *cakkaratana,* the jeweled disk also called the *arindama*),[7] while their concern for the religion was also Sakka's concern. King Kalancacsā stated in one of his inscriptions that Indra explained to the sage Bisnū, soon to become the king, that his (i.e., Indra's) role and those of the other celestial deities were to protect the religion: "In order to carry out fully the (good) works of my lord, up in heaven am I, King In, who wield(s) the *vajra,* the thunderbolt. Down below is the Nāga King, who is great in supernatural power (and) glory. . . . In the four quarters the four kings guarding the world shall keep (their) watch."[8] King Kalancacsā also described his palace as a "pavilion that is like unto . . . Wejayanta,"[9] and named his elephant Erāwan; King Narapatisithu enshrined relics in his temple, which he similarly named the Cūḷāmani; and Burmese kings dressed as Sakka when they performed the *laythwan maṅgalā,* the auspicious ploughing ritual to insure the arrival of the monsoons.

The ceremony that suggested the transformation of the king into at least an earthly manifestation of Sakka was the royal inauguration, appropriately called the *Indra-abhiṣeka.* The earliest record of this ceremony in Pagan is King Kalancacsā's eleventh-century coronation, and although the inscription is too fragmented to provide us with a complete picture, enough survives to suggest that similar if not identical rituals described later had been performed.[10] (The Rājāmaniculạ Inscription of 1649 describes in detail the *abhiṣeka* of Ṅā Thap Dāyakā, and the Great Chronicle of U Kala that of King Thalun in 1633.)[11]

The coronation itself was preceded by elaborate procedures that lasted several days. Sanctified water, obtained from politically significant parts of the kingdom, was placed in the *kalasa* vessel or "vase of plenty," which stood in an indentation at the center of what was called the *abhiṣeka* plaque. The rim of this plaque had engravings of twelve auspicious designs, most of which were the twelve signs of the zodiac.[12] The king sat on a throne made from wood taken from a *bodhi* tree, painted with the flower of the lotus, the *shwe padomma*.[13] After the king received his regnal title, the chief queen received hers ("Southern Queen"), the heir apparent his ("Lord of the Eastern [Front] Palace"), and the four chief ministers theirs (*cac sūkrī,* "commanders of the military").[14] Fiefs and other titles and gifts were then given to monks—who were conspicuously uninvolved in the anointing itself—soldiers, and local and regional officials, including the "umbrella-wielding kings" of the kingdom (fief holders and/or governors) who were required to attend the ceremony. All this occurred in the audience hall where the entire court was seated according to their appointed places, determined by rank. Then with great pomp and ceremony, the king and royal family, all the ministers, elephantry, cavalry, charioteers, and foot soldiers, proceeded to the "royal good deed," that is, the King's major temple, on which was placed the finial or *htī*. The placing of the *htī* on the royal temple and the crown on the king's head on the same occasion left few doubts as to their symbolic relationship—in fact both king and temple are referred to as *purā*—so that when the *htī* (which also means umbrella, a symbol of royalty) toppled during an earthquake, the political ramifications were similarly unambiguous. Once the *abhiṣeka* was completed, the king and his entire court embarked on royal barges to circumambulate via the moat the royal city, the earthly representation of Tāvatiṁsa, and to subsequently take formal possession of it.

The relationship of the *abhiṣeka* ritual to divine status was further suggested by the venue of the ceremony. The capital city that the king formally occupied upon his coronation was constructed to represent Tāvatiṁsa, Sakka's abode. Thirty-two small *prāsāda* (or *pya-*

that), pavilions with seven-tiered roofs, occupied at intervals the battlements of the city walls, while four major *prāsāda* loomed above the four main entrances located at the cardinal points. These special thirty-six *prāsāda,* all seven-tiered, surrounded the thirty-seventh, located exactly over the main throne of the palace, the Lion Throne, which had thirty-seven posts with lotus bases and was situated precisely in the center of the city. The attempt to associate the thirty-seven towers, each manned by a trusted lieutenant of the king, and the thirty-seven deities of Tāvatiṁsa (Sakka, the thirty-two lords, and the Four Lokapālas) is clear.[15]

In addition to this association, the *abhiṣeka* plaque was a microcosm of both the city and Tāvatiṁsa. Like the twelve signs of the zodiac that surround the inner sacred spot of the plaque where the *kalasa* vase stood, which held the sanctified water, the twelve gates, each of which also possessed a sign of the zodiac, surrounded the city's inner sanctuary, the Lion Throne, the counterpart of the *kalasa* vessel. The consecrated water in the center of the *abhiṣeka* plaque annointed the person who would legally take possession of the center of the capital city and the kingdom—the throne. The king was entrusted not only with the city of twelve gates and its contents (the basis for political power, for here were the treasury, the arms, the elite guards, the ministers, the records, and the queens) but also with life and time in general, because the signs of the zodiac on the city's gates represented the twelve-month and twelve-year life cycles of which the king was also custodian.[16] Clearly, the plaque was a microcosmic replica of the city, the kingdom, and (by extension) Tāvatiṁsa, and only the person that its water annointed might legally lay claim to its macrocosmic counterpart.

There was some ambiguity, however, as to who exactly the king represented at the inauguration. By sitting on a lotus throne made from wood ostensibly taken from the original *bodhi* tree under which Buddha attained enlightenment and "flanked by Brahmā and Sakka during the annointing," as the chronicler reported, the king, at least for the duration of the annointing ceremony, "became" the Buddha Metteyya, who sat between these two when preaching in Tāvatiṁsa. At the same time the coronation ritual seemed to be the political-temporal counterpart of enlightenment or Buddhahood, while other factors, mentioned above, linked the king to Sakka and, as we shall observe, even to the Mahayanist Buddha principle. King Kalancacsā's *abhiṣeka* palace was called a *pañcaprāsāda,* a five-point paradigm of four towers at the cardinal points with one (over the king's main throne) at the center, an arrangement that represents at least three different ideas: the Mahayanist, with Vairocana (the cosmic Buddha principle) residing at the center of the four Dhyāni Buddhas; the Theravādin, with its four Buddhas of this *kappa* who await Metteyya, the fifth and center; and the Brahmanic, with Sakka in the center of the Four Lokapālas. Perhaps the inexplicitness and ambiguity surrounding which divinity the king represents are in fact the very qualities that make the inauguration Burmese. This leads us to the truly Burmese *devarājika* component: the king as *nat*.

The Guardian Spirit (Nat)

*Nat*s are supernatural beings that range from Burmese versions of Vedic sky deities to terrestrial guardians of territory, institutions, and people. They are differentiated by relative status, function, and a precise place in the Burmese supernatural world. The general spirits of animism who inhabit nature are different from the household guardian *nat*, who is in turn a different deity from one who guards a particular village or forest. The guardian *nat* of the royal family is similarly different from one who "controls" a particular province in the kingdom; yet all are referred to as *nat*. Of these different types, there is a special group of mostly terrestrial *nat*s called the Thirty-Seven Nats, who are in essence, directly or implicitly, guardians of the state and royal family and guarantors of dynastic continuity. And it is the role of kings in the composition and function of the Thirty-Seven Nats where we find the third *devarājika* element of Burmese kingship.

In the nineteenth-century Burmese palace there were a set of images of royalty and a book of odes that were chanted before them. These figurines were made of solid gold, each stamped with its weight and with the name of the personage it represented. The rule was to make an image of a king at his death if he died on the throne and of a queen if she died while her husband was on the throne, but not of a king who had died after deposition or of a queen who had survived her husband. The regalia used by the dead personage was preserved along with his or her image. The images were kept in the treasury and brought out to the Zetawunzaung or Hall of the Ancestors (sometimes called the Hall of Victory) three times a year on the three great *kodaw* or homage days. As the king and queen made obeisance to their royal ancestors, their subjects similarly made obeisance to them.[17]

Belief in the presence of ancestors in the supernatural world is essentially a belief in the continuity of an individual's soul after death. The desire to propitiate ancestors stems ultimately from the concern of the living that departed kin not only have access to food and abodes made for them (*nat* shrines) but that they intervene on the behalf of the living. Propitiation was especially critical if the deceased had suffered a "green death," an untimely, unripe, and usually violent death. Throughout Southeast Asia—indeed, throughout much of the world at one time—such deaths have been a concern for the living, for the spirits of those who die green deaths, without a permanent resting place, are usually regarded as malevolent. When ordinary persons died such deaths, unless their spirits were propitiated with a shrine, lights, and food by people in the area, they created trouble for the inhabitants of that locality, and as such were only a local problem. When a king or popular hero died a green death, however, being "national," his potentially malevolent spirit could affect the entire culture. Unless everyone propitiated the spirits of violently killed persons of importance on the "national" level, the consequences would also assume "national" proportions. As such, the ritual could no longer be a local affair, it had to be treated as a "national" one, the collective responsibility of the entire society.

These types of concerns must have been responsible in part for the creation of the cult of the Thirty-Seven Nats, for the most important characteristic shared by all the members of the pantheon was their unnatural deaths, most of them victims of direct or indirect crown injustice. Though historically there were more than thirty-seven persons who qualified, the number itself has been meticulously preserved throughout Burmese history, which suggests that attrition from and additions to the list depended upon the most recent (usually political) concerns of the living.[18] Selection was accomplished not by any formal process but by a form of subconscious cultural pressure that changed the composition of the list when the cults were celebrated annually. In any case, the cult of the Thirty-Seven Nats, among other things, preserved deposed ancestors of royalty or near-royalty who, though no longer formally revered as royal ancestors, still needed to be meaningfully linked to their descendants and provided with permanent abodes. They thus constituted a "supernatural dynasty," an "outlaw" group of sorts, a counterpart to the current, temporal one, and one in which all historic dynasties were represented. (Indeed, reference to them utilized the same hierarchic language reserved for royalty.) In short, because the rules concerning proper ancestor propitiation prohibited honoring deposed kings and their queens on the one hand, and their green deaths needed to be accommodated on a "national" scale on the other, most in the pantheon were violently killed royalty or folk heroes who died at the hands of royalty.

To eliminate one's kin with virtual impunity one needed adequate rectification, however. That regicide was an invariable part of royal life was not to be taken as a license to kill, and, more important, one simply could not kill without *immediate* consequences. The fear surrounding the wrath of the green death victim was harnessed, therefore, by insuring that those who had died as the result of some sort of royal or government injustice—and were thus the source of guilt for some king—were included in the pantheon. It was an attempt to counterbalance the use of unmitigated power. Their presence in the pantheon in effect stated that justice had to be attained in this life without having to wait endless cycles of rebirth implied in kammic retribution.

But having created this pantheon, the society was faced with a monster (so to speak) that had to be continually placated. As early as the eleventh century, King Aniruddha—often regarded as the ancestor par excellence of the Burmese state—made the Shwezigon Pagoda the official abode of the Thirty-Seven Nats, in effect allowing this Buddhist temple to become also the ancestral stele of all Burmese royalty. Though apparently contradictory, this amalgam between Buddhism and supernaturalism—that is, of allowing spirits, which are essentially souls—is, as F. K. Lehman has pointed out, a contradiction inherent within the axiomatic structure of Buddhism itself.[19] Evil spirits are allowed places in Buddhism, and in a well-ordered·monarchical state they need to be placated, converted, subdued.

The pantheon was further subdued by allowing it a functional niche in integrative ideology, making it bridge the gap between many and diverse royal families, especially opposing ones. This was done in several ways. For one, different royal families, via members of the pantheon, were tied to the "first" Burman dynasty of Tagaung (Takoṅ). Since tradition was an essential criterion of legitimacy and justification for present action, whenever a dynasty or family ousted a ruling family, links with the latter (or an appropriate substitute) were made through the pantheon of the Thirty-Seven Nats. Sometimes, because members of royalty on the female side came from diverse ethnic groups and various parts of the kingdom (especially as tributary brides), representatives of those groups and places had to be included in the scheme. Among the Thirty-Seven Nats is a king from the Shan territories, as well as princes from the Mon areas; they represent two of the most significant cultural and political components that comprised the Burmese state.

Secondly, in the process of political and religious integration, where Buddhism emerged as the dominant belief system in a centralized state, the need to unify the rest of society's numerous and scattered ancestral spirits and their cults—like the dispersed humans devoted to them—became compelling. They also needed to be formally placed in a hierarchic scheme so that supernatural as much as temporal authority could be clearly delineated. To accomplish this, a member of the pantheon was "allowed" to represent (and in essence substitute for) one of the local ancestors and/or guardian spirits. But because there were only thirty-seven members of the pantheon and many more local spirits, the pantheon's authority had to be territorial as well as personal. Each member of the Thirty-Seven therefore "received" a fief from the reigning king. Any human living in the territory belonging to a particular *nat* propitiated that *nat* no matter where he or she moved to. While the king ruled the temporal world, his deposed ancestors watched over the supernatural as guardians in a realm the former could never hope to control while alive.

Finally, like its temporal counterpart, the supernatural scheme had a king and queen in Min Mahāgiri and his sister, who were guardians of every household in the kingdom. Mahāgiri alone was known as the *einhsaung nat,* or "household guardian spirit," but was seldom propitiated or represented in iconography without his sister Shwe Myet Nhā ("Golden Face"). Mahāgiri's special symbol was the coconut, whose cooling juices soothed the pains of this *nat* who was burned to death by a former king.[20] Both from Tagaung, the city of mythical Burman origins, their images came to guard the main (eastern) gateway of Pagan as well as the Lion Throne of the Konbaung dynasty in nineteenth-century Mandalay. That the actual king and queen were often half brother and sister; that the term *nhama* was used for both younger sister and female spouse; and that the king and queen were revered by their subjects on the same occasion in which they themselves honored their own ancestors further support Mahāgiri's and his sister's role as the royal couple of the supernatural dynasty. They offered protection against the guardian spirits of temporal opponents to the throne, something that the throne could not, by itself, do. In addition, Mahāgiri and Shwe Myet Nhā, who is the daughter of the *nagi* (female guardian of the underworld), may have served the same type of function that the Kauṇḍinya legend did in Cambodia and that the *kalok-bau* combination of the Mons (male house guardian and female ancestress associated with rights to territory) did in Lower Burma.[21] In this sense, Mahāgiri and his sister were more than the spiritual parallels of the contemporary king and queen: they were also the supreme and permanent ancestors of the spirit world, with a degree of permanency that their temporal counterparts could never offer to society.

Thus the Thirty-Seven Nats provided continuity to and organization as well as assimilation of disparate groups and individuals who otherwise would have been disconnected by time, by place, and by structure from one another, thereby bonding the society's past leadership with the present, its regional loyalties with the "national," and its supernatural elements with its human ones.

Dhammarājika and *Kammarājika* Elements

The Dhammarāja

Despite all his associations with the divine and the supernatural, the Burmese king was compelled to assume a human posture but most often succeeded in taking on the role of a superhuman. There were many human models he could use, but only a few specific superhuman ones were available: namely, the *dhammarāja*, the *cakkavattī*, and the *kammarāja*.

The concept of the *dhammarāja* functioned in various ways in Burmese history. It was used to justify the creation of new dynasties, particularly at times of disorder; it was used when the king's duties as defender of the faith were needed to control a powerful *sangha;* it was used when his role as preserver of the social and political hierarchy, particularly as custodian of law, needed to be invoked; and lastly, it was used when his role as provider of the material welfare of his subjects was required to claim the resources of the kingdom.

The first king of the world was a human, Mahāsammata, who, for a share of the crops, promised to establish order out of the chaos that then existed. As such he was a *dhammarāja,* whose role included the preservation of the political and social order. The disorder in Burmese history that occurred between the destruction of one dynasty and the emergence of a new one was an ideal time for the presence of a *dhammarāja,* and those who did restore order would invariably link their genealogies to the Solar dynasty, of which Mahāsammata was founder. Both kings Kalancacsā and Narapatisithu traced their genealogies in this manner after quelling forces of rebellion or unifying disparate groups.[22]

The *dhammarāja* was more than a provider of political order, however; he, like the Indian Buddhist king Aśoka, the *dhammarāja* exemplified, must secure moral order as well. Force could be used to subdue rebellious subjects instead of moral suasion only if no other recourse were available. Because kingship, like the kingdom itself, was a political institution that had to be justified by certain Buddhist precepts concerning unavoidable war and killing, wars of unification became efforts "to seek the holy relics," proselytize Buddhism, and acquire the "pure scriptures." These were *dhammavijaya,* "righteous conquests." Aniruddha sacked Thaton in Lower Burma in the eleventh century because he was refused the "correct version of the Tipiṭakas" that he wanted. Even the writers of the *Slapat Rājawaṅ,* the royal chronicle of the Mons, who were the victims, stated that Aniruddha had come down to dig up the relics in Thaton because Buddhism had been destroyed by heretics and the king needed these objects to restore the faith in his own kingdom.[23] His unsuccessful attack on the Nanchao area was "to seek the holy tooth," rather than to secure his strategic military bases; his destruction of Śrī Kṣetra, the capital of the Pyus, was not to pacify or eliminate a potential nucleus for future rebellion but "to obtain the frontal-relic" of the Buddha.[24] And his subsequent securing of the western frontier with labor raids on Arakan were predictably described by the chroniclers as attempts to obtain the sacred Mahāmuni image kept there.[25] Even if the contemporary inscriptions that recorded these events never claimed the motives that the nineteenth-century writers suggested, at least the actions of Aniruddha as described in those contemporary sources implied the inclusion of religious motives, for he did indeed build pagodas and temples and endow them with land and labor wherever his military exploits took him.[26] Each major effort at expansion by King Aniruddha was thus made to appear as the work of the *dhammarāja* spreading the religion.

In Burma, then, *dhammavijaya* as a concept of righteous conquest was exploited to its maximum potential and incorporated processes that may have had little or no resemblance to its original Indian counterpart. It was used as part of unification and consolidation after periodic decline of central authority as well as for expansion and conquest, and it was invariably justified as being in "the interest of the Religion." Instead of using the *aśvamedha,* the so-called "horse sacrifice," which Indian kings used to expand their territories, the Burmese kings employed what seems to be a unique innovation: where the king's elephant stopped (usually in a politically sensitive area) a temple or monastery was erected and endowed with land and labor. Lack of opposition to the act—who in a Buddhist society would oppose the building of pagodas?—confirmed the king's suzerainty, or at least his hegemony.

Several monarchs in Pagan and post-Pagan history stand out in this respect. It is fairly certain that until the accession of Aniruddha, Pagan remained the headquarters of a small but growing kingdom whose authority remained in Upper Burma, the economic and political "nucleus." There is little evidence of Pagan institutions spreading beyond that core area prior to the mid-eleventh century; nor does any contemporary account, indigenous or external, mention Pagan's expansion and growth in power and prestige until then. With Aniruddha, inscriptions began to record his conquest of distant Thaton, votive tablets inscribed with his title are found in both the extreme north and south, temples blossomed on the dry plains of central Burma, and he was recognized by King Vijayabāhu I of Śrī Laṅka as a great Buddhist ally who aided the Singhalese revolt against the Cholas.[27] Kings Kalancacsā, Aloncañsū, and especially Narapatisithu followed similar strategies. Kalancacsā was known for emulating Aśoka's legendary program of temple building in places as far from the capital as Mergui on the Tenasserim coast, and even sending a mission to India to repair the Mahābodhi temple at Bodhgaya. Aloncañsū similarly was known for his far-flung travel from the capital and building and endowing temples with land and labor in areas of political significance. When Narapatisithu ascended the throne in the late twelfth century after a period of disorder, as part of his reunification process he travelled throughout the kingdom, worshipping at and repairing important pagodas, especially those in areas of uncertain allegiance. Perhaps the most explicit statement came from Mingyi Swasawke of the Ava dynasty, who in 1365 justified his claim to certain lands by declaring that he was doing so as a *dhammarāja:* "The state paddy-land . . . has not fallen into my possession because I was elected king . . . but was secured by right of conquest in the interests of the Religion. . . ."[28]

If the *dhammarāja*'s use of the religion to justify his military exploits was less than candid, his assumption of control over the *sangha* domestically was even better disguised. It was part of his duty as *dhammarāja* to insure that the religion last the prophesied five thousand years, and the most important method to accomplish this was to periodically purify the *sangha,* the custodians of the religion. For this, he had ample precedent in Aśoka's example and the *Kammavaca,* the text that provided the proper and detailed methodology for purification. By a pure *sangha* was meant one that abided by the *Vinaya* (its code of conduct), which included a vow of poverty as well as a rejection of the secular world and its (especially political and economic) affairs. A wealthy, politically active schismatic *sangha* invited royal intervention and possible purification. At least from Aniruddha onward (and there is evidence of his grandfather purifying the church), the *sangha* was periodically purged and reformed, assuring the survival of the religion on the one hand while on the other enabling the state to recover or at least to slow down the outward flow of its wealth, which was continuously moving into the tax-exempt sector.[29]

Not only religious law but secular law as well fell within the *dhammarāja*'s purview. He was the custodian of custom and civil law and the legislator and enforcer of criminal law. He supervised the implementation of the *dhammasatham* (in Burmese, *dhammathat*), or civil code, by providing a system of courts and judges. Even though civil law was not normally his major concern—since he was more custodian than legislator—there were public assurances of his desire to see that civil justice was met. For example, and again in accord with Burmese perceptions of Aśoka's performance as a king, a bell was hung outside the Hall of Audience and by ringing it anyone could theoretically request royal judgment on a grievance.[30] But his real domain was criminal law, since by definition it referred to crimes

against the state, literally, *rājasat,* the "king's business," formally
known as *rājāthat* in Burmese, which was taken from the Sanskrit
rājaśastra. Murder, arson, and rebellion were in the domain of *rājāthat.* To continually supplement and clarify the law, kings issued
edicts *(amintō)* that met more immediate needs. From the Pagan
dynasty, only King Klacwā's (1234–1249) edicts survive today.[31]
They show a monarch attempting to live up to the Aśokan *dhammarāja* ideal, admonishing his subjects with high-sounding moral
aphorisms. He recalled how "kings of old" (meaning those of classical Indian tales) meted out punishment with boiling oil and iron
spikes, all taken virtually verbatim from the *MāllālankāraVatthu* (a
work on the life and legend of Gaudama Buddha) and the *Milinda
Pañha* (Questions of King Menander). He urged his subjects to live
by Buddhist values and avoid the reinstatement of such punish-
ments. He implied that he would prefer to rule by moral suasion and
referred to himself by the Burmese equivalent of the *dhammarāja—
taryā man (taryā*=law, *man*=king).[32] His edicts did not contribute anything new to the corpus of criminal law; they merely reiterated the
need to preserve social harmony by doing one's duty.

The *dhammarāja* was expected to provide for the material as much
as for the moral and spiritual welfare of the people. By keeping the
granaries full, he insured that the natural political and social order, a
necessary corollary of the moral order, was not violated. But in order
to be successful, the *dhammarāja* needed to receive celestial help of the
kind that enabled kings like Kalancacsā to promise that "the rain
shall fall 120 times, all men, women, and children shall have length
of life, (be) free from sickness, exempt from calamity, from misfor-
tune, eat plenty of food, enjoy happiness. . . ."[33] Royal righteous-
ness inspired celestial intervention to sustain nature's bounty. The
material productivity of the kingdom therefore proved to the public
that the king was indeed ruling justly. As intermediary between
heaven and earth, the *dhammarāja* had to possess powers beyond
those acquired even through exemplary moral behavior—he had to
have been an extension of celestial deities.

The Cakkavattī

Technically separate from but conceptually related to the *dhammarāja*
was the *cakkavattī,* the "world conqueror" or "universal monarch."[34]
Because *dhammavijaya* took the *dhammarāja* into neighboring states

and political centers, he in fact already assumed the role made for the *cakkavattī*. With his jewelled disk called the *cakkaratana* and his white elephant, he conquers with his four-fold army (*caturaṅgā* in Old Burmese) the four quarters of the world, eventually reigning over no less than the entire island of Jambudīpa, where Buddhas are made and the only place from where *nibbāna* can be reached. He prepares Jambudīpa for Metteyya's return to preach the *dhammacakka*, the ultimate "first sermon." And he is one of only four beings who can be honored at death by a *thūpa* (stupa).

The term *cakkavattī* was not used indiscriminately for every king of Burma but was reserved for the great unifiers and stabilizers in Burmese history. King Aniruddha was called "*cakravartiy* Aniruddha" by posterity;[35] King Narapatisithu referred to his capital as "Jambudīpa, the southern Island, *in* [emphasis added] the golden country called Arimaddanapūra," thereby equating the kingdom of Pagan itself with the universe, since Jambudīpa was *one* of four main continents in the universe.[36] By ruling Arimaddanapūra, he ruled by implication the universe—a *cakkavattī*. King Narapatisithu referred to himself as "the great king who resembles the flaming *Nat*, the color of the sun, who resides on top of Jambudīpa."[37]

After the political demise of the Pagan kingdom, these conceptions of the *dhammarāja* and *cakkavattī* continued to influence political thought. In the sixteenth century, even when the kingdom had shifted its economic base and livelihood to include intensive trade— a change not to be taken lightly since it meant transformation of some of society's institutions, at least temporarily—King Bayinnaung of the Toungoo dynasty continued to associate his conquests with *dhammavijaya;* and when Alaunghpaya sent a royal order to his generals in 1755, he addressed himself as "the great Alaungmin Taya [the Embryo Buddha, King of the Law] the lord of Jambudipa."[38] His grandson called himself "the authority who is the happiness of all the *yahans* [monks] and people in the entire country, lord of the hundred umbrella wielding kings [and] the entire expanse of Jambudipa Island. . . ."[39]

If monarchs perceived themselves as superhuman, the people sometimes were reluctant to do so, even in public documents. In such cases, the king was reminded of his humanity, at least while he lived. One donor recorded on her inscription, "I want all *human* [emphasis added] from the King downwards to acquire merit . . . , I want all *brahma* and *nat* from Sakka downwards to benefit,"[40] conspicuously excluding the king from the ranks of *deva*s and Brahmas. Of course, kings could do very little about what posterity wrote of them, and folk epithets of royalty continued to creep into royal histories. King Kalancacsā, as we noted above, made extensive efforts to link himself with divinity, but the term *kalancacsā* only means "soldier-official"; the name for King Kalāgya is a reference to his being "felled by the *kalās*" (Indians); and Narathihapade was known to posterity as Tarokpliy Maṅ, "King who fled from the Chinese," and during his lifetime as Panpwat Sañ Mlī, "grandson of the carver."[41]

Sometimes the king himself alluded to his human, indeed, paternalistic role: Kalancacsā declared that he was like the father who wipes away the nasal mucus from the noses of his children.[42] In court and tributary relations, kinship terms were used to further the image of human rather than superhuman relationships: the princes of the royal family would address ministers as *bhui bhui* ("grandfather") or *bha bha* ("father").[43] The terms *chuṁma* ("to punish") and *malimmā bhū* ("naughty") were used when King Maṅkhoṅ of Ava referred to a rebellion by one of his provincial governors, terms normally reserved for familial situations.[44] Kings also addressed tributary chiefs as *ññi tō* ("younger brother") or *noṅ tō* ("elder brother").[45] Shan or Mon chieftains were called "elder brother" by the Burman king, who was in turn addressed as "younger brother."[46] (The Four Buddhas of this *kappa* are often called "elder brothers" of Metteyya, who is considered the "younger brother," which explains the incongruity of the statement considering the relationship between the usually dominant Burmans and the less so Shans and Mons.) It was only at death, natural or violent, that kings came closest to being divine, for they were then said to have "departed to *nat rwā,*" the abode of the *nat*s. Because *kamma* can accumulate as well as dissipate, human attributes could be appropriate even for superhuman kings.

The Kammarāja

The term *kammarāja* is a relatively modern one, created most probably by Robert Heine-Geldern as an analytical concept. As such, it is not in the same category as either the *dhammarāja* or the *cakkavattī*. Yet it so appropriately expresses the components of a superhuman king that it is used here in that sense. The *kammarāja* was the person with the most abundant store of merit among lay people, and was therefore the ultimate (non-monk) superhuman.

Whether the king acquired his status by royal birth or at the persuasion of the gods, it was *kamma* that legitimized kingship and created the *kammarāja*. Success justified position. But as such, *kamma* was a double-edged sword, for it encouraged on the one hand the preservation of the political and social status quo—by saying in effect that one was born into one's position in life because of past *kamma* and therefore should not change it—while on the other, it allowed successful attempts at changing that status quo, justifying them ex post facto. One's birthright and hereditary succession were sacred social principles, but violation of those principles, if successful, was also acceptable under *kamma*'s logic. Kammic inevitability was actually changeable.

The story of Caw Rahan's accession epitomizes the process by which the *kammarāja* was made. He became king by having killed the reigning monarch, who had inadvertently plucked a cucumber from his garden. The chroniclers explained that "although in verity King Sawyahan [Caw Rahan] should have utterly perished, having killed a king while he was yet a farmer, he attained even to kingship simply by strong *karma* of his good acts done in the past."[47]

However, this idea created other conceptual problems that Burmese society had to address. Because one normally competed for the throne with one's kin, kinship ties—highly valued—and the political necessity of fratricide and patricide were always in conflict. The solution to the problem is illustrated by the following story. After King Aniruddha had killed his brother in fair combat for the throne, he could not sleep. Sakka consequently visited him in a dream and said:

> O King, if thou wouldst mitigate thine evil deed in sinning against thine elder brother, build many pagodas, *gu,* monasteries, and rest houses, and share the merit with thine elder brother. Devise thou many wells, ponds, dams, and ditches, fields and canals, and share the merit with thine elder brother.[48]

The political necessity of shedding kinsmen's blood could thus be atoned in part by meritorious acts. Murder, instead of being compensated by more narrow, tribal methods of blood vengeance, could be redeemed by good works that benefited not only the party wronged but the entire society whose laws it violated.

Usurpation could be similarly rectified. Because King Kalancacsā was not of the royal line, he gained partial legitimacy by completing the Shwezigon Pagoda begun by Aniruddha, thereby assuring his predecessor a place in the world of *deva*s by the merit acquired while also securing for himself certain rights to the throne. Legitimacy for those not appointed heir could be acquired by preserving, protecting, and promoting the religion and tradition as well as by pursuing temporal projects that enhanced the material needs of the people. Works of merit condoned the "sin" of regicide and justified one's present status. At the same time, building monuments and canals further reinforced the collectivistic tendencies and structure of economic redistribution and integrated them to the ideology of kammatic Buddhism.

Allowing success to be its own justifier meant, however, that hereditary right as a principle was being undermined. To solve this conceptual problem, the intervention of deities was considered relevant in determining the legitimacy of certain political events. The *Glass Palace Chronicle* records that when Kloṅ Phlū rode the magic horse and wore the ruby ring and ruby hairpin, carrying the lance and sword of royalty given to him by Sakka, who was disguised as an old man, everyone bowed down to Kloṅ Phlū as if he were the future king, for whom everyone, including Kloṅ Phlū himself, was waiting. It was then that the reigning king, Caw Rahan, demanding to know who dared to impersonate a king while he lived, was pushed down and killed by a stone statue. The people then bowed down to Kloṅ Phlū, according to the chronicle, because he "shone radiant with the ornaments of Sakra like the sun-child new arisen."[49] In other words, although Caw Rahan's rise to kingship had been originally legitimized by his *kamma* (from gardener to king), his deposition was similarly justified, but qualified by Sakka's intervention. When Aniruddha and his elder brother Sokkate battled each other for the throne, Aniruddha parried Sokkate's spear with the *areindama* lance, "Sakka's weapon," and won the battle.[50] In this case, both had been rightful heirs because of their royal birth—in fact Sokkate being the elder had prior rights—so the outcome was again left to the intervention of celestial deities.

The various conceptual dilemmas, then—of accepting successful usurpers while those legitimately installed still lived, of kin killing kin, and of settling disputes between equally legitimate contenders —were "explained" by invoking the Law of Kamma but also by insisting that the endorsement of celestial deities was needed. Kings were expected to behave in extreme ways, for their position was extraordinary; explanations were equally stretched.

Kingship and Charisma

Although ideologies were proclaimed in ritual, recreated in monuments, announced in titles, and confirmed by inexplicable and supernatural phenomena, the personality of the king was another highly important medium of expressing legitimacy. How did he show it in his personality? How was it manifest? This is where the supernatural, divine, and human characteristics coalesce, in the charisma of the *kammarāja*.

As discussed in chapter 2, a person who is believed to have a great store of merit is called *phungrī* "(one with) great glory," a term normally applied to monks. And, as we have noted, the word also has political and nonreligious connotations. A person with, shall we say, "political" *phun* (or *guṇ*) is recognized by his personality as much as by his position; that is, a monk already possesses *phun* because of his position and by virtue of his role as a "field-of-merit," whether or not he is drab and dull. But a layperson with *phun* in the political sense must be exciting, electrifying, with a magnetic personality and an intensity that is a little fearsome—what we have come to call charismatic. A truly legitimate king, in addition to possessing the correct hereditary credentials and supernatural signs, should effuse these qualities, should show evidence of an exemplary personality to fit his station. The charismatic leader in Burmese contexts is a political field-of-merit surrounded by the politically "unmusical"—who support and emulate him, who use him as a means to enhance their own status, who extract and share his *phun* merely by being in his presence—much as the monk is a religious field-of-merit surrounded by the spiritually unmusical.[51]

It has been argued that charismatic leadership is a form of crisis leadership, that charismatic leaders appear at times of crises, and they do so not necessarily because of the absence of leadership institutions but because of their default.[52] In early Burma, however, it was not so much the absence of leadership institutions—such as precisely defined rules of succession—or even their default at times when they were most needed that produced charismatic leaders. It was because legitimation in the context of *kamma*'s double-edged sword approved both proper succession and successful usurpation *at the same time!* Theoretically, kingship is an institution, a form of established, hereditary leadership accepted by the culture as legitimate, whereas charismatic leadership is derived spontaneously. It is supposed to be noninstitutionalized, at least to the same extent or in the same manner that hereditary kingship is institutionalized. Yet, in Burma, to have been an effective king, great in glory, one had to be more than just a prince in line for the throne, inheriting an office only by virtue of birth. In a court and kingdom where the conception of *kamma* encouraged successful action and where leadership had to be demonstrated in one's personality as well, the institution of kingship itself required noninstitutionalized (i.e., charismatic) criteria of leadership. The political culture demanded that leaders possess that magic found in charismatic personalities as unequivocal proof of legitimacy.

To add some historical facts to these perceptions, let us look at the most successful kings of the Pagan dynasty. In a political context such as Pagan's, the length as well as the stability of a monarch's reign were a fair indication of his ability. Of these monarchs, the most stable and longest reigns belonged not to those kings who had obtained their office necessarily by institutionalized means (appointment as heir apparent) but to those who had apparently seized it by force, in a manner characteristic of charismatic leaders. Of the nine kings of Pagan who ruled from the eleventh to the thirteenth centuries—the period of importance—on whom we have relevant inscriptional information, eight were, it seems, *not* in immediate or direct line to the throne. With one, at the most, two exceptions, those who obtained the office of king were neither clearly royal nor, if royal, relatively close to the order of succession and certainly not *de jure* heirs apparent.[53] The most successful of early Burma's kings were those charismatic mavericks who were most effective in a climate of political intrigue where success and personality played critical roles.

This pattern actually created more order than one might expect, for the mere existence of such a leader tended to stabilize Burmese politics, because the officeholder gave that ultimate proof of competence. Indeed, the existence of a dynamic king had the necessary effects upon the viability of law, morality, loyalty, and even on occasion the ownership of property—the legality of which became ambiguous once that type of leadership was perceived to have ended. It was ironic, though, that new kings had to persuade the public that edicts of past kings were to be considered valid, that the office not the person should be regarded as the ultimate authority. This contradiction or tension between the political system's creation of charismatic personalities on the one hand while there was a need for permanency of office that went beyond personalities on the other remains, I think to this day, a part of Burmese politics. In fact, the stability created by strong personalities itself may have fostered the kinds of chaotic conditions that inevitably erupted when such leadership waned, in turn creating precisely the kind of atmosphere that attracted the same kinds of leaders once more.

During such crises, another form of charismatic leadership ideology prevailed, the ideology of the *min laung,* Burma's version of a messiah or immanent king, closely linked to the ideology of revolt and rebellion. It incorporated the principal features of the different conceptions of kingship that have been discussed while challenging the established order's right to rule. In times of political chaos when central authority was effete; in times of social and economic stress when the rapacity of government exceeded its culturally defined share; and in time of religious decay when the symbols and indicators of a moral world were clearly meaningless and inadequate the society expected a *min laung* to appear and rectify the situation. Revolts and rebellions in these contexts were not true revolutions, for the transformation of the institutions in society were not the ultimate goals sought; rather the custodians of those institutions were to be replaced by more able ones. The concern of Burmese society was not so much the tyranny of leadership but the ineffectiveness of leaders to maintain order.[54]

A successful *min laung* had to possess features not only of a *dhammarāja* but those of a *devarāja* and *kammarāja* as well. For the *min laung,* too, the rules of *kamma* applied, and his success or failure was as much a measure of his legitimacy as that of the more established candidates. In fact, *kamma*'s double-edged sword, justifying the status quo as well as change, worked in the interest of the rebels (who were often princes) almost as much as it did for any heir apparent. What the *min laung* ideology did among other things was to make government accountable, for it knew that the *min laung* was the banner for legitimate revolts and that the *min laung*'s goals were, like those of the *dhammarāja, devarāja,* and *kammarāja,* in one way or another, also to create heaven or paradise on earth and thus equally salvationist, with the same appeal. In short, the ideology of dissent partook of the same ingredients that sustained the system.

In summary, it was essentially formal Buddhist ideology that kept the king human, while often contrary beliefs in the supernatural capabilities of dead royalty and other *devarājika* components bestowed semidivine status on him. The propitiation of ancestors who traced their lineage to the Solar dynasty to which the Buddha belonged and the deification of royalty who had died violent deaths as well as the belief in *devas*, who were either reincarnated as kings or intervened in royal affairs, continually pressured Burmese political ideology to deify the king. But Buddhism "insisted" that the king remain human, for even Buddha was man, not god. This amalgam —of being a deity, a human, and superhuman—may seem technically contradictory but was very much part of the political culture of Burma as legitimating and necessary components of Burmese kingship. For those who lived in a state whose raison d'être was established by the daily reenactment of this tripartite system and its ideologies, the similarities among the divisions were probably far more meaningful than their analytical differences are to us.

PART II

The Institutional Context: Organization of Human and Material Resources

4

The Division of
Socioeconomic Groups

IF, BEFORE THE EMERGENCE of cities and kingdoms in Burma, people living in the area that was to become the Kingdom of Pagan had organized themselves into communities linked by kin and other sociolinguistic ties, by the early days of the Pagan kingdom those associations had been superseded by political, religious, and economic ones as well, and their new relationships had been codified into law. The pool of human resources that made up the Kingdom of Pagan, estimated at one and a half to two million at its height, included Burmans, Mons, and Shans—who had the dominant political role—as well as Chins, Kachins, Arakanese, Karens, and Indians in less dominant positions.[1] This diverse conglomeration was organized according to a horizontal (class) and vertical (patron-client) structure.[2] The horizontal category had three major class divisions. The largest one consisted of commoners, followed by an upper and lower officialdom, on top of which was the royal family and the court. The vertical arrangement of patron-client ties cut across the horizontal one, according to roughly similar concerns—birth, occupation, political power, spiritual rank—and in the process gave the society its division of labor. The two most important features of Pagan social organization, the principles on which it rested, were hierarchy and cellularity. Thus social organization, like political organization in Pagan, was conical (like a cone) in that all the human resources of the kingdom were organized according to hierarchic, horizontal, and cellular principles (see Fig. 2). Rank in the society and the central position in the cell were determined largely, though not exclusively, by one's political, genealogical, and economic proximity to the throne on the one hand and spiritual distance from Buddhahood on the other. The court and officialdom as well as the *sangha*—patrons in Burmese society—are discussed in fol-

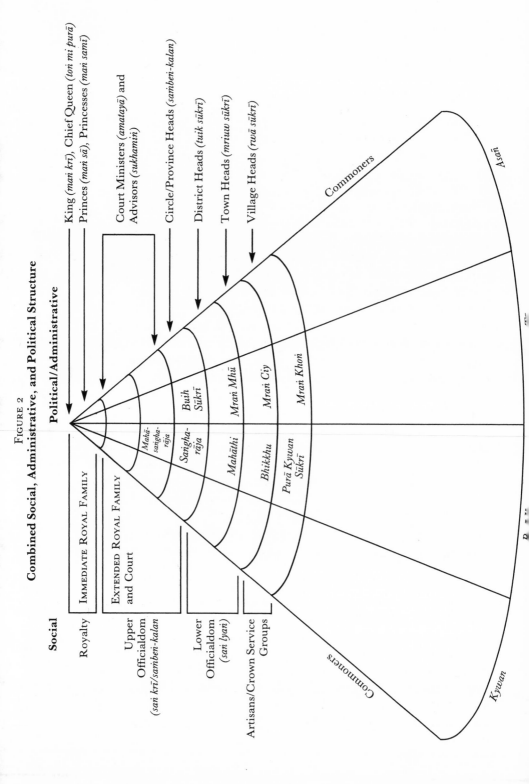

FIGURE 2
Combined Social, Administrative, and Political Structure

Social

Royalty

IMMEDIATE ROYAL FAMILY

EXTENDED ROYAL FAMILY
and Court

Upper
Officialdom
(*san krī/samben-kalan*)

Lower
Officialdom
(*san lyan*)

Artisans/Crown Service
Groups

Political/Administrative

King (*man krī*), Chief Queen (*ton mi purā*)
Princes (*man sā*), Princesses (*man samī*)

Court Ministers (*amatayā*) and
Advisors (*sukhamin*)

Circle/Province Heads (*samben-kalan*)

District Heads (*tuik sūkrī*)

Town Heads (*mruw sūkrī*)

Village Heads (*rwā sūkrī*)

Commoners

Maha-
saingha-
rāja

Saingha-
rāja

Mahāthi

Bhikkhu

Purā Kyuvan
Sūkrī

Buih
Sūkrī

Mran Mhū

Mran Ciy

Mran Khon

Commoners

Kyuvan

Asañ

lowing chapters on administrative and political structure. This chapter focuses on the clients and their organization, which comprised the commoners, the bulk of Burmese society.

Commoners had no genealogical links to royalty, little official rank or status in the administrative apparatus, and no real political or economic power as individuals. Most were cultivators or engaged in related agricultural pursuits, even though there was specialization of function in agriculture and a variety of occupations outside it. At the top sectors of the horizontal commoner class were artisans and elite crown service troops, enjoying a higher social ranking than most cultivators. Above them were their headmen, who, although of higher social rank, actually belonged to the same general class. In a social sense, the lower echelons of the *sangha* should be included also, for the ordinary monk who resided in the village monastery invariably came from this class. And like the ordinary headman of the village who was in most cases an elder among his peers, the monk's counterpart, the abbot of the village monastery, should be regarded in a similar manner. In a sense, however, the *sangha* belongs neither in this class—for as a class, it was more patron than client—nor in the social structure, for it was considered, at least theoretically, to be divorced from secular society. One can perhaps regard the diagram of the *sangha*'s structure as a separate section of dotted lines on the cone parallel to the others being described.

This large commoner class was linked to the very top of the structure, the royal family and court, by the upper ranks of what I have called the lower officialdom. These were township and district officials, who were ultimately responsible to the court through the provincial officials, most of whom were court appointees. In most cases, it appears that the township and district heads were local, probably hereditary, leaders who, however, had their offices confirmed by the center through seals and appointment papers. Their names were preceded by the title *san lyan* ("subordinate *san*") indicating their social rank. The personal names of those in the same class also ended with the suffix *san,* which revealed their social position. The provincial heads were part of what I have called the upper officialdom, consisting of the highest officials of the kingdom including those of the court whose names were similarly preceded by the term *san krī* ("big *san*"). Like their subordinates, they too had the suffix *san* attached to their personal names. Indeed, many royalty shared this mark of distinction. Some were members of the immediate as well as distant royalty who enjoyed their offices at the pleasure of the king. The class of district and township leaders that linked the commoners with the court was quite clearly very small, and some of them might as well have been high-ranking commoners. At this level too were its counterparts in the *sangha* hierarchy, the abbots of town and provincial monasteries, who were linked via their representative, the primate, to the top. (The administrative roles of these upper-level officials and monks will be discussed more completely in subsequent chapters.)

This entire horizontal section was cut vertically by several parallel patron-client columns of crown, glebe, and private categories, bonded and nonbonded functional specialists that provided the society with its division of labor. The patron-client structure was based essentially upon certain principles concerning obligation, what I have called kywanship, that will be discussed below. The entire commoner class was further provided with some concrete organization according to a third dimension: cellularity. This was the way in which people were geographically arranged mainly, though not exclusively, according to their occupational specialty, their social-spiritual status, and sometimes their ethnolinguistic backgrounds as well. This "cellular" pattern was used both on a large scale (organization of villages) as well as on a small scale (organization of work teams).

The Organization of People

The commoner class in Pagan was organized into four main groups: *asañ,* who were unbonded; *kywan,* those bonded to private individuals; *purā kywan,* people commended to religious institutions; and *kywan-tō,* those attached to the crown. These were legal categories that defined what were in essence economic functions but had social, political, and religious roles as well. This structure gave the Kingdom of Pagan its general division of labor, its method of harnessing its human and material resources, and the way by which its people were physically distributed.

Although there is virtually no evidence to shed any light on the exact numbers that served in each of these divisions of society—which could and did change with historical circumstances in any case—it appears that the bulk of the work considered important by the state and society was accomplished either by bonded groups or those temporarily under similar circumstances. Yet one should not conclude from this that the state therefore practiced a rigid, monolithic "Oriental Despotism" with no institutions to balance its power, or as a result that the lot of the individual in Pagan society was less than desirable. On the contrary, not only were there idealogical as well as socioreligious institutions that disallowed the abuse of power, the individual's lot in Burmese society was better in a patron-client context than it was in one without such ties. The reason for this lay in the meaning of bondage in early Burmese society.

The Meaning of "Bondage" in Burma

Since we invariably carry certain assumptions in our intellectual "baggage," it needs, on occasion, to be opened and inspected. These assumptions usually include conclusions about institutions such as bondage, what I have called "kywanship" in the case of Burma, that reveal a fundamental a priori democratic bias.[3] Let me be more specific.

If the ultimate value of a society rests on the political freedom of the individual, tyranny, more than anything else, becomes its major concern. The amount of political freedom from tyranny an individual has becomes the measure for the intrinsic worth of that individual. If, however, the ultimate value of a society rests on the *stability* of the *group,* then disorder more than tyranny becomes the primary concern. And under such circumstances, the condition and intrinsic worth of the group is measured not by the amount of individual freedom there is, expressed as disorder, but by the predominance of order, expressed as the preservation of group priorities. If the latter principle represents the assumptions upon which Burmese society was based—and so far, everything I have studied about Burma suggests that it does—then the amount of political freedom a *kywan* (a bonded person) possessed should not be either the measure or the focus of kywanship (obligation); rather, the extent to and way in which kywanship preserved the integrity and stability of the group should be. Kywanship asks the question "To whom are you bonded and for what purpose?" not "*Are* you bonded?" The answer reveals the individual's place in the hierarchy, determined by the importance of his or her function in the group rather than by the degree of political freedom that person has, on a scale ranging from full rights under the law to none at all. The issue, then, is not individual political freedom but the function that bondage played in the attempt to eliminate disorder or anarchy. The role of the individual in Burma, rather than "to go on his own"—which in a sense characterizes a person with no clear group ties, something undesirable—was to find a niche in the established order, for the ultimate goal of Burmese social organization was to preserve the group by *not* creating a society composed of individuals. (The rebel in Burma was the individual who rejected not so much these principles but his place in the hierarchy.) As order in a democratic society is preserved by balancing the rights and interests of individuals with those of society as a whole, in a society without inherent concerns about democracy or tyranny, order is preserved by maintaining an unambiguous hierarchy. In Pagan, it was the group that assumed, absorbed, and "redistributed," if you will, individual rights.

These rights were not the kind guaranteed in a democracy by law but privileges assured when an agreement between patron and client was reached. Kywanship promised social security, economic opportunity, family stability, social and political status, political mobility, and in some cases, even a better rebirth. One chose bondage ultimately for a better life. The critical distinction between bonded and nonbonded persons, therefore, was a difference in *modus operandi* for accomplishing one's general goals in life. Kywanship was expressed in the term *akyan ci,* which occurs appropriately in the law codes.[4] In Pagan, it probably meant "commendation" or "pledged," for the word *ci* of *akyan ci* (spelled *ciy* in Pagan) on numerous occasions was contrasted to the word *lhwat,* meaning "to redeem" or "to release," suggesting a context in which one is *not* redeemed or released; namely, legal obligation, indentureship, commendation.[5] King Klacwā's edict of the mid-thirteenth century confirmed the distinction between commendation and free agent status when it stated: "it is fitting for one commended (? *akyan sañ*) to gain one's livelihood . . . by 'eating' assigned (? *khla cā*) (land), (working on) streams, wet-fields, dry-fields, gardens, tanks, and businesses; or, by one's own industry . . ." (i.e., independently).[6] Kywanship in practice, then, was a situation whereby certain people had a legal, clientelistic relationship to others, mainly to perform economic services.

For those seeking bondage voluntarily, there were two forms of patron-client relationships: between individuals (known as a dyadic relationship) and between individuals and institutions (known as a corporate relationship).[7] There were no absolute dyadic relations of consequence in the kingdom, however, because the central authority had already established corporate relationships with everyone by categorizing society into the divisions already mentioned. Even if a person voluntarily commended himself to an individual patron as in a dyadic situation, it was in fact a corporate relationship, because the latter (the patron's) corporate status had already been defined by the state. For example, although a person commends himself in a dyadic relationship to a minister, the minister was already part of a corporate relationship vis-à-vis the state. Similarly with those persons commended to the *sangha:* although they were technically obligated to a head monk of a particular monastery and to a group of monks, legally they already belonged to a category of exempt (glebe) labor called *purā kywan* and were, therefore, organizational subordinates. Dyadic relationships in Pagan were fitted into an overriding corporate one.

What this suggests is that patron-client ties in general did not create a "feudal," manorial system, where independent lords and their retainers controlled and administered a particular territory in a politically fragmented atmosphere. Whatever political fragmentation patron-client relations may create in theory, in Pagan these relationships and their distinctions were meaningful primarily (if not only) within the context of an overarching authority, the monarchy, without which patron-client ties were of little legal or political consequence.

There was another form of kywanship: one that was formed involuntarily. It was usually the result of debt, conquest, or birth. Whether one became bonded voluntarily or involuntarily—someone brought back to the capital as a prisoner-of-war as opposed to someone who chose to become a *kywan* for whatever reason, ranging from poverty to ease of livelihood and merit making—usually made a legal difference. It was a factor in determining one's redeemability or the ability to legally change to non-*kywan* or different *kywan* status. (Redemption does not necessarily carry with it a moral judgment implying political freedom; here it is only a legal definition similar to today's "free agent status" of professional athletes who have been "released" from their prior obligations.) In short, kywanship was both personal and organizational (though largely organizational) as well as voluntary and involuntary (though largely voluntary).

The choice of patron for those voluntarily seeking kywanship depended upon general social, political, and economic conditions in the society as well as the client's own particular situation. In times of war, particularly if it were sustained and unsuccessful, people very likely preferred to be bonded to the *saṅgha* or even to private individuals rather than to the crown. But there were no more than a dozen occasions of statewide mobilization for war during the entire thousand-year precolonial period, with most of the evidence that showed a desire to leave crown service occurring at times of war or crises. Under normal conditions and in most cases, then, *asañ* who wanted a patron would not find it in their interests to bond themselves to private individuals, for under private patronage, artists and skilled craftsmen became no more than domestic servants. In contrast, the *saṅgha* and crown made far more attractive employers; they paid best, utilized and publicized one's skills most effectively, and offered their clients higher social, political, and in the case of the *saṅgha*, even spiritual status. That may further explain why many unbonded artisans and other skilled people preferred commendation itself over "free enterprise" in general.[8]

Such preference for royal and religious bondage has implications for certain theoretical concerns in Southeast Asian history. It has often been argued that large movements of people from the crown to the nobility tended to upset the balance of wealth in the Southeast Asian state, because wealth, hence power, was labor.[9] This interpretation needs some qualification on at least two points if it is going to be useful for other areas of Southeast Asia. First, the presence of a fairly large, economically independent noble or elite class with adequate landed estates to absorb the alleged influx of people into its domain must be documented. Second, there must be shown compelling reasons, defined by indigenous criteria of what was "compelling," for people to leave the crown sector for private sectors. Simply saying that crown obligation was onerous, usually at times of crisis, does not take into account its more favorable status under normal conditions.

The only two corporate "recruiters" (and possessors) of manpower in Burma, holding numbers that were economically and politically significant and documented by the most numerous examples of kywanship, were the state and *saṅgha,* not a class of nobility, whose existence itself is unproved. Certainly there was an elite officialdom in Burma, consisting of prominent families who may have owned some land and had servants, but that they were a permanently landed class and large enough to absorb significant movements of people is undocumented. The largest acreage and best lands that could sustain such a labor influx were held only by the state and *saṅgha*. This means that the issue of competition for labor in Southeast Asia is, in Burma, centered not between the crown and nobility but between crown and *saṅgha* and is therefore politically and economically meaningful only when these two groups are involved. Whatever elites, nobility or not, there may have been, they were in any case not an independent corporate group that competed (structurally or ideologically) with the state—they were *part* of the state.

Finally, in a society governed by a semibureaucratic central government not normally characterized as a "feudalized" system where politically and economically independent nobles provided the only government there was, and one where the economic and social benefits were better in government service, neither personal nor political "security" were compelling reasons for individuals to seek shelter, protection, and wealth with private individuals. Bonded status per se did not imply inferiority to nonbonded status, essentially because the real concerns in Burma—disorder and anarchy—placed a higher value on bondage. Economic and social independence not dependence was conceptually synonymous with lawlessness and inferiority. The "escape from bondage" thesis thus rests on a priori conclusions about bondage itself and derives its evidence mainly from times of crisis, not representative of normal conditions.

Asañ: Nonbonded Commoners

Because democratic proclivities often compel one to automatically categorize any person not bonded as "free," nonbonded persons in Pagan, known as *asañ,* had always been regarded as freeborn persons. Along with that conclusion a value judgment was invariably made about that status; namely, that they must have been superior to those not free. Yet, the word *asañ* does not mean free, nor were the people it described freeborn persons in a feudal sense. *Asañ* is, rather, a neutrally descriptive term, and its meaning in the context of "medieval" Burmese society may be best recaptured by simply presenting the functions and characteristics, the status and rank, and perhaps even discussing briefly the etymology of the word.

One who bakes is a baker, one who drives a driver, and one who

sells, a seller. Just as the suffix "er" attached to bake, drive, and sell
makes a noun out of these verbs and one becomes the "doer" of each
verb, in Pagan—and later Burmese history—such a doer in general
was called *asañ,* the *a* representing the noun that the *sañ* modifies.
Thus, with *kun* or "merchandize" it becomes *kun sañ,* "merchant";
with *mun,* "baked goods," a *mun sañ,* baker; with *kuhā,* "wash," a
kuhā sañ, "washerman," and so on. Midwives were *lak sañ;* "boat-
men" *lhawkā sañ;* palanquin carriers, *sanlyañ sañ;* preserved fish pro-
ducers, *pi sañ* (from *ṅga pi*).[10]

On a higher economic and probably social scale, but still classified
as *asañ,* were artisans and craftsmen. Some were no longer simply
sañ or doers, but *smā,* "experts" at whatever occupation the *smā* was
attached to, such as carpenters *(lak smā)* and masons *(puran smā).*
Asañ craftsmen and artisans were extremely independent, working
on contract and paid well in cash and kind. We find in the inscriptions woodcarvers *(panpu sañ),* artists *(panklī sañ),* woodturners *(panpwat sañ),* brickmakers *(ut sañ),* blacksmiths *(panphay sañ),* sculptors
(purā sañ, literally "doer" of the *purā* or Buddha), temple-finial
makers *(htī sañ),* and gold- and silversmiths *(rhuy sañ* and *ṅuy sañ).*[11]
But not all *asañ* were craftsmen, artisans, or skilled laborers; many
were engaged in agriculture. Their occupations did not determine
the difference between them and bonded groups, for there were
crown and glebe cultivators, artisans, and craftsmen as well.[12] This
was determined by their tax obligations: *asañ* normally paid per
capita tax in cash or kind, computed by a complex system of households and occupations, but not in service, while the crown bonded
groups, usually in lieu of tax, paid in service. In return, the latter,
especially if in the military, received choice royal lands to work, live
on, or "eat."[13] Those bonded to the *saṅgha* were, of course, exempt.

Asañ status varied. Socioeconomic distinctions existed as much
between different levels of *asañ* (village headman and salt-fish producer) as between *asañ* and bonded persons of the same general class
(salt-fish producer and cavalry soldier). Thus, some *asañ* were headmen and some the lowest hawkers of wares while others owned land
with the potential to become upper officialdom, even to marry into
the royal family. But the latter were an exception. Moreover, by
most accounts those who worked for the crown as bondsmen, particularly those who were in the military, were considered superior in
status to *asañ.*

Asañ status was also related to ethnic background. Although there is no certain method to determine whether *asañ* were always non-Burmans—and if so to which ethnic group they belonged—the words for artisan skills (such as *panpu*) were either Mon in origin or Mon adaptations of south Indian words. This relationship may have stemmed from Aniruddha's conquest in the mid-eleventh century of the Mon kingdom of Thaton in Lower Burma, when he brought back with him the bulk of the Mon population, including large numbers of the artisan class. Also in Pagan and post-Pagan Burmese society, the personal names of most *asañ* suggest a non-Burman background, while those of crown servants were largely ethnic Burman names. Even during the late eleventh century when Mon cultural influence was at a peak, ethnic Burmans enjoyed the highest social and political status. It seems, therefore, that *asañ* as a category within the larger class of commoners (not necessarily as individuals) held a status *lower* than that of crown bondsmen precisely because of their conceptual proximity (racially, culturally, physically) to the crown.[14] The criteria for rank and status—and as a result, presumably for happiness and well-being—had little to do with personal economic or political freedom of the kind with which we are familiar.

Kywan: Private Bondage

The origin of the word *kywan* is obscure. It may have come from the Mon word *klon,* "to work," in part verified by an early spelling of *kywan* on the Myazedi Inscription of A.D. 1112, where it was written as *klon.* G. H. Luce has suggested on phonetic grounds that the word may have been derived from other Tibeto-Burman words meaning "captive."[15] Others, like Hla Pe, have tied it in a similar sense to the word *chum* in Maru, another Tibeto-Burman language.[16] By the sixteenth century, a Mon inscription recorded that "the whole country of the Mons became subjected [*kywan phrac*]" when Lower Burma was conquered.[17] Under a monarchy with a king who was considered "lord of land and water," everyone in the kingdom was theoretically a subject (therefore *kywan*) of the king. By the immediate precolonial period, the word had come to mean "slave." Although in Pagan, its general meaning may have been "servant" or "subject" (as one donor stated, "I too am a servant [*kywan*] of the Three Gems"),[18] the word had several more specific meanings, depending upon the context.

The precise obligations of ordinary *kywan* to their individual patrons of course varied—dependent usually on the *kywan*'s skills—but the essence of the relationship between *kywan* and patron was based on what was known in European history as the prebend: service in exchange for a share of or rights to produce and/or land. In Pagan, this included domestic services of *im̀ kywan* (household servants) in a type of relationship Marc Bloch has described with regard to Europe: one takes the man (whose service is desired) "into one's household, to feed and clothe him . . . to grant him in return for his services an estate, which, if exploited directly or in the form of dues levied on the cultivators of the soil, would enable him to provide for himself."[19] Most ordinary *kywan* were domestic servants, bodyguards, or members of the general entourage of a rich person—or partners and co-workers in a situation where both patron and client were poor. If they were skilled in a craft, however, their obligations were sometimes transferred by their patron to the *sangha*. The transfer could be permanent, in which case the *sangha* became the patron, or it could be temporary—that is, only the services of the *kywan* would be given while the owner retained the legal rights to the *kywan*. In such cases of transfer—whether permanent or temporary —the *kywan* in practice, though not legally, became a *purā kywan* (glebe bondsman) and for all other purposes ceased to be an ordinary *kywan*.

Whether or not *kywan* status was hereditary depended upon the circumstances surrounding the nature of the bondage itself. Simply because a *kywan* could be moved like property from one owner to another or from one village to another did not necessarily mean that the status itself was hereditary.[20] It is true that on the death of a patron, his *kywan* could be passed on to his descendants,[21] but the *kywan* could still redeem *(ruy)* himself if he were willing and able or have someone else redeem him, as one king redeemed three sons of a woman for thirty irrigated fields.[22] In fact, inheritance law disallowed children of debtor *kywan* to inherit their parent's status, stating in effect that a person's obligations ceased with death and could not be perpetuated, at least in these types of cases.[23] *Kywan* and their descendants derived from the spoils of war and *purā kywan* and their descendants were the only ones whose heritable status seems relatively clear.

In exceptional instances (about two in two hundred years), magnanimous patrons absolved their *kywan* of all obligations by simply releasing them. As one woman stated: "I did not dedicate these *kywan* to the Three Gems; I did not give them to my relatives. . . . When I am dead, let them go to where the grass is tender and the water clear."[24] She then placed a curse on those people most likely to violate her wishes, namely her relatives. The curses were backed by laws that explicitly forbade such violations: "Those who have been . . . [released] by their master," noted one law, "cannot be . . . [bonded] by their children."[25] Whatever the case may be, hereditary status in general implied security and stability.

That economic difficulties sometimes drove people to seek security in bondage is seen in the following case. When a toddy-palm climber in 1228 "commended his wife and two daughters to a minister," it was because, he stated, "I had become poor and broke."[26] In return, the toddy-palm climber received "the price" from the minister, who also settled accounts with the former's creditors and redeemed the toddy-palm climber's own *kywan,* who then became servants of the minister. By paying the price for redemption of any *kywan,* one became a patron, as testified to by the person who stated that he "got the *kywan* . . . by redeeming" them.[27] In another case, because their parents had died, two brothers sought a patron and became his *kywan.*[28] In these types of cases resulting from poverty or debt, the agreement made between a voluntary *kywan* and his patron usually stipulated the nature of the service to be performed and the exact amount to be paid for it. It was legally binding, complete with written contracts, witnesses, and an exchange of money. In fact, there were people called *kywan sañ,* brokers apparently, who specialized in the business of *kywan.*[29]

Sometimes, the inscriptions record people being bought and sold. Our immediate reaction is "slavery!" Closer scrutiny, however, suggests that whether one was bought or hired had little to do with one's relative status, for people who were clearly hired for wages were also called *kywan,*[30] while in one case a man even referred to his wife and children as "my *kywan.*"[31] Buying also involved a legal contract made between the *kywan* and his buyer, stipulating that the *kywan* remained with the patron until the price of redemption had been paid. It was more an employer/employee rather than master/slave relationship, suggesting that the words "to buy" *(we)* or to hire *(ṅhā)* were meant to clarify the type of bondage and conditions involved and did not imply a distinction between "free" persons and "slaves." It described mainly a legal obligation as well as general

obligation and explains the use of the term *kywan* in different clientelistic situations.

Another major difference between those bought and those hired
was that the latter were free to work for others at the same time,
whereas those bought (or redeemed from someone else) could serve
only their patrons until the price of redemption was paid or the
patrons released *(lhwat)* them from the obligation of kywanship. It
would be similar to an employer today who insists that his employee
not hold another job. Just such an issue—specifically, whether or not
a *kywan* had been employed *(ciy* or *ciy-ṅhā)* for wages *(lak-kha-ṅuy)* or
sold *(roṅ)*[32]—triggered a court case recorded in an inscription of
1226. The suit involved two parties, in which one side, Minister
Anantasū, claimed that a particular *kywan* named Ṅga Mway
belonged to him. The other consisted of two persons who claimed
that a third party, a husband and his wife, had sold Ṅga Mway to
them instead. Witnesses were brought before the court. The husband had died and the wife testified that she "never sold" the *kywan*
to the party contesting Minister Anantasū's claim but had hired him
out for wages. Other witnesses privy to the transaction were called
and testified that they did indeed see the money and goods being
exchanged, but whether or not these were for the price of the *kywan*
or for his hire, one admitted, "I do not know." Consequently, the
judges declared that the words of Anantasū and the wife "were in
agreement," that "it is true that the *kywan* Ṅga Mway was indeed
given to Anantasū by . . ." the husband and wife. "Let Anantasū
have the *kywan*," the judges declared, and with that formally
announced Anantasū the "winner of the case" and affixed their seal
on the document that recorded the decision.[33] The testimony and
questions asked of the witnesses stressed precisely those distinctions
between hired and sold, on which the outcome of the suit depended.

In today's modern, democratic, and egalitarian context, not only
is there a significant difference between hiring and buying someone,
but because we assume, in addition, that everyone is legally free and
equal, legal obligation should have nothing to do with personal subordination and monetary responsibility need not imply *personal* servitude. If a person defaults on a mortgage, the bank can repossess his
house and other assets but not his body. Yet in a society where the
principles of obligation rest on *personal* servitude, one's "body"
becomes collateral. Default means personal servitude, and obligation means subordination.[34] Thus although terms in Burma such as

"to buy," "to hire," or "to redeem" made a difference in determining the specific types of bondage and obligations involved, they cannot be used as evidence to distinguish free from slave labor. The difference between a nonbonded person and a bonded one was not a case of one individual enjoying certain rights and the other none (or few) but one where everyone's rights were redistributed according to their rank and role in the hierarchy, so that ambiguity in status might not create conceptual disorder (or individualism).

Purā Kywan

Those permanently bonded to the *sangha* were known as *purā kywan*. They were "servants" or "subjects," that is, *kywan* of the Buddha/temple/monastery/monks. Their formal title in most Theravāda Buddhist countries was *kappiyakaraka*, though it was only occasionally used in Burma. By serving the Buddha or his disciples—a form of denial and asceticism that rejected the secular world—they acquired a superior social-spiritual status, although that status denied them civil and political rank. On the other hand, because monks were forbidden to even touch money, the headmen of *purā kywan* (who could be *purā kywan* themselves or laypersons) oversaw the administration of religious endowments and *sangha* property in general, which placed the right to produce and land squarely in their hands, and along with it economic power.[35]

During the Pagan period, glebe bondsmen like other bondsmen comprised a variety of types of skilled and unskilled people. They were dancers, singers, musicians, scribes, scholars, masons, carpenters, gold- and silversmiths, along with farmers and sweepers of floors. They supplied daily food, lights, water, and other amenities and saw to the continuous upkeep of the monasteries, temples, and other buildings. Many were *asañ* hired on a temporary basis, others were *kywan* dedicated by their patrons as part of an endowment.[36] Those *asañ* who worked for the *sangha* on hire were not legally considered *purā kywan*. Because they fulfilled what were in essence *purā kywan* functions among other *purā kywan*, however, there must have been few conspicuous features distinguishing the two. Only their written, legal contracts would disclose that difference. To avoid such confusion, especially at tax time, each permanent *purā kywan*'s name, along with those of his or her offspring, was inscribed on the

donative stone, whose contents were duplicated on palm leaf and
kept by the government. It would have been tempting for *asañ* on
hire to pose as permanent *purā kywan* and thus avoid capitation tax.
This would be particularly easy, since most *purā kywan,* other than
sweepers of temple floors and those with similar jobs, did not reside
at the monastery or temple to which they were obligated. Most lived
on or near their "fief."[37] If a donor endowed an entire village of (say)
mainly cooks—over whose revenues he in turn had been given rights
—to a particular group of monasteries,[38] the tax collector would
have a difficult time determining, in such cases, who else in the village owed capitation.

It appears that bona fide *purā kywan* status was hereditary. The
clearest indication of this was the periodic rededication by various
kings of glebe property, which included their attendants. Like religious gifts, *purā kywan* were transferred to the religious realm in a
formalized ritual; and like religious property, they were given in perpetuity.[39] This should not have applied, at least legally, to those who
were either already bonded to the crown or private individuals
whose patrons had temporarily donated their services to the *sangha*
nor to *asañ* who were working for the *sangha* on a temporary basis.
The hereditary status applied only to *purā kywan* whose ancestors
were, for some reason, themselves hereditary *purā kywan,* prisoners-
of-war who had been dedicated in perpetuity, or political opponents
the king wished to eliminate from the scene—as in the case of three
ministers who were donated to the *sangha* by the king.[40]

Hereditary or not, compared to private—and, in some cases,
crown—bondage, *purā kywan* status offered more economic and
social-spiritual advantages. *Purā kywan* were exempt from government service or capitation tax, yet enjoyed a piece of tax-free land
(or rights to it).[41] Their domestic duties were probably less onerous
than those of other *kywan* (the monks did not eat after noon and
meditated much of the time), and their livelihood was certainly considered more noble than most, as they were servants not of ordinary
mortals but of the Buddha. In addition, their offspring were guaranteed security as well. In times of war, moreover, monasteries were
probably some of the safest places to be in. Realizing these advantages, many sought to become *purā kywan,* such as the woman who
dedicated her husband and children to the *sangha,* or the couple who
dedicated their four daughters to a particular monastery, and the
court official who dedicated himself, his wife, and their two sons to
the *sangha.*[42]

The meticulous record keeping of the names of *purā kywan* and their offspring has often been interpreted to suggest a desire of *purā kywan* to escape bondage. But, as we have observed, the economic and social security of *purā* kywanship, particularly if translated in terms of permanent rights and ties to land, was extremely valuable for Pagan citizens. It was a desire to preserve their exclusive rights to tax-exempt land and the government's inclination to prevent others from usurping these rights rather than a desire to escape bondage that such precise records were kept. It was with pride, not shame, that a *purā kywan* would say, "I am the *saṅgha*'s man," in the same spirit that a *kywan-tō* or crownperson would say "I am the king's man."

Kywan-tō

People legally commended to the crown were known as *kywan-tō,* literally meaning "royal *kywan*" or "royal subjects," the *tō* an honorific used (in this case) with royalty and suggesting a meaning similar to the term "government servant" used today. But because everyone in the society, whether or not legally obligated to perform crown service, was theoretically a subject of the king in any case, everyone was a *kywan-tō.* A more precise term was thus needed to distinguish the general populace from crown servicemen. Subsequently, the word *ahmudan* ("bearer of the duty") replaced *kywan-tō* in the fourteenth century, while *kywan-tō* became the personal pronoun "I," still in use today, indicating everyone's relative status within the context of a monarchy.[43]

Although the word *ahmudan* as such was not used in Pagan, the context in which the words *ahmu* (duty or service) and *than* (or *dan*, "to bear") appeared in thirteenth-century inscriptions suggests that the institution was already in existence.[44] (Certainly *ahmudan*'s structural counterpart, *asañ,* was already present.) An edict of 1367 also clearly indicated that the predecessors of *ahmudan* were in fact *kywan-tō.*[45] Another, two years later, associated the term *kywan-tō* with military service, the major function of later *ahmudan.*[46] References to the term *ahmudan* itself in three edicts of the seventeenth century showed that their functions had been preserved well into the eighteenth and nineteenth centuries. In the seventeenth century, *ahmudan* had to perform specific crown duties, received royal land for their service, were not promoted outside their group, and were considered to be of hereditary status. Meticulous records were also kept of *ahmudan*—their births and deaths, those disabled by age or sickness, those who were able-bodied, and those who had been ordained as monks.[47]

It is this kind of information of later *ahmudan* characteristics that has given us a picture of their predecessors in the Pagan period, for the Pagan records are mostly religious donations, not the normal place to mention crown service groups. It appears that *kywan-tō* similarly owed military and/or general corvée to the crown in return for exemption on capitation tax and the use of good crown lands. In most cases, these lands were given as permanent fiefs and although technically inalienable, on occasion, especially in later centuries, were sold.[48] In times of war, *kywan-tō* probably served as soldiers and support troops. In peace time, they served as policemen, toll collectors, and general security forces and must have taken turns (as later *ahmudan* did) at palace guard duty, their maintenance provided by their units who derived their revenue from their fiefs. Although most *kywan-tō* probably cultivated their own land, military officers with larger allotments could have just as easily hired tenant cultivators composed of both *ahmudan* and *asañ*. There were, in addition, non-military *kywan-tō*—crown serfs, crown artisans, crown scribes, and a host of others who, like other bonded persons, performed services for the government in exchange for some form of payment, usually rights to or in some instances outright ownership of land. *Kywan-tō* also repaired irrigation works and royal temples and harvested, collected, and stored grain in *ki tō* (royal granaries).

During times of military conquests (not war per se) the ranks of the crown service groups probably swelled, since all prisoners-of-war, regardless of occupation, became the property of the crown. This principle is reiterated in one of the laws on kywanship, which stated that "one . . . becomes a *kywan* for having incumbent danger warded off . . . (and) shall pay a sum becoming his rank for his redemption."[49] A person whose life one saves—by taking him captive rather than killing him—becomes one's *kywan*, for the crux of the matter was still obligation. Prisoners-of-war awarded to princes or ministers as alienable property became ordinary *kywan;* if inalienable, they remained *kywan-tō* but controlled by the recipient. Those captives awarded to the *sangha*, being normally permanent, became *purā kywan*, exempt from government revenue and service obligations. *Kywan* often became *purā kywan* also. A person not wishing his own property to be mistakenly "returned" to the state with other temporary gifts of the crown or used by his descendants for their own salvation would, before his death, donate all his *kywan* to the *saṅgha*.[50] Such donations, particularly those of considerable size that might include crown property, needed permission from the crown. But since these requests were usually made in public, no good Buddhist monarch concerned about his image and accumulation of merit would refuse. In short, most prisoners-of-war eventually became *kywan-tō* or *purā kywan* but not ordinary *kywan*.

The influx of labor from war meant that certain adjustments had to be made with regard to rank and status vis-à-vis the established groups. Captives, although initially placed in lower positions, could, after a generation, assume the same level as their Burmese counterparts. The descendants of Mon craftsmen taken in the mid-eleventh century from Thaton became a much respected group in the early and late twelfth century. Craftsmen and artists obtained from Thailand in the sixteenth and eighteenth centuries similarly became a significant part of Burmese society and culture, while even racially and culturally distinct Portuguese mercenaries of the sixteenth and seventeenth centuries and Manipuri cavalrymen of the eighteenth century in a short time became respected *ahmudan*.

Kywan-tō like *purā kywan* status, with its ties and rights to crown land, was probably a major economic and political incentive for most people, especially because under normal circumstances the crown was the richest employer, its jobs the most prestigious, and its path the most mobile politically. In terms of economic security, it is likely that the crown shared its appeal with the *saṅgha* also, although in terms of political mobility, crown service may have been more attractive. There were problems, however, not so much for the *kywan-tō* themselves as for the government. For instance, *asañ* who worked for the crown and paid with rights to produce or land, would not be ordinarily distinguishable in terms of function and obligations from other *kywan-tō*, except from those in the military. Yet as *asañ*, they would be technically required to pay capitation tax in lieu of service. Like those *asañ* who worked on hire for the *saṅgha*, many *asañ* on government payroll were tempted, especially at tax time, to disguise their *asañ* status and pretend to be *kywan-tō* instead, thereby avoiding capitation. Even among bona fide *kywan-tō* there could be similar problems. A *kywan-tō* family that owed service to the crown in exchange for land would, over time, regard their rights to that land as hereditary, even if it was still technically crown land. The crown would have to make certain that the service to which it was entitled continued, and that the status of those grants of land being used as hereditary property be clarified periodically.

One of the ways the government sought to solve these problems was to encourage bondage (at least crown bondage) to remain hereditary as well as conspicuous. *Kywan,* and perhaps even *purā kywan* (although the evidence is not clear here), were tattooed according to their categories and in the case of military *kywan-tō,* even according to the regiment to which they belonged. The Pagan government kept and maintained meticulous records of all kinds of kywanship, requiring the names of all bonded persons, their marital status, occupations, places of residence, number and names of offspring (even "suckling babes"), and, of course, deaths.[51] More specifically, some of these records were meant to determine who among crown employees were permanent *kywan-tō* and who were really *asañ* with obligations of capitation.

This fastidious keeping of records and tattooing, especially of crown bondsmen, may have been mistakenly interpreted as suggestive of the undesirability of crown service, instead of what I believe was an attempt, in the context of crown fiefs tending to become hereditary, to insure the continuity of those *kywan-tō* services that were required of anyone holding crown fiefs.

Other factors also helped preserve the status quo among crown service groups. Since occupation and ethnic background were often synonymous, ethnicity and hereditary function were linked, which in turn tied the styles of dress often affected by various ethnic groups to occupations. Those who "bore swords . . . wore white *kuchon* [bottom garments], shirts, and hairbands . . ." were Burmans, stated one inscription.[52] Dress and insignia that distinguished rank and function in Pagan had, by the seventeenth century, become law. An edict of that century noted that "an official who neglected to use all the paraphernalia given to him by royal order as insignia of his rank was . . . criminally liable. Using insignia of a higher rank was also a crime."[53]

It is not certain when precisely inheritance of office, property, and titles, emerged as a written, legal right; but by the period of this study, it was already an accepted custom. From the officialdom down to the wet nurses of kings, from lay overseers of religious property to military officers and headmen, office and titles were being inherited by their descendants.[54] Even *asañ* who were not normally subject to these regulations, were nevertheless controlled by them, being confined to their respective occupational villages, which hindered mobility and thereby facilitated the collection of capitation tax. This critical development, of inheriting one's office and property, had profound economic and political implications for the balance of power in Pagan society, for making status hereditary was a double-edged sword. It changed the essence of power from that based on personal ties to that based on institutions, as we shall observe more fully in chapter 9.

Finally, to better administer all these groups, the government specified that residences were to be arranged according to category and often occupation: *purā kywan* in one village, *kywan-tō* in another, and *asañ* elsewhere, an arrangement that has been called cellular.

Cellular Organization

Most of the people of the commoner class worked in guildlike units, arranged into what Edmund Leach has called "cellular" organization: "localized groups of technical specialists [who] form a work team centered in a leader."[55] However, unlike Śrī Laṅka, which was Leach's primary concern, cellular society in Pagan did not imply political fragmentation or village autonomy. On the contrary, cellular arrangements, particularly on a scale larger than the work team, seemed to have been part of Pagan's efforts at centralization and unification in order to better control disparate groups, their obligations and occupations.

It is not certain what the origins of cellularity were in Burma; that it had socioeconomic and political functions by the Pagan period is clear. Groups with similar occupations resided in villages or sections of towns named after their particular craft. Drummers lived in Cañ Sañ Village; Panthyan Village was for masons and Pumnā Village for Brahmans; silversmiths lived in Mapañcara Town at Ṅuy (silver) Village; goatherds lived in Chip Thin (goatherd) Village and cowherds in Nwā Thin (cowherd) Village; while "earth diggers" (i.e., construction workers) lived in Mle Tū ("earth digging") Village. Potters resided in their own village, called Uiw Thin (potter) Village, and the bulk of artisans and skilled craftsmen such as musicians, painters, woodcarvers, and blacksmiths were found in Cakuiṅ (Sagaing) in their respective sections of town. Hunters were located in Muchiuw (hunter) Village, while those who produced salt resided in Chākhyat ("salt cooking") Village, and boat and raft makers made their homes in Phoṅ Chaṅ Village. Some villages acquired names descriptive of peculiar local customs, such as Chaṅthwan Village, "where they plough with [apparently dwarf] Elephants," or Kwaṁ Ma Sā Village, "village where betel is not eaten," and Kulā Mañ Village, "village of dark-skinned Indians." An entire village of prisoners-of-war, in this case Tai *(Syaṁ)*, who were classified *kywan-tō*, settled in Syaṁ Kaṁ Puiṅ Lay. Villages named for their ethnic inhabitants included Mon Village, Poṅ Loṅ (Palaung) Village, Syaṁ Village, Talop (Chinese) Town, and Lawa Village. (People were also named after their ethnic background; there were "Miss Poṅ Loṅ," "Mr. Shan," "Mr. Mon," "Mr. Arakanese," and "Mr. Chin.")[56]

This pattern of socioeconomic arrangement persisted throughout premodern Burmese history and accounts for G. E. Harvey's description of nineteenth-century Burmese society as "tribal not territorial . . . , [with] organization not of local communities but of occupation guilds, and authority vested in the head of each class, not the head of each village."[57] In Myingyan district, he continued, there were still Talaing (Mon) colonies, claiming origin from prisoners taken at Thaton in A.D. 1057 and during attacks made on the delta by the king of Ava, Minhkaung, in the fifteenth century.

> They were settled according to their craft . . . for instance, Shwega, the village of the shield makers; Sinkha, the village of the *howdah* makers; Kabyu, Kamye, Kani where saddles were made, white for commoners, black for junior officials, red for senior officials; Thintabaw, Thintaya, the villages of hairdressers; Pontha, the village of musicians.[58]

Crown workers seemed to have been similarly arranged into specialized groups who lived together in their own villages or localities according to their specialty. Among the military, for example, cavalry men often resided in villages with the word *mraṅ* or "horse" attached to it: Mraṅ Pagan, Mraṅ Khuntuiṅ, and Pak Lak Mraṅ. Chinese cavalrymen lived in the town called Talop (Chinese) Mriuw. Nagā Buih, men who carried shields, were similarly grouped. Lands given to the military often assumed names such as Lak Way Ray Chu Mliy ("communal military land of the Left") and Lak Yā Ray Chu Mliy ("communal military land of the Right"). Although distinctions were made between conscripts and the standing army, both were provided land on which to live.[59] Conscripts, who were probably required to join the military forces once orders had been sent to mobilize, were drawn from specific towns and villages obligated to send a stipulated number of men. Although we have no precise figures for the Pagan period, the *Jatatawbon,* a fifteenth-century history, listed 127 towns and villages designated to supply a total of 21,426 fighting men.[60] Pagan, a far wealthier and more centralized kingdom than its immediate successor Ava—the period to which the *Jatatawbon* refers—probably commanded a greater number of troops. Indeed, one inscription of King Narapatisithu mentioned his command of 30,000 cavalry.[61]

In these cells of technical specialists, loyalties were focused on the leaders or foremen, and nothing better describes the relationship than the terms used for them: *sūkrī* and *khoñ,* "big person" and "head," respectively. When the word *sūkrī* was attached to one designating an occupation, such as *rhuy* ("gold"), for instance, it indicated that the *rhuy sūkrī* was the leader of a group of goldsmiths; if attached to *mle tū,* "digger of earth," it meant a foreman of a group of construction workers; and with the word *kywan,* as in *kywan sūkrī,* it identified the person in charge of a group of *kywan.*[62] Similarly, the word *khoñ,* as in *mrañ khoñ,* "head of cavalry," referred to an officer who led a platoon of riders. In both cases, *sūkrī* and *khoñ* suggest authority over people, not over places. But if a group of say, cavalry, comprised an entire village, its leader would in fact become a headman of persons as well as one over territory, assuming both personal and territorial authority. If both *asañ* and *kywan-tō* (cavalry and goldsmiths, perhaps) resided in the same village, each leader would be responsible only for his own group. However, since only *asañ* were obligated to pay capitation tax, whose computation invariably involved land, the *asañ* headman, responsible for the tax, may have assumed a territorial jurisdiction as well. If *kywan* and *purā kywan* resided in the same village, the responsibilities of *kywan sūkrī* and *purā kywan sūkrī* would probably be made separate.

In turn, the *sūkrī* or *khoñ* had superiors to whom they were responsible. In the case of *asañ,* the government tax assessor was probably the highest authority a headman had to deal with, unless the revenues of his village had been given to a fief holder, in which case the tax was turned over to that person. In the case of *kywan,* their *sūkrī* was directly responsible to their patron or his appointed overseer. In cases where revenues from *asañ* villages had been dedicated to a monastic establishment by the fief holder, the *asañ sūkrī*'s superior may well have been the abbot of the religious establishment. *Purā kywan* came under the authority of a *purā kywan sūkrī,* an overseer designated to a particular monastic estate. *Kywan-tō* leadership was more structured: military men were ranked under various levels of officers until the conical structure reached the *mahāsenāpati* ("great general"), who was a member of the king's court—in essence his cell.

Even though there was personal responsibility at the level of the guild or platoon and between clients and patrons, the government, through such requirements as capitation tax on *asañ* and military service from *kywan-tō,* integrated these various networks under one supreme umbrella. This meant that territorial jurisdiction had to supersede personal authority above the district level, where a crown officer was always in charge and who carried the title *saṁbeñ-kalan* or a variation of it.

This office has long perplexed scholars of Burmese history, and the question of exactly what it entailed has never been resolved satisfactorily. It has been suggested on the one hand that the title, which is Old Mon, was given to a "high government official . . . [with] civil functions," and on the other that it referred to those in charge of land surveys.[63] Neither explanation is very explicit. The evidence appears at first glance to be contradictory. In some inscriptions, the officer is a judge;[64] in others he is referred to as a *buih sūkrī* (headman of the troops), clearly a military person.[65] Indeed, the *mahāsenāpati,* the highest military officer in the kingdom with the exception of the king, was often given the title *saṁbeñ.*[66] Other *saṁbeñ* were conspicuous because they carried swords.[67] Governors of towns were also called *saṁbeñ.*[68] There were also *saṁbeñ* who dealt with land and labor and with granaries who were witnesses at religious donations and recorders of inscriptions and "death registers" *(siy cā rañ).*[69] Some *saṁbeñ* had place names attached to their titles indicating their territorial jurisdictions.[70]

However, when we realize that civil and military functions were often merged in ancient Burma, where a single official may be a judge as well as a military governor; that neither *asañ* nor *kywan* had military responsibilities, were governors of provinces, and certainly were never commanders-in-chief; and that *kywan-tō,* in addition to their military duties, often performed what seemed like general administrative functions such as land surveys, granary protection, and justice, *saṁbeñ* were very likely kingsmen, high-ranking crown officers whose authority was clearly superior to that of *asañ* and *kywan* in the administrative structure and whose authority was both personal (vertical) and territorial (horizontal). He may have been the Pagan equivalent of the *myo wun,* the viceroy or provincial governor of later times, whose Burmese title had replaced the Old Mon *saṁbeñ.*

The arrangement of people into villages organized by occupation, which was hereditary, and the use of elaborate procedures to maintain the political, social, and economic status quo suggest and give credence to the traditional assumption that labor control was indeed a major problem in labor-scarce, precolonial Southeast Asia. Moreover, it shows that this problem had its roots as early as the ninth century, when, as we observed in chapter 1, Nanchao raided central Burma and transported back to Yunnan after the conquest some three thousand Pyus. As long as service remained a basic ingredient of wealth, control of labor was the key to political power, reason enough to legalize hereditary occupation. Although *purā kywan* and *kywan-tō* sometimes attempted to change their status by joining the *saṅgha,* it was a move to a sphere of life and type of status quite different from what is expected of true secular mobility.[71] Perpetuating the economic and social status quo only intensified an already differentiated and highly specialized socioeconomic structure, resulting in persons of essentially similar rank and function—such as gardeners, planters of *padi* and betelnut, reapers of *padi,* climbers of toddy palms, tenders of goats, cattle, buffaloes, and ducks—attempting to distinguish themselves from one another socially. Such elaboration and preoccupation with similar categories and concern for distinguishing between somewhat redundant functions suggests an "involuted" structure, at least in the agricultural sector.

The persistence of this form of artificially elaborate social arrangement into the nineteenth century suggests further that the population of the kingdom must have remained relatively stable prior to the colonial period—the estimate ranges from one to two and a half million people—a characteristic not uncommon to other medieval societies.[72] (England's population between the time of William the Conqueror and Elizabeth I remained at two and a quarter million, and China's population until the 1600s remained between sixty and one hundred million for nearly thirteen centuries.)[73] That is not to say that within a particular dynastic cycle or period of growth population did not increase, only that throughout the entire precolonial period population fluctuations were subject to stabilizing demographic factors that kept maximum increases within certain limits beyond which the population did not climb until the early nineteenth century. (Even today Burma is one of the few if not the only country in the Third World with a pronatalist policy.) Without the type of pressure to which increasing populations subjected postcolonial societies and their economies, the ratio of cultivable land to labor would have remained stable. In other words, the continuity of Burmese institutions was tied as much to the perpetuation of certain ideologies related to salvation, social status, kingship, and the state as it was to the absence of the kinds of geodemographic pressures that normally stimulate and create profound changes in a society.

In summary, society in Pagan can be described as conical: horizontally divided into three major classes, vertically organized around both dyadic and corporate patron-client relationships formed voluntarily as well as involuntarily, and arranged according to a cellular pattern of occupational teams and residences. Yet patron-client ties did not create a feudal situation in the European sense, where a host of humble folk were economically subjected to a few powerful men, epitomized by the manorial system and backed by one of the most distinctive features of that system—the heavily armed horseman. Rather, the protective capacity of the state in twelfth- and thirteenth-century Burma was a strong one; it was not a violent or chaotic society but an ordered and hierarchic one, concerned not with individual political freedom as a measure of happiness but with social and political order, ruled not by independent lords and armies but by a sovereign and his officials, and pacified by a primate and his monks. In this ordered society, slavery as we know it played no significant economic, social, or political role. Instead, the material substance of the Pagan kingdom—the large tracts of irrigated land; the canals, sluices, and dams; the granaries that helped stave off famine; the outposts that collected taxes and kept order; the capital and provincial cities that provided the state's strength and grandeur; the magnificent temples and monasteries that were an indispensable feature of the classical Burmese state— were the work of paid, common folk, not forced, slave labor.

5

The Administration of
Material Resources

A SYNCHRONIC STUDY, even if only in part, often creates inconsistencies or contradictions because change and the passage of time are excluded from it. The characteristics of institutions in existence during a certain period may often be at odds with those found later in the same institutions; or it may appear that there is a complex definition for something quite simple. In the two hundred years of the Pagan period under study here, administrative terminology suffers from precisely this problem of imprecision. At first glance, the ambiguity in Pagan administrative terminology suggests a confused state of affairs, a decentralized state and society not quite certain of its power, what it represents, or where it is headed. On further diachronic analysis, however, it becomes clear that this imprecision exists in the reconstruction, not in the society itself. Since Pagan society was dynamic, vestiges of older forms of terminology remained, especially in parts of the kingdom where change was slower. Old and new meanings were sometimes used interchangeably, the speaker taking for granted that everyone knew what was meant and therefore providing no explanation. It was only through an analysis that allowed one to "become a contemporary," so to speak, that the sources yielded the assumptions held by the people of Pagan. The conclusions reached in this chapter are the result of such "subjective" though absolutely necessary analysis; however, the steps involved may not always be provided. To do so would take too much time and space.

Although located in the dry zone of Burma, with approximately 45 inches of rain a year, Pagan, like the majority of Burma's dynasties, harnessed a system of perennial rivers using dams, weirs, sluices, and channels, managing to provide water to a rich but thirsty land and thereby cultivating almost three crops a year. Most of these intensively cultivated areas lay within easy reach of the capital city and once under central control, supplied more than the necessary wherewithal for the survival of a powerful state, so that whatever human or material resources that were acquired in addition to this base in central Burma was pure surplus. Most of the coastal cities and towns heavily involved in the trade of India, Southeast Asia, and China were lucrative prizes for the inland, agrarian powers. The Kingdom of Pagan controlled most of these cities, usually with direct garrison rule headed by a governor who was sometimes the crown prince himself. As the coastal cities were the windows to the international world, materially as well as intellectually and culturally, the inland agrarian capitals seldom destroyed these coastal cities: they would instead seek to control them. (In fact, the inland states sought to destroy other inland states.) In return, the coastal cities rarely seriously challenged the more powerful agrarian states. It was a matter of self-interest: the inland states, more concerned with and vulnerable to domestic issues and problems, needed the luxury goods, the ocean products, and the "latest" goings-on in the international world, while the coastal-trade oriented cities, whose existence depended upon international rather than "national" affairs, needed the rice and other inland products about whose production they knew or cared little. It was a material and psychological equilibrium understood for millennia.

The units with which the Pagan kingdom administered these territories, both in the heart of the kingdom in central Burma as well as the plains carved out by the Irrawaddy, sometimes even the hills on either side of this valley, were the circle *(khwan)*, town/fortress *(mriuw)*, and the village *(rwā)*. The mechanism by which this system operated was the fief, based on principles of economic redistribution, which executed the extraction of revenue—mainly irrigated rice or *padi*—in a culturally acceptable manner.

The Kingdom and Its Material Resources

The physical configuration of the kingdom may be likened to several concentric circles: the capital and its immediate environs consisted of the first ring; the second was composed of the first as well as another, larger ring measuring approximately 100 miles in radius from the capital city. Together they comprised the central region. A third ring encircled the first two, circumscribing the effective limits of Pagan's immediate political authority. The extent of this territory —particularly northward and southward—was roughly equivalent to Burma's present-day north-south boundaries (see Map 2). In actual geographic terms, Pagan's administrative authority remained in the flat, alluvial plains on both sides of the Irrawaddy River, from Bhamo (near Nāchoṅkhyaṁ) in the far north, widening in central Burma between Mandalay and Pagan, then narrowing again as the river moved south, until it emptied into the Gulf of Martaban. The cities on the western Tenasserim coast remained, on the whole, under Pagan's hegemony for roughly two hundred years. Graphically, then, the area of control resembled more a tube with a "bubble" in its middle than concentric circles. The bubble was the heart of the kingdom, the area called Tampadīpa Prañ, Pugan Prañ, and in Pali, Arimaddanapūra Prañ, as well as Mranmā Prañ (kingdom or country of the Burmans).[1] The *prañ* included the first and second rings while the third referred to *nuiññaṁ* or the "conquered territories." As the *nuiññaṁ* were settled, they slowly became part of the *prañ* also. The social organization described in chapter 4 was found to be particularly effective in this central region.[2] Areas distant from the capital may have retained local idiosyncrasies, but the primary categories of bonded and non-bonded groups also applied equally to them.

Nucleus

In the center of the first ring was located the capital city and suburbs of approximately 25 square miles, with the court and palace, myriad temples, monasteries and some of their endowed lands, a walled town where the palace was enclosed, and possibly the residences of the high-ranking members of court. The inscriptions mention a *prañ sūkrī* ("headman of the *prañ*," in this context, "capital") in whose hands most of the city administration must have fallen.[3] As in later Burmese history, the capital city was further divided into four *arap* (wards or quarters) corresponding to the cardinal points, each the responsibility of a prince of that "direction."[4] The capital city was the seat of government—the religious, cultural, and ceremonial center of the kingdom—but not necessarily the heart of its economic resources. It was the conceptual and physical source from which political patronage and redistribution of goods and power commenced and the source from which merit flowed. This role is illus-

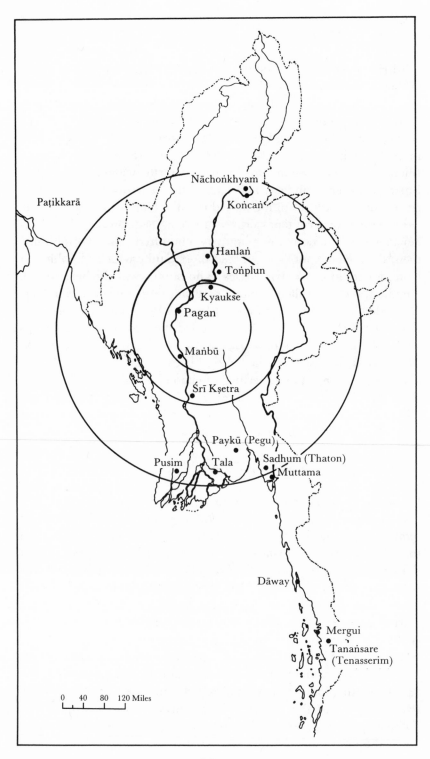

Paṭikkarā

Nāchoṅkhyaṁ
Koṅcaṅ

Hanlaṅ
Toṅplun

Kyaukse
Pagan

Maṅbū

Śrī Kṣetra

Paykū (Pegu)
Pusim   Tala   Sadhuṁ (Thaton)
Muttama

Dāway

Mergui
Tanaṅsare
(Tenasserim)

0   40   80   120 Miles

MAP 2
Burma and the Kingdom of Pagan

trated by the physical composition of the city, which consisted primarily of the palace and the temples around it. Most of the material wealth—the thousands of acres of wet-rice fields—and human wealth—the conscript segment of the army with its various corps, much of the actual labor force that built the temples, and the craftsmen and artisans who designed and decorated them, the majority of all the tangible components of the kingdom—was not to be found within the capital city itself. The people who built it, fed it, and protected it did not, for the most part, live in it. The capital city was the showcase of the kingdom, and perhaps even a "theatre state" in many respects. In the center, the *prañ*, the majority of the inscriptions were found; the bulk of the temples were built there; most of the lands that were endowed and the people donated belonged to the central region; the *kammarāja* ruled from this inner core; his palace, his temples, court, concubines, and ministers were there. It was, after all, Tāvatiṁsa, and in Tāvatiṁsa neither the miseries of *saṁsara,* the tragedies of *niraya* (hell), nor even the realities of *kama rūpa* (the material world) belonged.

The nucleus also consisted of three critically important agricultural areas, approximately 100 to 150 miles from the capital and surrounding it on three sides. To the north and northeast was Klokcañ (Kyaukse) and Toṅplun; and in the southwest, Maṅbū (see Map 3). They all possessed extensive irrigation networks, were watered by perennial streams and rivers, and were referred to as *kharuin*. The precise meaning of the word *kharuin* varies with the context, but it generally connotes "the heartwood," or "core," the "central part on which other parts depend" (i.e., the hub or nucleus), a rather appropriate term for the economic basis of Pagan's existence. The striking absence of *asañ* from Kyaukse inscriptions leads one to conclude that *kharuin* (at least Kyaukse) were crown lands, inhabited by *kywan-tō* probably residing in fortified villages.[5] Presumably, too, the other two *kharuin*, like Kyaukse, were ruled directly by an appointed member of the royal family who held the title "chief minister of the royal granaries" *(kī tō).*[6] The word *kharuin* subsequently—perhaps by the fourteenth century—became an administrative term proper, but during the Pagan period it was reserved only for these three geographic areas, the nuclei of crown wealth and the material basis of royal power.

Tuik were new settlements that emerged around the end of the twelfth century and were located on the western side of the Irra-

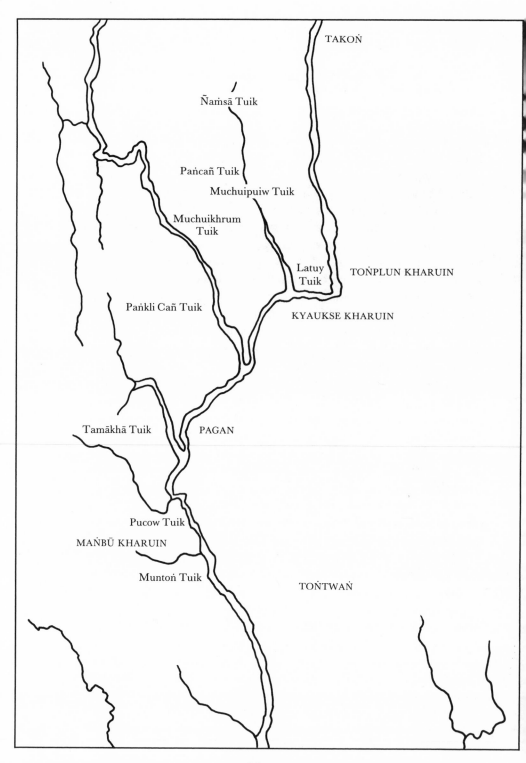

MAP 3
Central Burma and "Frontier" Settlements

waddy across from the city of Pagan, spreading from Maṅbū in the south northward almost to Takoṅ near the Nanchao border (see Map 3). Their appearance at that particular time in Pagan's history coincides with the great burst of energy engendered by King Narapatisithu, during whose reign and after most of the monumental construction occurred.[7] His reign was a watershed in Pagan's history, an acceleration point in state development where most of the evidence of quantitative change is found: the codification of law, the zenith of temple construction, development of the military, increased activity in foreign relations (notably with Śrī Laṅka), agricultural growth, and, as attested by the creation of *tuik,* administrative innovation and territorial expansion. It was Narapatisithu's successful conquests that brought much needed laborers, who settled these new *tuik* areas, into the nucleus. The kingdom, having clearly expanded beyond its original agricultural base of the eleventh and early twelfth centuries, needed additional land relatively close to the capital to support and sustain a growing economy, population, and burgeoning state. The *tuik,* then, became part of Pagan's second ring.

Moreover, the locations of *tuik* suggest military and strategic reasons for their establishment. The capital city's location between Maṅbū in the southwest and Kyaukse in the northeast, meant that it controlled the only natural crossing to the west bank of the Irrawaddy available for miles. All of the *tuik* lay on that side, thereby giving protection to the rich Maṅbū Kharuin. Building *tuik* on the western shores protected Pagan's western flank, both northward and southward; the eastern side was already protected by a line of forty-three fortresses situated on the Irrawaddy stretching northward as defense against invasion from that direction.[8] Altogether, the founding of fifteen *tuik* was recorded during the twelfth and thirteenth centuries, each *tuik* providing the seat of central authority in its respective location.[9] Tamākhā Tuik, for example, was probably the headquarters for the defense of Pagan's western flank as well as the center for royal administration in that area. Pucow Tuik protected Maṅbū, while Paṅkli Cañ Tuik to the north of Pagan controlled that particular area, as well as the area that continued up to Ñaṁsā Tuik in the far north. The function of *tuik* as essentially defensive posts further suggests the presence there of *kywan-tō,* governed by *tuik sūkrī.*[10] Like the *tuik* they governed, the *tuik sūkrī* were new elements in the administrative hierarchy with both territorial and personal jurisdiction. *Tuik,* in short, performed a role similar to that of the fortified outpost in the frontier history of expanding states.

Extremities

The extent to which society in areas away from the center was organized in the same manner that *it* was depended upon the extent to which central control extended into these areas. The basic division of Pagan society into independent, crown, and religious categories seems to have been widespread, found as far away from the center as Lower Burma, where even the price of a *kywan* (as in the capital city) was "fixed" at 30 *klyap* of silver. Society outside the central region was certainly not vastly different, but it may have been less structured than at the center. Although there is little data on this area except for the important towns at the extremities of the third ring that were governed directly as fiefs by favorites of the king, it is likely that towns and villages in the intervening areas maintained a system of village administration similar to that of the center. With the exception of some of the riverine towns situated at strategic places on the Irrawaddy (which, if they supplied the crown with war boats and men, were considered *kywan-tō* towns), most of this area must have been inhabited by *asañ* cultivators. Certainly, there was less of the "cellularity" here than was found in the center, and there were no large populations of artisans and craftsmen, which only the capital's economy could support well.

These areas outside the two inner circles were initially known as *nuiññaṁ*, effectively "conquered [territories]," which implies "foreignness," distance in physical and cultural space, and something outside the familiar conceptual world. The term *nuiññaṁ* means having dominion over, as in "I wish to be great in dominion."[11] Pagan, basically agricultural and inhabited by people socialized by Burmese culture, must have viewed nonagricultural, trading (market) towns inhabited by people of an international class, not all Buddhists, as indeed foreign. Towns like Thaton, Mergui, Tala, Pusim (Bassein), and Pegu (Paykū), when conquered by King Aniruddha in the mid-eleventh century,[12] were inhabited mainly by Mon, Indian, and other ethnic groups. Before being sacked, they most likely existed as "neutral ports of trade" (in Karl Polanyi's sense of the term) providing to inland, agrarian Pagan a window to the outside world of trade and commerce—to the Chola and Malay regions in particular.[13] With Pagan's subsequent growth and expansion, this neutrality must have given way to control by titular heads who promised loyalty and military levies and/or material tribute.[14] By the twelfth century, especially after King Narapatisithu's reign, these commercial towns had become fiefdoms, some ruled directly by princes of royal blood and in some cases even settled by people from the central region.[15] The term *nuiññam* by the late twelfth and thirteenth centuries no longer applied to areas foreign or strange, for the more familiar, administrative terms that were in use in the central region began to be used in this area as well.[16] Places in the delta came to be described in phrases that conveyed geographical and cultural proximity, such as "downstream in Tala."[17] The change from "conquered territories" to "a place downstream" was symptomatic of the growth, expansion, unification, and integration of central administration over the bulk of the kingdom.

Units of Administration

The whole kingdom was administered as three distinct units: "circles" or provinces *(tuiñ* and *khwañ); towns (mriuw);* and villages *(rwā).* The kingdom had at least fourteen circles or provincial units called *tuiñ* and/or *khwañ.* They were dispersed over the kingdom, as far south as Tala and Pusim on the coast and as close as Calañ in Mañbū and Mrañkhuntuiñ in Kyaukse.[18] The governor of each circle probably resided in its major town, whose function and importance varied according to the province itself. Governors, often entitled *sambeñ,* administered their domains as the king would the kingdom: they were chief justices, commanders-in-chief, and tax collectors, much like their eighteenth- and nineteenth-century counterparts, the *myo wun.* The port cities in the south that were headquarters of the southern provinces seem normally to have been reserved as fiefs for high-ranking princes of royal blood. Klacwā (1234–1249) as crown prince enjoyed Pegu as a fief and was called Pakuiw (Pegu) Mañkrī, "lord of Pakuiw"; Klawcwā (1287–1300), while heir apparent, enjoyed Tala's trade revenues and was called Tala Sūkrī; Co Lu (Sawlu), Aniruddha's heir, was given the town of Mergui on the Kra Isthmus "to eat."[19] King Kalañcacsā also assigned several of his ministers to this area as governors.[20] Evidence also suggests that some provincial capitals were not "eaten" in absentia but in situ: Klawcwā, the Tala Sūkrī, was also called Tala Pyam Mañ, indicating that he died in Tala. In the north, Koñcañ,

Nāchoṅkhyaṁ, and Takoṅ (all near the border) served as major defensive headquarters, protecting Pagan from its traditional northern enemies. Here, too, governors "ate" in situ and were chiefly of ministerial or princely rank. We hear of "Maṅ Matkrī Koṅcaṅ" ("Great Royal Minister of Koṅcaṅ") as well as "the Great Left [Hand of the King] who fought [and won] the Takoṅ War," namely, Prince Nātoṅmyā, commander of Takoṅ under whom were ten thousand households.[21]

Mriuw, fortresses that had grown into towns, functioned as garrisoned strongholds of central authority in areas distant from the center. If large enough, they were divided further into *arap.* Makharā Arap, for example, was a ward within Mraṅkhuntuiṅ Town; Mapañcara Arap was in Calaṅ Town; Añā Arap was in Talop Mraṅ Town; and Sacmatī Arap was in Pagan Town.[22] The official head of a town or *mriuw* was a *mriuw sūkrī,* but the title was descriptive not prescriptive; that is, since military commanders of varying ranks ruled the *mriuw, mriuw sūkrī* was simply a general term to refer to that headman.[23] If, for instance, the *mriuw* had not yet grown into a town proper and had remained a fort, the *mriuw sūkrī* was in all likelihood a *mraṅ khoṅ* or *mraṅ mhū* (cavalry officer), and the *mriuw* was inhabited not by people of different occupations but by *kywan-tō.*[24] If, however, the *mriuw* had grown into a larger town like Koṅcaṅ, with various categories of people living in it, the *mriuw sūkrī* would be a governor of ministerial rank.

The basic unit of administration was the village *(rwā).* The importance of a village depended on its location; similarly, the importance of village headmen differed according to type of appointment, the kind of village concerned, and where the village was located. If, for example, the village happened to be in Kyaukse, its importance to the state would far exceed that of one located elsewhere. Yet both the Kyaukse village leader and those of ordinary villages were called *rwā sūkrī* ("headman of the village"). Like the term *mriuw sūkrī, rwā sūkrī* was a general, descriptive term that did not indicate rank or function. Thus a *rwā sūkrī* of Mlacsā, the headquarters of Kyaukse, was a member of the royal family, while *rwā sūkrī* of other villages, as were those of *asañ* villages, might be hereditary leaders of commoner status. Those of artisan villages were leaders of cells of skilled craftsmen, and *rwā sūkrī* of *kywan-tō* villages were military officers and foremen of crown serfs or similar groups of crown workers. Unlike the nineteenth-century *rwā sūkrī,* who were subordinate to the *mriuw sūkrī*—since *mriuw* had become large and important towns while *rwā* remained villages—Pagan *rwā sūkrī* were often superiors of the Pagan *mriuw sūkrī*. In the Pagan period, for the most part, *mriuw* and *rwā* were administrative units distinguished not so much by quantitative criteria (size) as by qualitative ones (function and importance).

As there is a problem in precisely distinguishing one *rwā sūkrī* from another, so too did other administrative terms vary in meaning. The term *rwā* often referred specifically to those villages found in the well-irrigated plains of Kyaukse, which must have produced in the minds of Pagan people images of entities far more significant than any ordinary village would have been. Because *rwā* also meant "abode," as in *nat rwā*, "the abode of the *devas*," where only kings and people of great merit ascended upon death, it clearly had connotations beyond the administrative unit. The same was true with the word *mriuw*. Originally it meant a fort possessing a wall, moat, and belfry.[25] But when some *mriuw* grew into towns proper and others less strategically located did not, two essentially distinct administrative units evolved: one a fort, the other a town, each with a different type of *mriuw sūkrī* with different ranks and functions. Yet the words used to describe the units as well as their headmen were exactly the same. The word *tuik*, which originally referrred to frontier outposts found only in specific areas, in post-Pagan times came to mean "district," monastery, as well as "brick enclosure." Similarly, *kharuin* originally referred to three large, intensively irrigated areas, the core of royal lands and the treasury of the kingdom. Culturally, too, the term *kharuin* implied "the nucleus," the hub of Burmese jurisdiction and power. Yet subsequently, *kharuin* became administrative units proper, equivalent to provinces. *Prañ* could mean at once "capital," "kingdom," or "country," as in Mranmā Prañ, country or kingdom of the Burmans. It could like *rwā*, however, also mean "abode," as in Nat Prañ, "abode of the gods." *Nuiṅnam* in the early Pagan period was the designation for conquered territories or "domain," but in the thirteenth century it referred to areas within the boundaries of royal hegemony where people were being settled and to where administration was being extended.[26]

The terminology used for the officials of these entities was also imprecise in terms of application: a *mriuw sūkrī* during the Pagan period may have been the commander-in-chief of the army controlling a highly important northern Burma town with a large population and revenue base, or he may have been a junior cavalry officer in charge of a small fort. A *tuik sūkrī* in Pagan had authority over a frontier outpost, not, as in later Burmese history, over a circle of villages. In short, if we simply defined *rwā* as "village," *mriuw* as "town," and their administrators as "village" and "township" headmen, the critical differences between these units—the fact that this period was a time of ferment and the degree to and manner in which these institutions later evolved—would never have been revealed.

The Fief: The Basis of Administration

In general, human and material resources in Pagan were organized according to principles found in systems anthropologists have labelled "leveling" or "redistribution." The basis of this administrative system was the fief, epitomized by the term *cā*, "to eat." One "ate" the produce of a piece of land in return for service of some sort. Crown land was cultivated, irrigated, and maintained by crown serfs who ate part of the produce. Imperial troops ate the produce of lands designated for them, in return for duty as palace guards in peace time and military service in war. Military governors, government administrators of towns, and other clients of the king were given the revenues of provinces and districts, towns and villages to eat, either in return for administering those units or at "the pleasure" of the king. Private individuals gave their clients lands or produce of lands to eat in return for services of a personal nature. And religious estates provided for the payment of its *purā kywan* and their overseers with either land or its produce for services such as maintaining religious property, feeding the monks, and general upkeep of temples and monasteries. Independent *asañ* were the only group that received cash as well as fiefs to eat.

Produce was shared among those responsible for cultivating it, each portion determined by the person's relative rank in the sociopolitical hierarchy; the largest portion was submitted to the government as tax. It was either collected and moved to the capital or left at the place of production, in which case the rights of disposal were given to whoever was in charge. Technically, all non-crown persons paid a per capita tax, either in silver or in kind, but were not required to provide corvée. For the most part, the religious sector was exempted from obligation to the government in terms of both produce and service. The effectiveness of the centralized power structure, then, lay in its ability to harness revenues in the most efficient way: in terms of crown land and labor, this meant retaining as much of it as possible in government hands; in terms of non-service groups, it required keeping accurate registers of people, their births and deaths, and limiting their movements from the taxable category to the exempt (i.e., the *saṅgha*); in terms of the tax-exempt, religious sector, it called for regulating its growth to controllable proportions. At the top of this organization was the king and court, the sources of patronage, the hands that "fed" those who "ate."

Because labor was a scarce commodity in precolonial Southeast Asia, service had always been a major ingredient of wealth. By and large, it was the service of crown laborers (as military, administrators, or serfs) that constituted the state's wealth and, to a lesser degree, the capitation tax imposed on *asañ*. Similarly, it was the service of *purā kywan* that made up the *saṅgha*'s wealth and the service of *asañ* and *kywan* that supplied private individuals with their wealth. Wealth in land was realized only by the service of a variety of workers who were either sharecroppers enjoying rights to a percentage of the produce or owners holding pieces of land in return for hereditary service. Most rights to land were subsumed under the concept *cā*, a fief given for services performed. This term applied as much to monks and students who enjoyed the produce of endowed lands as to favorites of the king and the provincial military governors who administered his kingdom.[27]

There were essentially two categories of fiefs: those given outright, alienable and irrevocable, and those given "at the pleasure" of the king (*sa nā tō*, literally, "[at the] royal compassion"), which were theoretically inalienable and revocable. Normally, the former comprised gifts given by the king to subordinates who had performed well in the military and other similar capacities or to members of the religious order, both of which were called *mahādan*, the "great gift."[28] The revocable category included grants of crown land given to *kywan-tō* (soldiers, serfs, and other crown service groups) who lived on and cultivated these lands, "eating" the produce and submitting part of it or providing military and other service. Such crown lands granted to *kywan-tō*, although in theory inalienable and revocable by the crown, were in practice regarded as hereditary estates, since their holders' occupations were also hereditary, and were sometimes, even if illegally, sold. Inalienable and revocable gifts of the king also included revenues from *asañ* and crown lands given to governors of provinces, queens, concubines, and other favorites of the king. These gifts were good as long as the recipient stayed in the king's favor. When the king died, their status might have to be reaffirmed by the new king, for which special occasions were reserved, such as the *abhiṣeka* (coronation) and *kodaw* (fealty or homage) days. There was one exception to the inalienable and revocable status of fiefs given at the king's pleasure. If the fief was in turn donated by the recipient as a religious gift, the revenues of that fief became in perpetuity the property of the *sangha,* and the rights to the revenues that the "eater" would have enjoyed were instead transferred to monasteries. The amount of revenue a new governor of a province could expect to receive depended on what his predecessor had donated to the church, a situation that created frequent conflicts between provincial governors and those in charge of religious lands in that territory.[29] What had once been revenue due the crown from exempt or crown villages—the basis of state power—could, under these circumstances, have become for all practical purposes "private," ancestral property that was irrevocable, alienable, and hereditary.

Revenue

The mainstay of any government, its ability to collect revenue, rested upon essentially two sources in Pagan: the service of its *kywantō* and the produce or money from *asañ*. The method used to collect both was also based on the principle of the fief, either in the form of a tenement or a portion of the revenues collected. That is, a person responsible for collecting revenue received a fixed share of that revenue or a piece of land outright. The portions, beginning with the state, were determined in order of the recipients' rank, from the farmer whose bullocks were used to pull the plow, the reaper of the grain, the guards of the fields, the tax assessor and collector, and the headman to the governor and his staff.[30] Such an arrangement implied the presence of a storage system and a class (or group) of government officials to carry out the program of collection.

The amount of grain production was predictable because the bulk of crown land was watered by perennial streams or by nonseasonal sources such as reservoirs (tanks). Monsoons had little effect in the dry zone where the capital was located—the rainfall did not exceed forty-five inches a year—and the state was more concerned with permanently irrigated lands in any case. This means that supply was presumably stable, and the concept of a fluctuating supply stimulated by an equally unpredictable demand, creating price, was on the whole absent. Prices, particularly of certain essential types of commodities, were thus "fixed": *padi,* land, and labor of equal quality cost virtually the same in the eleventh century as in the thirteenth (see note 8, chapter 9). With the price of the two major economic products (land and labor) also fixed, other values in relation to them tended also to remain stable. The price of elephants, for example, was in a fixed ratio to the price of rice; silver to gold, with one exception; and lead to copper and other metals. Moreover, the ratio itself did not change over the years.[31] That the supply and demand of labor—a major *casus belli* in precolonial Southeast Asia—failed to establish itself as the principle upon which prices could be determined, shows the degree to which price-making, "market" mechanisms were uninvolved, even in an economic situation potentially ideal for them.

Even if market principles were at work, prices would have remained stable (despite Pagan's growth) primarily because of the fixed socioeconomic relationship between the expansion of cultivated land (supply) and the increase in population (demand). That is to say, the extent to which the Kingdom of Pagan could increase production by cultivating more land (increased supply) depended upon the addition of labor (increased demand) in the agricultural sector, the one off-setting the other. Moreover, supply as a concept was perceived as fixed, and anticipated, stable, supply determined distribution proportions, while lower supplies did not mean higher prices but smaller shares.

Similarly, surplus did not mean lower prices but larger shares, especially for the state, which stored it and used it as much for famine relief as for the glorification of itself and the religion and more strictly for purposes of patronage. Thus no conceptual or institutional relationship need exist between large supply and lower prices or small supply and higher prices. Predictable, maximum, supply decided ultimate value, as illustrated by the following donor's inscription: "As for this estimate of mine [of rice allotted to the *sangha*], if there is *padi* in excess [large supply], let these . . . [shares] remain as I said. But if there is less [smaller supply], let the proportion be calculated before dividing it out."[32] These calculations allowed the allocation of precise portions for all those involved with little or no concern for the fluctuation of supply and demand, at least on a large scale. The donor allotted "one *cā rwat* [a unit of measure] daily" for the monks; "one *prañ* [basket] for the *pitaka* [library, i.e., paying for those who maintained it]; thirty baskets of unhusked rice for the school; twenty *prañ* of husked rice for twenty monks per day; one *tañ srak ta khway* [another unit of measure] went to the 'law' [preaching of the Law] every three months of *si tañ* [Buddhist 'lent']." The rest went to those who worked the land.[33]

Because occupation was hereditary—especially in the government sector—population increases during periods of obvious growth did not necessarily imply agricultural expansion. If, for example, the agricultural sector needed more cultivators but population increased among the artisans instead, this additional supply of labor did not necessarily affect the expansion of cultivated land directly. And vice versa: If population increased in the agricultural sector, but labor was needed in trade, workers in the former simply became more specialized rather than moving to sectors where they were needed, for mobility was forbidden between classes (*kywan-tō* or *purā kywan* could not become *asañ,* although the reverse was allowed). The result was that population increases per se need not imply increased production; demographic and other pressures tended to be resolved by specialization of function within a class. Rather than changing economic roles, individuals created more niches in traditional forms of livelihood, making elaborate distinctions in essentially homogenous groups. Thus we hear of cowherds being distinguished (in ways more significant than the obvious) from goatherds, buffalo herders from tenders of ducks, elephant keepers from those in charge of horses; planters of *padi* from reapers of *padi,* guards of the fields from gardeners.[34] Hereditary occupation, in other words, limited the choices available for people to find new modes of living.

The capital enjoyed easy access to the royal granaries dispersed throughout the crown lands via perennial streams and rivers, which allowed grain to be transported to the capital where much of it would be deposited. Not all royal grain was physically moved from crown lands to the capital, however, since rights of disposal given to fief holders and other administrators accomplished much the same goal of distributing economic and political patronage. The "headman of the granaries of the eleven *kharuin*" (Kyaukse), a minister at court,

apparently oversaw the operation.[35] A similar parcelling of the grain
or extraction of other revenues as tax took place in non-crown areas
also. It is not certain, but likely, that *asañ* ancestral lands were not
subject to produce tax, but a per capita tax, known later as household tax, was probably imposed on their owners. In the eighteenth
and nineteenth centuries, communal (ancestral) holdings by *asañ* villages were exempt; in the fourteenth century they were required to
pay a miniscule one–sixty-fourth of their crops, probably imposed as
a token since the ancient texts sanctioned it. Because the state
already held the best lands in the kingdom, far more revenue could
be acquired by imposing per capita tax on independent persons than
by levying a produce tax on people who were largely in nonagricultural occupations. As noted earlier, if *asañ* villages had over them
an "eater," the revenue due the state was instead taken to that person, after government assessors and other officials had claimed their
stipulated shares.[36] Thus one inscription declared that "the fees of
the assessor shall be a piece of cloth and 25 pieces of lead in the case
of a field having a sowing capacity of half a basket; 50 pieces in the
case of *muryañ* [a type of rice] paddy-lands."[37] *Asañ* villages that
earned their living in ways other than cultivation paid a form of
fixed "occupation tax"; for example, fishing villages paid according
to the number and size of each fishnet they possessed or were subject
to *añ khwan* or "fisheries tax," which may have been a fee for the use
of government fisheries.[38] In addition, there were "the usual court
fees, harbor dues, cart tolls, stall rents, and petty taxes," including a
sales tax on the transactions over sale or hire of labor, the rights to
which probably lay either in the governor of the province or the
eater.[39]

Trade too was apparently administered by the state. There is little
contemporary evidence on external trade, partly, it seems, a result of
the type of sources available and partly because of the subordinate
role trade played in the kingdom's economy. Only a few nonindige-
nous items such as coral, pearls, and imported (and expensive) cloth
are mentioned, and very rarely, in the inscriptions. Although this
may suggest some commercial relations with Śrī Laṅka, known for
its pearls, and India, for its cloth, Pagan already had substantial religious contacts with both.[40] Furthermore, linguistic evidence illustrates the minor role that trade played in Burmese society: the word
for oceangoing vessel *(sañphaw)* is of Malay origin, while the word
for pearl *(pulay)* is Mon.[41] Moreover, the bulk of the occupations

mentioned in the epigraphs are agrarian in nature; seldom are commercial occupations mentioned. However, the fact that traders and trading towns were distinguished in an organized fashion from non-commercial villages and towns suggests at least the existence of administered trade. Indian merchants were located together in colonies where they lived and worshipped according to their own customs.[42] The word for "rich man" *(seṭṭhi)* is Tamil and was used often as a title, suggesting that these Indian merchants were a select group. The government also directly administered the nerve centers of trade in Lower Burma and the Kra Isthmus when it could: Pusim, Pegu, Tala, Muttama (Martaban), Thaton, and Mergui's economic affairs were regulated by appointed governors of the Pagan court.[43] As labor was often acquired from India,[44] that trade had to pass through some of these Lower Burma ports, notably Pusim, the east-west gateway, and under direct control of Pagan.

On the whole, Upper Burma throughout its precolonial history had little need for external trade. Everything it needed for the functioning of its economy of redistribution, the development of the fine arts, and for temple and monastery construction was available there. Irrigated lands, fruits and vegetables, fisheries, marble, iron, alabaster (for sculpture), gold, silver, rubies, emeralds, clay, bricks, timber, and stone were all products of Upper Burma.[45] Internal trading activity seems also to have been under state regulation, since all occupational groups, traders as well as non-traders, were organized by the state into guildlike communities, thereby allowing central control over most economic activity. "Trade," to use Marc Bloch's description of Medieval European society, "was not nonexistent, but irregular in the extreme. The society of this age was certainly not unacquainted with either buying or selling. But it did not, like our own, live by buying and selling.[46]

Sluices, canals, dams, and weirs, along with a variety of other methods, were used to tap the perennial rivers that fed dry but rich central Burma, dominated by three large irrigated plains that surrounded the capital. Many crops were grown here but it was *padi,* the mainstay of the Kingdom of Pagan, that allowed Pagan to grow from a fort on the Irrawaddy to the capital of a mighty Southeast Asian kingdom. *Padi* paid the soldiers and government officials who administered the state from Bhamo to Thaton, the artisans who built the (nearly) four thousand temples that dotted the landscape, fed the monks and their attendants as well as the population, which must have numbered between one and a half to two million, and provided the wherewithal to perpetuate all of these for three and a half centuries. Trade may have been important, but it was not vital to the state. It was land and the labor that were vital. Using what were probably natural units of administration—village, town, and circles —ruled by local, regional, as well as central officials, appointed by the center at times and elected by their own constituents as well, the kingdom "fed" these officials who "ate" their share of the grain in return for service. Through a system that is now called redistribution, the material resources of the Pagan kingdom were harnessed, then transformed into political power, social rank, and spiritual status, all intimately embedded in one another. Land, labor, and water turned the dry plains of central Burma into the center of a bustling, thriving, dynamic kingdom that convinced the ordinary man and woman that indeed Pagan was earthly Tāvatiṁsa, paradise-on-earth.

6

The Articulation
of Social Behavior:
Justice, Hierarchy, and the Law

THE ADMINISTRATION of civil and criminal justice in Pagan was based on codified law, which in Burma was expressed in two major genres: the *dhammathat* and the *rājāthat*. The former was essentially a collection of civil laws that normally dealt with marriage, inheritance, property rights, and the status of people. The latter, mainly a collection of royal edicts *(amintō)*, was concerned primarily though not exclusively with crimes of a political nature such as theft, arson (often a signal for rebellion), murder, and treason. Although it is not certain precisely when the term *rājāthat* emerged, this distinction between criminal and civil law seems to have existed as early as the Pagan period. For our purposes, however, the emphasis will be on civil law; *rājāthat*, though certainly important, is a subject that received little attention in donative inscriptions.

The concept of justice, furthermore, was not detached from other concerns of society but was embedded in the social, political, and religious institutions of Pagan as well. In fact, civil law upheld religious ethics, social status, and political rank, while criminal law, dealing with crimes against the state, was meant to insure political order. This chapter will discuss several major issues of civil law: the uniformity of the system, that is, that law was indeed codified and applicable to both commoner and minister, to city dweller and villager, and to those in the capital and those outside it; and how this law explicitly upheld the hierarchic (therefore kammic) conceptions of society.

Sources

With a few notable exceptions, like the now rare works of E. Maung, Emil Forchhammer, and Sir John Jardine, few works based on original source material have been published in the West that deal with either the history of legal institutions in Burma or the development of its laws.[1] R. Lingat's article on the subject in the *Journal of the Siam Society* was derived from secondary sources and was occasionally factually incorrect. A 1978 article by M. B. Hooker on Southeast Asian law is one of the few analytical treatments in English to include Burmese law since the works noted above, which were completed in the early 1900s.[2] The problem is not lack of sources, however, for there are many *dhammathat* available that were compiled during the course of Burmese history. There are numerous edicts issued by various kings as well as a countless number of *sittan* (administrative records) from which could be extracted information on law as it was practiced. The inscriptions of Pagan yield some data, too, in the form of several legal cases, and although they are of one kind (usually disputes over ownership of land), they nevertheless throw considerable light on the structure and sometimes principles of thirteenth-century jurisprudence. The problem is rather one of analysis: of the development and relationship of civil law to other institutions in Burmese society.

Emil Forchhammer's study, entitled *King Wagaru's Manu Dhamma-sattham,* attempted to show by internal analysis that many of the various law codes found in Burma had been based on this thirteenth-century work, which, although commissioned by King Wagaru of Martaban in Lower Burma, was compiled by a jurist of Upper Burma. Forchhammer felt that there were sufficient differences among the law codes in his possession to suggest that they had been compiled not only independently of one another, but at different periods in Burmese history. Of these law codes, the *Wagaru Dhamma-that* had preserved basic civil law, while the other legal codes of a later age, such as the *Wonnana* and *Manu Kyay,* increasingly justified secular customs and laws by appealing to what Forchhammer called "Buddhist metaphysics."[3] My research has shown that in addition to the *Wagaru Dhammathat,* there are at least two other codes that can be used to represent Burmese society in the thirteenth century, if not earlier. The oldest of all the *dhammathat* that survived in Burma appears to be the *Kungya Dhammathat,* ostensibly compiled in four volumes in A.D. 713 by Minpyan, a Pagan prince, which had as its basis an even older one (that does not survive) whose copy was said to contain more rules than the *Kungya* and was allegedly written in A.D. 649. (The Sadaw Maha Saṅgharājādhamma, who resided at

Pagan in the gilt monastery built by Mohnyin Mintayagyi of Ava in 1426, possessed a copy of the latter *dhammathat.*) The *Kungya* is also referred to as the *Pagan Pyanchi* and the *Lezaudwe.*[4] The title *Pagan Pyanchi* is a clue to its authenticity, because there was a family of scribes in Pagan whose title, *Pyanchi,* was mentioned several times in the contemporary inscriptions.[5] (Normally, persons excelling in literature or scholarship had their titles attached to their works.) Despite the existence of these various, perhaps, older law codes, Forchhammer chose—for reasons that we cannot deal with here—to use the *Wagaru Dhammathat* as the example par excellence of Burmese civil law.

The other *dhammathat* that is important to this discussion is the *Dhammavilāsa Dhammathat,* probably compiled sometime in the latter half of the twelfth century by a Buddhist monk named Sariputta, who subsequently received the title *dhammavilāsa* for completing this work.[6] In 1650, the code was recopied under the auspices of another king.[7] In 1781, it was copied again and renamed the *Minkun Dhammathat Lanka;* and was also analyzed by Forchhammer, who stated that it was "in good order containing 86 leaves, eight lines to the page."[8] This is apparently the same code that Father Vincentius Sangermano included in an appendix to his history of the Burmese empire, although the title by which Father Sangermano knew it was not the same.[9]

In 1893, the British government concluded that Burmese law was in fact significantly different from Indian law with its emphasis on caste (especially that concerning marriage and inheritance) and assigned Wundauk U Gaung, the Kinwun Mingyi under King Mindon, the task of compiling a work of Burmese civil law based on all the then extant law codes in Burma. U Gaung managed to collect thirty-nine law codes and consequently produced two large volumes dealing with marriage and inheritance. Each law in the compilation was accompanied by a reference in the margin to the particular *dhammathat* from which it was taken. This detail was especially useful, for it enabled the reader to determine not only the approximate age of a particular law but also its source.[10] Of the thirty-nine codes collected, twenty or more were compiled after 1750; no more than three or perhaps four before the fourteenth century; while the rest were written between the fourteenth and eighteenth centuries. Most of the law codes in Burma that survived, then, were compiled under the energetic King Alaunghpaya. Several were written or copied after his reign, from about 1842 onward. Of the latter, about eight are copies of older works and are not originals. The codes relevant to the discussion here are those belonging to the fourteenth century and earlier, along with, of course, contemporary inscriptions. These are Forchhammer's thirteenth-century *Wagaru Dhammathat* and Sangermano's edited version of the twelfth-century *Dhammavilāsa Dhammathat* (the *Shwe Myañ* ["golden"] *Dhammathat,* as we shall see), both of which also appear in U Gaung's digest.

Codified Law in Pagan

The authenticity of these two codes can be substantiated in three ways. One is to verify, through contemporary inscriptions, the existence of the monk Sariputta of Pagan said to have compiled the *Dhammavilāsa Dhammathat.* Another is to analyze Pagan epigraphs for mention of codified law. A third is to assess the extent to which actual court cases recorded in the inscriptions reflect the principles found in these laws and the extent to which these principles corroborate our reconstruction of Pagan society. Because law expresses the concerns and characterizes the structure of a society, the hierarchical organization, hereditary status, and embedded nature of the economy in Pagan should be evident in its legal principles; and specific institutions, such as fixed equivalencies and indentured labor, should have some mention in the codes.

For having compiled the *Dhammavilāsa Dhammathat,* the monk Sariputta received the honorable title *dhammavilāsa* from King Narapatisithu and was similarly honored by his successor, King Nātoṅmyā.[11] It follows, then, that whatever evidence might exist of this monk Sariputta in the inscriptions of Pagan should be found in the reigns of Narapatisithu and Nātoṅmyā. The earliest reference to Sariputta comes in an inscription erected by the monk himself in 1187 during King Narapatisithu's reign.[12] In 1211, another inscription, this one by King Nātoṅmyā, mentioned the monk by title: " . . . our Master, great king of glorious future, at the time when Master Mahathī Thammavilāsa paid respects with ornaments to the Pagoda, the Master (also) offered these *kywan* . . . ."[13] In 1231, a monk entitled "Dhamma rājā vilat" erected a pagoda, and in 1238, among the important religious personages present as witnesses to a dedication was one identified as Dhammavilat.[14] Moreover, an anonymous monk in Śrī Laṅka, upon his return from Pagan to Mahānāgakula (near Polonnaruwa), a contemporary kingdom in Śrī Laṅka with which Pagan had relations, sent a letter to a colleague in Pagan in which Sariputta was mentioned with great reverence. The letter began with a panegyric of the splendors of Pagan, then followed these lines: " . . . about this time there was a distinguished friar in Pagan, Sariputta surnamed Dhammavilāsa . . ."[15] In the fifteenth century, King Dhammaceti acknowledged the role Sariputta had played and described him in the Kalyani Inscription as "a *sāmanera* [novice] called Sāriputta, who . . . went to Pukām and received the *upasampadā* ordination at the hands of Ānandathera . . . (and later received) the title Dhammavilāsa Thera."[16] Finally, in 1661, an author with the title Shyaṅ Mahā Silavaṁsa mentioned in a small historical treatise called *Parāyanavathu* the *rahan* (monk) Sariputta who had compiled the *Dhammavilāsa Dhammathat* and received the title of *dhammavilāsa*.[17]

That a civil code was functioning in Pagan is clear. In 1249, King Klacwā issued a series of edicts inscribed on stone pillars that were dispersed over the Pagan central region, of which a few survived. Included in these edicts is a brief description of legal procedures and jurisprudence as it was practiced.

> If a thief is caught, the King, before proclaiming, [this man] "stole," gives him to the persons who consider theft cases. And these persons, having carried out an investigation, should [he] not be [a thief], release him. But if he is, they cause the *Amanwan Cā* ["Collection of Old Rules"] to be read. In the *Amanwan* it says that a thief, if he has committed such and such a transgression, must pay such and such a penalty. [Then] the King matches the thief's transgression in the *Amanwan* and exacts the penalty incurred by that crime.[18]

In the same edict, King Klacwā added that his words were not merely of the present moment but laid down in the law *(ya khu ti sā ma hut, taryā twaṅ le ī suiw min e mat lo)*.[19] In the same year, a person by the name of Jeyyapikraṁ and his wife erected an inscription in which another reference to the (apparently) same treatise was made even more explicit. A civil case had been brought under investigation, and when the judges had reached a decision, King Klacwā declared: "If that is the testimony, you [judges] arrange [the verdict] according to the *Golden [Shwe Myaṅ] Dhammathat*."[20] A legal document explicitly referred to as a *dhammathat* and used as a basis for legal decisions is nothing less than codified law. As early as the Pagan period, then, it appears that a law code called the *Golden Dhammathat* was already in use. The context of the latter court case concerned the ownership of *kywan,* which further testifies to its civil nature, while the *Amanwan Cā,* concerned with theft, may have been the origin of the criminal code, the early equivalent of the *rājāthat.*

It is my belief that the *Shwe Myañ Dhammathat* mentioned in the inscriptions is the source for the later *Manuthara Shwe Myañ Dhammathat,* which Father Sangermano appended to his book. The names are identical except for the prefix *Manuthara* ("Laws of Manu"), a common title affixed to many legal codes of Burma to give them classical Indian credentials, a practice that appeared early rather than late in Burmese history. Moreover, the original title of the code Sangermano included in his book still survives in the British Library —*Manu Manaw Dhammavilāsa Shwe Myañ Dhammathat*—indicating that the compiler was indeed Dhammavilāsa.[21] By the seventeenth century, the *Shwe Myañ Dhammathat* was treated with great respect and regarded as the ultimate source of Burmese legal principles. When King Thalun issued two edicts setting guidelines for jurisprudence, he instructed his judges that if one could not reach a decision based on contemporary law, then "let him take in hand the four volumes of the *Manosara* [*Manuthara*] *Shwe Myañ.* . . ."[22]

Many features of Old Burmese orthography in these codes further strengthen our view of their Pagan origins. Spelling of such prepositions as *kuiw* ("to") was still retained; *tō* (honorific) was spelled in a transitional manner, between Old Burmese and nineteenth-century Burmese; *phurā* ("lord" or "Buddha") was still spelled with the *pha* or *pa* and not the later *bha;* the "high" tone, represented by consonants or not at all in Pagan, appears in the codes more frequently as the *visarga* (:); the *ai* sound was represented by a relatively new symbol (`), instead of the older use of a "y"; "three" *(sum)* was spelled as in Pagan, with an *m* final; *syañ* (an honorific) remains the same and had not yet become *rhañ.*[23] Many of the names given to *asañ* craftsmen retained their older forms, such as *khawā sañ* (washerman).[24] Titles such as *senāpati* or *cac sūkrī* (commander-in-chief) continued to be used, while *sūthi sūkrway* ("rich man") had undergone a change, from *ṭh* to *th,* although pronunciation appeared to be the same.[25] Finally, the content of the laws themselves reveal their own origins, for the principles that they express almost always echo the important social and economic concerns and institutions of Pagan.

Most of the lawsuits recorded in inscriptions concerned the ownership of land and rights to labor. They are recounted in minute detail, naming every owner, who sold what to whom, who inherited what, and whether or not a seller had the legal right to do what he did. More important than purely legal matters was the way in which the facts that were brought out in court tended to confirm the principles found in an embedded economy. One case, for example, revolved around "interest" on borrowed money, limited to double the principal.[26] In another, the costs of land included fees that were irrelevant to the land itself (such as food and drink for the parties involved), and whenever there was default, the costs were double those set in the original transaction. When the deal was finally closed, the total costs were about three times those first agreed upon.[27] Such thirteenth-century practices are echoed in the *Shwe Myañ Dhammathat,* which declared that "whosoever takes money from another, promising at some stated time to give him some merchandise, but afterwards breaks his word, is bound to pay double the sum he has received;" or more important, the *Wagaru Dhammathat* stated that the price of a full grown male *kywan* was set at exactly 30 *klyap* of silver.[28] Similarly, the purchase price of other important commodities was fixed: elephants were worth 100 *klyap* of silver, a horse 50, a buffalo 3, an ox 2, and a pig 2. The equivalents of precious metals, especially gold to silver and silver to lead, were similarly fixed. Wages for laborers were set at "a quarter or the eighth part of a [*klyap*] for a woman, and twice as much for a man." And, according to Sangermano, "these prices represent ancient standards."[29]

Law also mirrored social organization. We have discussed how a person pledged to a patron as a *kywan,* was actually on contract, that kywanship was a legal status; this status was recorded in a document called a *cā raṅ* or *cā khup,* which was stamped with a color-coded official seal *(taṁ chip).*[30] A *kywan,* though on rare occasions, could alter his status by joining the *saṅgha,* after which, even if he decided to leave it, he could no longer be legally considered a *kywan.*[31] This practice is confirmed by the *Shwe Myañ Dhammathat,* under the statute called "the Law on the Seven Kinds of *Kywan,*" which states: "Those who having been *kywan,* have, with the consent of their master, put on the habit of a *Talapoin* [monk], these, even if they afterwards lay aside the habit, cannot again be reduced to *kywan* status."[32]

The categories of *kywan* set out by the *Shwe Myañ Dhammathat* also apply readily to the situation at Pagan. But even more significant, the definition of a *kywan* echoes the Pagan situation almost exactly.

There are seven species of *kywan* who are bound to render personal services to their masters. 1. Those who are bought with money. 2. The children of a female *kywan* living in a family. 3. *Kywan* by birth, that is, those whose parents are *kywan*. 4. *Kywan* given as presents. 5. Those who make themselves *kywan* to deliver themselves from some trouble. 6. Those who in times of scarcity are dependent on others for support. 7. Those who hire themselves out for daily or monthly labour.[33]

The last three categories especially explain how one in fact became a *kywan* in Pagan. The *Shwe Myañ Dhammathat* then makes it even more explicit: One can become a *kywan* if "a father . . . sells himself [as?] a *kywan,* and at the same time gives his son *in pledge* [emphasis added] to the same or any other master. . . ."[34] It goes on to categorize two kinds of *kywan,* one temporary and the other permanent, whose counterparts in Pagan we have already noted as debtor *kywan* (with the option of redemption) in contrast to those captured in war (whose status was permanent).[35]

The mere presence of such laws in the *Wagaru Dhammathat* and *Shwe Myañ Dhammathat* is convincing proof of their antiquity, if not of their Pagan origins. Moreover, these laws as well as the codes were not simply models from which moral aphorisms could be extracted and pronounced but were a fundamental part of everyday life and its processes throughout the twelfth and thirteenth centuries and those after Pagan's political demise. That the *Wagaru Dhammathat,* compiled in Mon Lower Burma, upholds institutions that could be described as Pagan's testifies to the extent of administrative uniformity even in distant places. More importantly, that codes thought to be written in the twelfth and thirteenth centuries were used continually in later Burmese history, both as contemporary guides as well as sources of legal precedents, indicates the strength and continuity of Burmese legal and social institutions.

The Justice System in Pagan

There were at least two, possibly three, administrative levels of justice in Pagan: a preliminary investigative body known as *tamkra,* the

lower court or *buih taryā,* and the superior and appellate court called
the *ataṁ taryā.*[36] Their functional distinctions are to be seen in a case
(among others) involving rights over ownership of *kywan.* The litigants had taken the case to the appellate division because, as one
stated, no satisfactory decision had been reached at the first two
levels. Witnesses were called to testify, having sworn on the *Abhi-
dhamma,* and "pleaders" for both the state (called *man khraṅ*) and the
defense (called *khraṅ cayā*) presented their arguments.[37] The decision
was subsequently declared, written down by the judges in palm-leaf
books called *atuiṅ phrat cā,* and affixed with a seal of the court as well
as those of the individual judges, then stored. These decisions were
collectively called *amū kwan* or *amhat kwan* ("legal records") and
must have been the basis for later expansion of the legal code.[38]

The lower court may have represented the village or town judicial
system, while the appellate court may have been concerned with
those matters not settled at the first level. Although there may have
been appellate divisions at various designated towns throughout the
kingdom, the inscriptions describe only the one at Pagan. It is
unlikely, however, that appeals from as far away as Bassein or Tala,
for instance, would have to be tried in the capital. More probably
appellate courts away from the central region were simply ad hoc
arbitration sessions agreed upon by the litigants (as the *Shwe Myañ
Dhammathat* in fact states)[39] or called by the governor of the nearest
major town, as was done later in Burmese history.

In the capital, cases were tried in a building called "the pleasant
palace of the law" *(taryā kon sā yā)* in which resided judges who were
given the title *taryā saṅ pha ma* or simply *taryā* ("the law") or *saṅ pha
ma* ("justices").[40] Sometimes they were called *taryā sūkrī* ("headmen
of the law").[41] Like other members of the king's court, outstanding
jurists received additional titles from the crown such as *manu rājā*
("Lord of Manu," i.e., expert on legal matters).[42] While the positions of the judges on the superior court seemed permanent, those of
the lower courts were apparently ad hoc, filled primarily by different
categories of headmen.[43] However, since most positions in Pagan
society were hereditary, such ad hoc functions probably became permanent. The mere existence, not to mention the functioning, of various judiciary levels such as the investigative body, lower courts, and
appellate divisions indicate the extent to which Pagan's legal structure and thought had evolved. Moreover, that the concept of "appeals" was in operation is an admission that even governments led

by "Embryo Buddhas" could be fallible, for the concept recognizes "fairness" in contrast to arbitrary judgments, a structural contradiction to the institution of Burmese kingship itself.

The richness of legal terminology used in Pagan further illustrates the relative complexity of the system: there were terms such as "litigant" *(amu sañ)*, "suits" *(taryā chan)*, and "to sue" *(taryā cway)*;[44] and also legal phrases such as "the bench of the magistrate" *(taryā plañ)*[45] and "judges that appear at the court house" *(kwan plok* [court house] *htwak tō mū sō* [that appear] *san pha ma suiw* [judges]).[46] "Barristers" or "attorneys of the state" were called *rhiy tō niy amū chan khran sō san pha ma suiw*, literally meaning "pleaders who reside in front of the King."[47] The inscriptions record legal jargon such as "fell into dispute" *(min kra)*; "winning (and) losing the verdict" *(oan* and *ma oan* or *taryā oan* and *taryā whum)*; "to bring suit (or) legal action" against someone *(taryā chan kra)*; "court's formal (sealed) decision" *(taryā tan chip tap liy)*; "to have a hearing" *(kra ra kā)*; and "judicial decision" *(taryā htuy tao tān lat)*.[48]

Law and the Belief System

In simplistic terms, the underlying concern in twelfth- and thirteenth-century Burmese law was hierarchy. Rank in society was confirmed by law, in effect legalizing the social position one acquired at birth.[49] Hereditary status was a legal principle upon which conceptions of justice were based. Justice was not impartial, blind to birth and rank nor did it assume that all individuals were equal before the law. Social status rather than objective factors determined punishment. As the *Shwe Myañ Dhammathat* stated:

> if a man, free born and of a respectable state in life, kills a poor man, he must pay the price of ten *kywan;* and the fine is the same in (the) case (of) a poor man who kills a *kywan:* but if he kills a person superior to himself he must pay the value of fifteen *kywan*. The murderer of a Talapoin or a Brahmin must pay a fine of fifty ounces of gold.[50]

The legal motto in Burmese law might well have been "Let the punishment fit the man" rather than "Let the punishment fit the crime." That equality was not a valued legal concept is attested by most of the cases that have been analyzed here: no *kywan,* as far as can be ascertained, brought suits, and they were probably restricted from doing so. Even credibility as a witness was determined by status.[51] "If," stated the *Wagaru Dhammathat,* "all evidence is equal regarding property, the King and his ministers' claims shall get the preference, as he is the Lord of the Land . . . ," a position frequently echoed in the inscriptions. Trial was conducted by ordeal only if the litigants were of similar rank and the evidence in such cases less than compelling.[52] Trials-by-ordeal in fact confirmed ex post facto the belief that man was inherently unequal, with differences in past *kamma.* This principle of "inequality" was only mirroring what was a major component of the belief system—unequal merit.

As equality before the law suggests egalitarianism, inequality before the law implies the presence of hierarchy and subjective judgments. And where law is personal and subjective, it is embedded in institutions not necessarily legal in nature. Western concepts and values that uphold individuality are as often reflected in impersonal and egalitarian legal principles as those supporting collectivism are mirrored by personal and hierarchic legal principles. In Burma, when one's relatives were legally held responsible for one's actions, collectivistic not individualistic priorities were being affirmed.[53] Yet, because politically and socially superior people had to behave in ways that reflected their station in life, as did those under them, inequality before the law did not necessarily imply injustice per se, for often the inferior in rank, because of that rank, benefited. "If the offender does not possess . . . (the) amount, then the fine inflicted shall be proportional to his means," stated the law, or "If a man were hungry there shall be no fault in his eating fruits and other things" that belonged to another.[54] Even in the business sphere justice was subjective: "When a person puts out his money to interest, if he be a poor person, he may receive monthly one per cent.; two per cent. if he be of the class of Mandarins; four per cent. if he be a rich man; and five per cent. if he be a merchant."[55]

Thus guilt or innocence, fine and punishment were not treated as though they were divorced from the kinds of social considerations that might, in a Western court of law, be seen as "irrelevant and immaterial." Even the buying and selling of one's own property had social, kinship, and community considerations. Empirical factors had less to do with the criteria for determining what constituted justice than harmony and community good will did. Values regarding kinship ties, religious morality, personal relationships, social status, and political power were all involved as factors in defining what was legal.

Law in Burma then, was personal, subjective, hierarchic, and embedded in institutions not necessarily legal in nature. Because morality and hierarchy were synonymous, and hierarchy was the principle upon which Burmese law was based, legality was synonymous with morality. Merit and glory *(kutho* and *phun)* in effect defined what was legal.

Several conclusions are suggested by this evidence. First, legal terms, such as "bench," taken for granted and abbreviated without explanation suggest their already established status by the thirteenth century. Furthermore, the presence of barristers, however inchoate, corroborates the existence of uniform, codified law at least for a substantial period of time, for there must first be written, uniform law before there can be a distinct group or category of experts whose profession rests largely upon that uniformity. Moreover, the presence of lawsuits instead of justice through vengeance from kin and other familial groups implies that Pagan society recognized by then a central, uniform authority and perceived of itself, order, and justice in terms that transcended the personal, tribal, or familial. Society no longer consisted of the fiercely independent groups of kin, tribes, or fortified villages of pre-Pagan Upper Burma. That stage of development had been reached where a higher authority was recognized not simply as a military power uniting disparate groups by force of arms but as a social, economic, and legal force integrating society. In fact, lawsuits decided on the basis of uniform, codified law among members of society from different social and economic levels suggest that the concept as well as the reality of "belonging" rested upon concerns reflecting a unified polity. In effect, the autonomy of subgroups had been compromised for a higher order of stability—that of central government.

Marc Bloch aptly wrote of European society:

> The consolidation of societies into great states or principalities favoured not only the revival of legislation but also the extension of a unifying jurisprudence over vast territories. . . . [It reflects] an era in which society tends to organize human relations more strictly, to establish more clearcut divisions between the classes, to obliterate a

great many local variations, and finally to allow change only at a slower rate. For this decisive metamorphosis . . . the transformation of
legal thought . . . was a very important contributory factor.[56]

Uniform jurisprudence in any given area within Pagan's political
boundaries meant centralization of the political and economic forces
there. Indeed, the late twelfth and thirteenth centuries witnessed a
process whereby those disparate traditions that went into forming
the Kingdom of Pagan were made permanent. It was a time when
weights and measures, currencies and monies were standardized;
when a norm for language and literature was being articulated;
when art and architecture became classic models to be emulated by
posterity (even if poorly); when Theravāda Buddhism was institutionalized and integrated with a variety of beliefs; and when customs
were codified and legalized.

But because the legal system of Pagan was not made for a trade-
oriented society but an agrarian one, not for the merchant but for
the artisan and the cultivator classes—whose political, social, and
economic presence was indispensable to the heartbeat of the civilization—the artisan and cultivator classes remained predominant in
the social, political, and economic life of Pagan, reinforced by their
"ally," the Buddhist *saṅgha*. Instead of changing the priorities held
by these nonmerchant classes, the legal system reaffirmed their
established values and traditions and codified them into law—allowing these principles to prevail and to be perpetuated well into later
centuries. The irony was that by the sixteenth century the conditions
in Lower Burma were ripe for the merchant and trading classes.
Instead of becoming a major force in post-Pagan Burma, however—
and perhaps altering certain priorities of Burmese society—these
incipient merchant classes were subjected to laws that confirmed and
perpetuated the interests of the artisan and cultivator classes, thus
allowing society to retain its fundamental agrarian nature. Had the
merchant in Pagan, instead of the artisan, taken the role that he did
in Europe, the history of post-Pagan Burma might have been different.

Like the society and culture, the state must also have been going
through similar trends and transformations toward establishing a
permanent tradition. This is the subject of discussion in the next
chapter.

7

The Arrangement of
Political Power

To THE HISTORIAN, the importance of ideology lies in the realm of intellectual history, where beliefs, having been absorbed and internalized by the society, shape behavior, which in turn helps create events. Like C. C. Berg's picture of the relationship between Javanese mythical culture and its political structure, Burmese political ideology has been no less important in shaping the course of "objective" events in its history,[1] and the Pagan court was no less a structural realization of political ideology.

But deciding exactly where the political structure ends and the social or administrative structure begins is largely arbitrary. In the conical scheme already described, those with the highest social status were also those with the highest administrative authority and political power. The only exception was probably the primate, whose status was strictly religious, though even he was not without political, economic, or social influence. Nevertheless, viewing the Pagan kingdom from the political dimension, one finds at its very top the king and his court, which consisted of princes, princesses, and queens, all members of the royal family, and royal advisors, some of whom were former monks, some trusted elder members of the royal family.

At the apex was the king, a sovereign, not *primus inter pares,* whose right to kingship rested on a variety of factors—especially performance and, of course, birth. The king was the cell leader, the *khoñ* or head of his cell, the court, which was in turn the "head" of Burmese society. The entire political structure was a matter of relationships: between the king and his primate, his princes, his queens, his ministers, and his advisors, each of whom headed a segment of Burmese society. How he managed each relationship often determined his legitimacy as well as his survival—in some cases, the survival of the kingdom itself.

Much of the data for the following description, mostly of the Pagan court, is derived from King Nātoṅmyā's reign (1210–1234) and represents a form that was fully developed only by the mid-twelfth and early thirteenth centuries. Because Nātoṅmyā's reign immediately succeeded King Narapatisithu's era of immense growth, understandably, it enjoyed many of the fruits of that period: it had the stability, the peace, the leisure to allow growing institutions to take root and mature. There are, however, gaps in the knowledge of this period because of the paucity and type of evidence at our disposal. Data from the immediate post-Pagan period where the same or similar institutions were being described have been used to fill some of these gaps. Moreover, our sources do not allow a full analysis and description of every office at court, but those that were of paramount importance to the power of the king will be discussed, however briefly.

The Court

The court was a microcosmic replica of the larger socioadministrative pattern—a small cone to be more precise—which has been described in an earlier chapter. It was the highest-ranking cell in the kingdom, whose leader was the king. Though the court was substantially more complex than the unit upon which it was probably founded, it nevertheless retained the basic principle of the cell—centricity. The crucial factors upon which power rested were in part institutional and in part personal. Buddhist conceptions of the universe and of kingship with their directional appellation and symbolism were a basic part of the structure of the court. Buddhist terminology articulated, in what was then an international jargon, an essentially Burmese sociopolitical and economic unit.

The members of court may be divided into three general categories: royalty; administrators of ministerial rank, who may or may not have been members of the former; and subordinate officials of the above. At the top was the *maṅ krī* ("great king"), under whom were *maṅ sā* (princes), *maṅ samī* (princesses), *ami purā* (queens), and *moṅ ma* (concubines). Below this group were ministers, called *amat* or *amatayā,* who were primarily but not always more distant relatives of the royal family. Under them were their subordinates, apparently non-royal but probably belonging to the top officialdom and perhaps even to the commoner class. Titles, ranks, insignia, fiefs, and other such rewards helped maintain the loyalty-patronage structure of the court.

By the mid-thirteenth century the Pagan court had evolved through at least two intermediate stages. Three inscriptions in particular record its development, as presented in Figure 3.[2] Although the ranking of court members in all three seems to be basically the same, the differences indicated among the members themselves were determined by different sets of criteria. For example, *A* is a *functional* view of the officials; *B* is concerned with *generic* or basic distinctions (that is, kinship relationships between the king and other members of the royal family); and *C* denotes *titular* distinctions between the members.

FIGURE 3
Political Structure

A Functional (A.D. 1192)	*B* Generic (A.D. 1235)	*C* Titular (A.D. 1271)
man krī (king)	*man krī* (king)	*man krī* (king)
man nay (lesser king)	*man sā* (son of king)	*man sā* (prince)
amat (minister)	*man ñī* (brother of king)	*ami purā* (queen)
prañ cuiw (governor of capital?)	*man samī* (daughter of king)	*man samī* (princess)
cā khī (scribe)	*man mliy* (grandchild of king)	*mon ma* (concubine)
asañ (non-bonded commoner)	*man nhama tō* (younger sister of king)	*amat* (minister)
	ami purā (consort of king)	*kalan-samben* (crown official)
	akrwan may ("leftover," i.e., non-royal commoners?)	*buih pā* (troops)
	prañ sū (civilians?)	
	buih pā (troops)	

These different perspectives of the court, recorded for identical purposes but by people of three different classes (a chief queen, a well-to-do couple, and a commoner) and at different periods in Pagan's development, provide us with information on the various components of its structure. The lists may also reflect changes in the court structure, indicating the path it took from a relatively streamlined organization *(A)* to one that became rather complex *(B)* and top heavy, eventually reverting to a less complicated but still elaborate structure *(C)* toward the close of the dynasty, perhaps suggesting the success of some needed reform.

In the context of the study as a whole, the word *maṅ sā* in *C* should be translated as a title ("prince") since the rest of the list consists of titles. In *B*, the same word should be translated literally, that is, "son of the king," for the words that follow it, such as *maṅ ñī* and *maṅ mliy* ("younger brother" and "grandson [or grandchild] of the king," respectively) are also kinship terms. In *A*, however, the corresponding word is neither "king's son" nor "prince" but *maṅ ṅay* ("lesser king"), indicating neither a kinship nor a titular relationship with the king but the functional distinction of a person who performed certain administrative duties at a level subordinate to the king. A similar case can be made for the word *ami purā*. That *A* failed to list it suggests that the queen did not play an administrative role in the court. In *B*, a kinship distinction is made between *ami purā* and *maṅ nhama tō*, both queens, the latter being the "younger sister" of the king. She was, in actuality, the chief queen, for the inscription from which *B* was taken states that "starting with the 'younger sister' of the king *(maṅ nhama tō)* . . . (were) all the queens *(ami purā),*" specifying her superior position among the other queens.[3] The chief queen's status was related directly to her particular consanguineous tie to the king.[4] In *C*, however, *ami purā* should be regarded as a title that separated queens from concubines *(moṅ ma)*, as *B* has separated consanguines from affines and kin from non-kin.

The same distinction applies to the official called *amat;* in *A*, he should be regarded as a "companion" of the king (the term's original Sanskrit meaning), albeit inferior in rank, whose functions distinguished him from others on the list. In *B*, *amat* is not mentioned because it is a kinship list. Yet we know that *amat*s existed at court, and we know that royal princes, more often than not, held ministerial positions. Thus in list *B* one should assume that male members of the royal family—particularly brothers *(maṅ ñī)*, (elder) sons *(maṅ sā)*, and perhaps even talented grandsons *(maṅ mliy)* of the king— were understood to have been *amat*s.

Below the level of royalty and court dignitaries, the political structure seemed to have been organized according to similar criteria. The *praṅ cuiw, cā khī,* and *asañ* of *A* were all functionally distinct terms, describing the governor of the capital city (?), his secretary, and the non-bonded worker, respectively. In *B*, distinctions were again generic, based on non-royal, that is, commoner, status; some of those listed were civilians while others were military. Admittedly, although the latter can be regarded as a functional distinction, it was made in a context that distinguished between two segments of one general class in the same way that different members of one royal family were distinguished from each other. The listing in *C* records only those given titles (such as *kalan-saṁbeñ*) normally held by crown officials. Apparently, *buih pā* (troops) was both a generic term as well as a title, appearing in both *B* and *C*. That they were not mentioned in list *A* suggests that most of the commoners in the eleventh and twelfth centuries must have served in the military (therefore their role was taken for granted) while *asañ,* being novel and apparently uncommon then, were explicitly mentioned. Indeed, the number of craftsmen, artisans, and traders (all *asañ*) must have increased only with Pagan's need to develop the arts and acquire labor from other areas, whereas people who served in the military must always have been part of the state, particularly at its inception when it was attempting to consolidate the various ethnopolitical elements in the vicinity.

Significantly, categories for neither the bonded *(kywan)* nor the "other worldly" *(saṅgha)* were included in the three lists, suggesting the largely political way in which the court was perceived. Leaving *kywan* out implied, among other things—such as a lack of civil status in law—that political power, in the eyes of Pagan society, was seen as an absence of obligation to a patron, and obligation was precisely what gave the patron political power. Members of the *saṅgha* were simply not viewed in a political context, regardless of their eventual role as a countervailing power to the state, for they were perceived to have left the secular world for the spiritual realm. When all three lists are combined, hierarchic separation in court appears to have been accomplished by titles, whereas division of power corresponded to functional distinctions. Below the court level the latter seems to have been the rule, for there were few titles.

Thus the court apparently evolved from a unit that in the eleventh and twelfth centuries had functionally separated its officials, into one that in the early thirteenth century stressed birth in a family that had acquired the exclusive distinction of being royal, and finally into one that distinguished its members by title, reflecting both function and proximity to royalty. Because of this change, titles such as *maṅ sā* in the late thirteenth century no longer applied exclusively to "sons of kings," a category that had apparently grown to uncontrollable proportions with the practice of concubinage. Such titles could now apply to anyone granted one, including brothers, grandsons, and uncles of the king—perhaps even to non-royalty recognized for distinguished service. And so it was with the title *man samī,* which no longer referred to the king's daughter, but to anyone holding that title, including nieces, granddaughters, sisters, and sometimes even concubines of the king. Similarly, *ami purā,* once a title reserved for those born of or marrying into the royal family, now applied to those *given* that title and was used primarily to distinguish a "queen" from a "concubine," rather than kin from non-kin. As for the term *man nhama tō,* what was once the king's "younger sister" now included other "terminological equivalents" such as the king's cousins as well. This type of development affected even the king's title *(man),* which was once reserved exclusively for him but by the thirteenth century was being used by several high officials while the king assumed increasingly grander titles. Because the court and royal family had apparently grown so large, proximity to the king had also become ambiguous. Kinship and functional titles that once had special meaning in a small court and royal family could no longer command the explicitness they once had enjoyed.

This is not to say that function or royal birth ceased to determine kingship or position in the court, but by the latter half of the thirteenth century the emphasis had changed from one particular set of criteria to another. Nor does it mean that kings did not possess elaborate titles earlier; they did. What it does mean is that the king's role as a governing *functionary* was more important in the eleventh and twelfth centuries than were his titles; that his royal birth was more significant in the early thirteenth century than his functions had been earlier; and that the possession of titles in the late thirteenth century had become more important in determining the composition of the court than either function or birth. Function and birth certainly continued to play a role in deciding elitism, but their relative importance had changed along with other transformations in the society—changes such as the growth in population, dispersion of political and economic power, and development of a larger officialdom—all of which in effect rendered earlier criteria for determining political rank not only less important but at times even anachronistic. In other words, the functional criteria that had originally distinguished one member of the court from another had become established to the point where the title, once merely a symbol of those criteria, had become the distinguishing criterion itself. The court's development, consequently, is an account of the institutionalization

of hereditary claims to offices that once had only functional requirements.

The King

As Pagan grew from a strategic fort on the bend in the Irrawaddy in
the ninth century to a kingdom that in the thirteenth century ruled
virtually the entire plains area of Burma, its political structure
became more and more complex. By the twelfth and at the latest the
thirteenth century, Burmese kingship had become regularized as the
top position on the cone. The Burmese king was a suzerain; he had
become a territorial as well as a personal head; he was guarantor of
justice and legislator of standardized laws, not simply perserver of
local and regional customs; he was guardian and ex officio "owner"
of the entire realm, not one of many territorial lords, "owners" of
their respective domains; he was defender of the faith and protector
of a "national" religion, not simply patron of the local bishop and a
participant in a universal Buddhist church headquartered elsewhere.
Pagan had become a centralized state, one that transcended the
ruler's personal authority. The royal army was the only army, the
royal courts were the only legitimate systems of justice, the royal tax
collectors were the only legal gatherers of revenue, and the Burmese
Buddhist church was the only recognized religious authority. No one
but the crown had military power backed by regular troops; no justice but crown justice was ultimately valid (with the exception of
ecclesiastic law for monks); no one but the crown could legally
impose taxes or make exemptions; and no other religious organization but the national *sangha* was considered the vehicle to salvation.
Burma by the thirteenth century was an embryonic nation-state, in
that its members perceived that they were related to each other
through common bonds of heritage and culture strong enough to set
that group off in significant ways from others.

As "lord of land and water," a descriptive phrase frequently found
in contemporary records,[5] the king enjoyed a suzerainty well established in concept as well as in fact by the period under study here.
Whether or not specific individuals, even as kings, succeeded in
asserting their power effectively at all times is not the issue. Some
individuals were certainly more able than others. What is at issue is
the recognition that the officeholder had the legal right to do the

things the office allowed him to, even if he were unsuccessful. That it was the institution of kingship that legitimized the office over the individual holding it is attested by the presence of succession rules (among other factors). Succession rules imply that an office should preempt the person holding it (regardless of violations of the rules), the assumption being that the office will remain intact while persons filling it come and go. The appointment of—and, one might add, even the desire to appoint—an heir apparent is testimony to the regularization of Pagan kingship. Clearly demarcated, ranked, and enfoeffed titles and positions subordinate to the king are further evidence that this assumption was in operation. Princes had their designated posts, as did queens, ministers, and advisors.

Furthermore, the title "lord of land and water" expressed suzerainty over both territory and the people in it, which made a king the owner—for as long as he held the office—of all the lands in the kingdom designated as "crown," of all the people designated as *kywan-tō,* and of all the other rights over non-crown people and territory to which his office entitled him. The king's political and economic power, then, rested upon control of land and labor, their use, and their tenure. Any rights to lands, people, and revenue that the king gave as fiefs, called *mahādan,* "the great gift," were given "(at the) royal compassion" *(sa nā tō);* they were revocable when that compassion waned. As a result, no contract was signed between king and subject that stipulated the extent and nature of service in return for the use of the land and its laborers. This favored the king's position, for the definition of "loyal service" (the basis for continued compassion) was left ambiguous, making that position even more absolute.

In other words, there were no other significant powers within the kingdom to compete for these resources—except the *sangha,* which will be discussed below. As noted earlier, there is no evidence in Burma of a feudal nobility, a landed class comparable in scope and significance to those of medieval France, England, or Japan. Of the few individuals who might have met those criteria, their numbers and share of the wealth of the kingdom have never been shown, much less their threat to the existence of the throne. Suzerainty, on the other hand, did not mean there were no political opponents; it meant that the ultimate aim of opponents was to secure the throne, not break away from it, for it was control of the position at the top of the cone that was the desired objective. The only class with the power and wealth, with the structure and the common interest to pose a balance to the government's control of the kingdom's wealth, was the church. It took a variety of methods and a great deal of ingenuity on the part of Pagan monarchs to keep the sources of power in crown hands.

The King and *Saṅgha*

Technically, the *saṅgha* was not a part of secular society, though in practice it was intimately integrated into the social, political, and economic life of Pagan. Virtually every male, at least once, entered the Order to experience a status spiritually above that of the laity. Those who decided to remain permanently in the clergy had to cut all secular ties—with family or political office as well as previous economic and legal obligations. For example, *kywan-tō*, if they joined the Order, would no longer be required to provide military or corvée service to the crown (and for this reason were often discouraged from joining the monkhood on a permanent basis); *asañ* under the same circumstances would no longer have to submit capitation tax. Those who became monks would instead be on the receiving end, so to speak, as both material and spiritual rewards were bestowed upon them by the public and the crown. Moreover, although immune from civil and criminal law, they could nevertheless use lay trustees to protect their temporal property, even in the secular courts, without directly giving up their privileged position. In criminal cases, they could throw their robes over condemned persons to spare them from the executioner's blade. The political implications of such action could be significant: a contender to the throne reprieved in this manner could enter the monastery under the protection of the monks, where, with potential political opponents of the king knowing exactly where he was, he might become the nucleus for a future rebellion, simply waiting for the opportunity to strike. Lastly, the *saṅgha* was, in terms of sheer numbers, probably as significant in Pagan society as it is today.[6] Thus, even though the *saṅgha* may have been technically divorced from secular society, in many ways it played a significant role in it.

The *saṅgha* seems to have been organized according to the following ranking system. *Bhikkhus* (monks), or *ariya saṅgha* as they were referred to in Pagan, and novices formed the most common level of monks; abbots or *mahāthī (mahāthera)* were apparently heads of village or town monasteries; *saṅgharāja*s apparently presided over monasteries of major towns or famous monasteries, for instance, those built by royalty; and the *mahāsaṅgharāja* was the appointed, technical supreme patriarch of the entire legitimate Buddhist church in the kingdom. The *mahāsaṅgharāja,* not technically a minister, nevertheless held a position in court and presided over those monks who were heads of major monasteries in Pagan and who were responsible to him on matters of discipline, enrollment, and other religious affairs.[7] Although the *mahāsaṅgharāja* may not have been formally given the title *amat* reserved for secular officials, his role at court must have been included in the cosmological scheme implied by the arrangement of religious buildings. We know that the *mahāsaṅgharāja* and his subordinates were present at major dedications, invariably reciting the *paritta* (incantations) to properly release donated lands from other possible spiritual ties.[8] It is difficult to say whether major monasteries similarly displayed the directional symbolism for which the rest of the court was noted, but there were mentioned northern, southern, and western monasteries in the contemporary sources.[9] The venerable Mahākassapa, one of the most important abbots during the thirteenth century in Pagan, headed the so-called "southern monastery." (Kassapa, one of the Buddhas of this *kappa* whose name the abbot assumed, is invariably represented in the iconography of Pagan on the southern face of temples.)[10] We also know that certain important temples and monasteries were built around new capital cities in a pattern that did fit into the cosmic design of a center with four cardinal points.[11]

Some scholars suggest that the *saṅgha* in Burma was never unified under one supreme head, the presence of sects or "branches" being given as evidence for this claim.[12] Although the question is still to be resolved, there are some reasons for disputing this view. Branches or sects *(guiṅ)* in Burmese history have been known more for their similarities than for their differences; they can be essentially distinguished by the degree of strictness by which they interpreted the *vinaya* or by their adherence to another, minor code of behavior or way of dress that symbolized that behavior. The schools around which differences in sects have tended to coalesce are traditionally two: the Mranmā Saṅgha (Burma *saṅgha*) and the Sīhala Saṅgha (Śrī Laṅka *saṅgha*). The latter represents the stricter of the two and is traditionally considered the "purer," at least in Burmese historiography, and is not a foreign church but an indigenous organization whose claims to legitimacy go to Śrī Laṅka.

There were also other sects, particularly orders of "forest monks," that disdained the wealth and worldly behavior of the main Order. There have always been such anti-establishment groups, but by and large, they have been small and without political or economic power. It was not uncommon, in fact, for a king to invite a highly renowned forest monk considered extremely pure by the public to serve as head of the Order. If the monk refused the king would of course be embarrassed, but there was reason for the monk to accept such an offer: it would on the one hand give him a chance to restore the "worldly" *sangha* to a state he could live with (its worldliness being the crux of his objection in the first place) and on the other provide him an opportunity to oversee a kingdomwide purification. It would play on his devotion and his belief in the necessity to return to purer origins. The king, for his part, would accomplish his desired goal of reducing the power of the main Order, in effect, creating a new sect. Purification, once achieved, however, was not permanent; public and royal largesse in time made the purified *sangha* again wealthy and hence "impure." It was then up to the next generation of kings to reduce that *sangha* by establishing another sect that was "purer" —that is, attracting another famous monk, sending a group of monks to Śrī Laṅka to be reordained (discussed below), and once more conducting purification.

This ebb and flow from purity to impurity—from Sīhala to Mranmā proclivities—should not be taken to mean that there were two structurally irrevocable, unchanging, and omnipresent branches or sects in Burmese Buddhism; rather there was one large *sangha* until such time that the king (or members of the *sangha*) thought that reform was needed. The king then "created" a purer branch, which became known as the Sīhala Saṅgha. The significance of the Sīhala Saṅgha in Burmese society lies in its *periodic* surfacing as a counterbalance to a church that had become uncontrollable, not as an entity that was structurally permanent. It was very much a part of the indigenous *sangha,* distinguishable—or rather made conspicuously distinct—only when reform was needed. The presence of smaller, doctrinally variant groups of strict adherents to the *vinaya* (or for that matter, to "heretical" doctrine) does not necessarily contradict the existence of a Burma-wide *sangha* nor the Mranmā-Sīhala paradigm either. Nor should the presence of diverse groups analytically contradict a hierarchy in the major *sangha,* for it was not a matter of absolute control where sectarian differences no longer existed, but one where a main church with a hierarchic structure was manipulated by the state. The success or failure of this manipulation depended upon a variety of factors, including the strength of the monarch and the particular circumstances surrounding his reign.

Purity and impurity of the *sangha,* therefore, are relative terms, depending upon the king's ability to control the Order. Reform-minded kings sensitive to the economic and political (ideological) power of the *sangha* (or purists within the *sangha* itself) manipulated the system by using the *sangha* in Śrī Laṅka itself as a tool to control the Order at home. In fact, it was the king's duty as defender of the faith to do so periodically. But in effect, what it did was reduce the power of the Mranmā Saṅgha by allowing the king to legally cut back its wealth, pare its size, and create a new hierarchy staffed on top by his own appointees. Kings Caw Rahan, Aniruddha, Kalan-cacsā, Narapatisithu, and Klacwā all used this tactic. They played one "branch" of the *sangha* against the other in public; and monks patronized by the king invariably rose to the top of the system, with the king's appointed supreme patriarch as its head.

As for *sangha* organization, certainly the term *mahāsaṅgharāja* itself, existing coterminously with the term *saṅgharāja,* is clear enough evidence, both semantically and institutionally, to suggest a hierarchic structure in the church. This is even more convincing when we know that the *mahāsaṅgharāja,* who was usually the king's personal teacher under whom he studied as a prince, was given elaborate and special paraphernalia of office, such as a white umbrella, normally reserved for royalty, along with titles indicative of his rank not only in the society but in the church.[13] The argument here is that there was not only a hierarchy, but its creation and recreation were an attempt by the state to control what was in fact a true, horizontal class (with similar interests and common economic resources), involved in virtually every institution of Burmese society and the only significant countervailing power to that of the state. Yet the *sangha* saw itself as belonging to the system, not as a force that wished to eliminate or replace the monarchy, with which it was, after all, structurally and ideologically related.

During the tenth, eleventh, and twelfth centuries, the devolution of land and labor to the religious sector was not a significant problem because land was plentiful and people immigrated voluntarily to a growing kingdom that paid well for skilled laborers. At times when demographic pressures outstripped the natural or voluntary means by which such problems were avoided, kings conquered neighboring polities to acquire what was needed, especially labor. King Aniruddha took Thaton in the mid-eleventh century for just that reason. Kings Kalancacsā and Narapatisithu also followed expansionistic measures. But the amount of cultivable land and corvéeable labor was not limitless. There were times when reform of the internal structure was more feasible than conquest, especially when neighboring states also experienced scarcity of labor or when the state's military machine was unable to perform successfully against other states. This meant essentially—in the absence of a large, land-owning nobility, whose resources might have been manipulated—that the crown asserted control over the process of land and labor devolution to the tax-free sector, the church. There were two main ways in which Pagan kings accomplished this. One method was simply to exercise the royal right to grant permission for donations to the church. Another more effective, elaborate, and extensive way was *sāsana* reform or purification of the *saṅgha*.

The first method, limiting religious donations before they became sacred property, was probably easier and perhaps less exhausting and time consuming than religious purification. The king's permission was needed whenever a major contribution to the religion was to be made, particularly when it involved land and labor.[14] Monarchs exercised this prerogative most often in the dedication ceremony, wherein only they (or their appointee) could pour the sacred water of consecration that would not only recognize such donations as legally religious (and exempt) property, but by cutting all secular ties "released" *(lhwat)* the donation into the religious realm. The king in essence controlled the procedure by which donations to the *saṅgha* were made tax exempt.

The ritual was elaborate. After the correct alignment of stars in the constellation and other astrological calculations had been carefully considered, the precise hour was fixed and then the ceremony was commenced. The monks purified and sanctified the objects to be released by reciting the *paritta*. Then the water was poured in the presence of official witnesses, who were said to "hear" and "see" the dedication. The ritual severed all prior claims to the land to be donated, spiritual as well as secular. King Narapatisithu's 1183 dedication illustrates the essential steps involved in this ritual:

> (first) he built a *kū,* and when it was finished, he entered it and in front of the Buddha statue, called forth the Mahāsaman Krī and poured the

Water: (and) so that for the 5,000 years of the Religion, this would
last, he dedicated lands and people. . . .[15]

In 1241, another inscription describes the same sequence involved in
the ritual: "on this date, the property was released *(lhwat)*. While
being released, the royal water was poured and (the gifts) were
donated *(lhū)*."[16] The word *lhū* is used only with religious and not
secular gifts, and therefore the "ceremony of release" had to precede
it, to transform material things, such as bricks and mortar used to
build the temple, into sanctified and holy objects. It was this part,
the *lhwat* or release, that was the king's prerogative. Normally, the
king was concerned only with large donations, while small gifts to
the *sangha,* such as flowers or petty cash, apparently needed no royal
"approval." The whole ceremony was performed in a very conspicuous manner, as King Nātoṅmyā did: "with the beating of drums and
blaring of trumpets, in front of his officers, ministers, *rahans* [monks]
of the *sangha* . . . [he] poured the water of consecration."[17] The ceremony publicly reiterated his authority to release gifts to the church
before they could be considered legally valid (and in effect sacred).

In time and during weak reigns, however, kings became bound by
the ritual. Almost every new king in Pagan performed a water-
pouring ceremony during his reign. Depending upon the monarch's
power, the ceremony could be a promise that he would maintain the
validity of royal deeds done in the past. That is, what one king had
declared legal was to remain legal. It was, moreover, a statement
that the office and the rights and prerogatives of that office pre-
empted the person occupying it. Each new king wanted to reaffirm
the legitimacy of the present as well as the preexisting social and
political order, for he was the preserver, not changer, of tradition. In
fact, one of the titles of the king in Burma was Śrī Nitya Dhamma-
dhāra, "Fortunate Possessor of the Principle of Permanence," suggesting that the king was an agent of continuity in a belief system
that taught discontinuity—impermanence. Consequently, immediately following a royal accession, all property dedicated to the *sangha*
by his predecessors was publicly declared legally valid, assuring the
various political and social forces in the society that, although leadership had changed, tradition would be upheld.

On the other hand, the ritual could have been used by the king as
an expression of power; in other words, only because there was a
king to personally declare the state of things was there in fact social

and political order. In that vein, King Aloncañsū in 1124 rededicated and thereby reaffirmed the validity of Aniruddha's donation to Gavampati; while in 1200, King Narapatisithu acknowledged the validity of donations previously released by King Kalancacsā.[18] A year after his accession in 1211, King Nātonmyā confirmed as valid those lands "offered by Great King Cañsū,"[19] and subsequently in 1229 hinted that his act of reconfirmation was in fact what made these past donations valid. "Since they were released in the reign of these kings," he asked rhetorically, "why should it not be released during my reign also?" and proceeded to perform the ceremony of water consecration.[20] In 1235, King Klacwā declared: "I will rededicate this land," and so saying "poured the ritual water in the presence of his ministers. . . ."[21] Long after the Pagan dynasty had ended and rival factions had split the central plains into various camps, each in essence tracing his legitimacy to a unified empire, Mingyi Swasawke in 1369 managed to reconstruct some semblance of a cohesive kingdom, and the ideal of unity began to materialize once more. One of his first acts was to rededicate the religious lands offered by "the ancient kings."[22]

The reconfirmation ceremony struck a balance between the personal nature of kingship and its institution, for although it could imply that legality, legitimacy, and even ownership of property were operative only when personally assured, such acts of assurance were virtually mandatory for those who occupied the office that gave one that right. It suggests that conceptions of legality must be defined within the context of kingship (particularly laws that were of a political nature), and that part of the king's function was to uphold and guard the laws of the land. Reconfirmation of previous claims, then, can be viewed almost as an oath of office, an inaugural promise that, as king, he would uphold the religion and preserve the traditional order, precisely because power based solely on personal allegiances could disrupt otherwise institutional continuity. For the various political groups in court that wished to display publicly their loyalty and endorsement of the king, the reconfirmation ceremony provided the occasion at which they could be present—or absent, depending on their sympathies.

Yet, although the king reserved for himself certain regulatory rights over the flow of land and labor, because he was promoter of the religion his role was not to hinder but to uphold the well-being of the *sangha*. How could he, a *kammarāja* or a *dhammarāja*, forbid donations to the clergy? Indeed, to be commensurate with his status, his donations should surpass everyone else's in a society where duty to the *sangha* superseded duty to the state, and it was more righteous to give to the religion than to the state.[23] The prevailing morality declared that the religion came before and above the state when conflict of loyalty occurred and that church and state were *not* separate. In fact, one of the measures of the king's morality was the well-being of the religion. When the religion flourished, the historians would argue, the king was good, and when it waned, the king was evil.[24] Translated into political terms, the less the king hindered the growth of the *sangha* materially, the better he was; the more he disallowed donations to it, the more evil he became.

In terms of effectiveness, then, this method of control over the flow of land and labor to the *sangha* only managed to regulate the speed at which it took place. The king could delay and obstruct the flow temporarily, but in the long run he could not deny the means to achieve salvation or accrue merit to the people or to himself, nor could he reclaim lands already lost through donation. If these lands had remained with his secular clients, at least they could be taxed, but once they became glebe lands—and they did so in perpetuity—the "returns," in administrative terms, were irretrievable. As a consequence, some kings resorted to another desperate measure—confiscation—an action apparently taken with some frequency, since the curses at the end of many donations were often directed at those people likely to violate their integrity, namely, "future kings, princes, ministers, and relatives. . . ."[25] Here too, the king had to follow procedure. As protector and promoter of the religion, the only justifiable reason the king could give for confiscating religious property was to charge the *sangha* with impurity, determined by behavior contrary to the tenets of asceticism and austerity and corroborated by the large amounts of property it held. Thus when it became necessary to confiscate land, it happened that the *sangha* was also conceptually impure (wealthy) and ready to be purified.

Although purification of the *sangha* was invariably characterized as a religious concern—an attempt to purge the Order of undesirables and to keep the *sangha* doctrinally and structurally unified under one head—it nevertheless had profound political and economic ramifications. It was the function of the *dhammarāja* (as defender of the faith) to see to it that the Order retained its purity and orthodoxy so that it could survive the predicted five thousand years of its existence. Periodically, as the *saṅgha* would become impure (secular), specially chosen monks were sent to Śrī Laṅka to be reordained in the "pure" Mahāvihāra tradition there, which was thought to be the most orthodox Order in the Buddhist world at the time. After a designated period of study in Śrī Laṅka, the Burmese monks would undergo reordination. At the beginning of the ceremony the initiates were given white robes to signify their status as novices. Only after this symbolically purifying process of wearing white robes were they permitted to don once more the saffron robe, indicative of their full status as monks now reordained in the Mahāvihāra tradition. The monks who had ordained them, regardless of previous rank, were now superior to the newly reordained monks.

The Burmese monks then returned home and proceeded under conspicuous royal direction to reordain those monks in Burma who desired the "pure tradition." With the realization that refusal could result in loss of material as well as moral support, from the public and the state, reordination became compelling. With public and state support lavished upon those monasteries that had the reputation for orthodoxy (for peoples' merits depended upon the purity of their monks), it was in the interests of those who were not in any wealthy or established position to accept purification. Moreover, seniority was determined not by previous rank but by the order in which reordination was received. Monks therefore wished to be reordained as soon as possible. Through this ingenious method the monks who first went to Śrī Laṅka under the king's auspices would become senior to any other monks left in Burma, for they were the first to be reordained. The king would thus have under his own *mahāsaṅgharāja* the most senior monks, loyal to him.

Reordination did not continue indefinitely, however. A date was set to end all reordinations, unless specifically approved by the king's committee. As King Dhammaceti, whose fifteenth-century example epitomizes the procedure, declared:

first inform us (so that the case can be) examined in the *sīmā* here . . . [with regard to new applicants]. When definite arrangements have been made, we will present the monastic requisites and will support the ordination. But if (you) do not act thus, but confer the *upasampadā*

ordination privily, the mother (and) father of those who receive such
. . . ordination, as well as their relatives, and likewise their lay sup-
porters, will be visited by us with royal penalties.[26]

By such an order, the state could thus limit the number of validly
ordained monks allowed in the Buddhist *saṅgha,* thereby controlling
the movement of otherwise taxable labor into the Order and keeping
it relatively small.

Dhammaceti also made it clear what kind of behavior was expected from those who joined the *saṅgha* and how he felt about the possession of property and a divided *saṅgha.*

> Let there be a single sect! Let not divers sects arise! Having caused a
> message in these terms to be drawn up His Majesty caused investiga-
> tion (and) search to be made throughout the whole extent of his . . .
> country regarding slaves, female slaves, cattle or buffaloes, and His
> Majesty caused word to be sent to them in this wise: "My lords, give
> up and surrender your goods if you would observe the conduct of
> monks. If my lords fail to do so, then with your goods follow the life of
> laymen."[27]

Finally Dhammaceti announced that "servants of the King, com-
panions of the King. . . ." should not be taken into the Order and
effectively eliminated a much-used sanctuary for political exiles.
Dhammaceti was known to have constructed close to 350 *sīmā*s
(ordination halls) to carry out his program of purification. His aim
was to create a situation wherein land and labor could be retrieved
either directly or indirectly as taxable secular property, while the
saṅgha would be compelled to once more return to its austere,
ascetic, and other worldly nature, stimulated by the new reformed
atmosphere.

Thus, by exercising his religious function as a *dhammarāja* who was
supposed to be concerned with the piety of the *saṅgha,* the king could
stop, at least for a while, the process of land and labor devolution
into the untaxable religious sector by using a socially and religiously
acceptable ritual. Moreover, by controlling the "admission policies"
for applicants desiring reordination and forbidding private ceremonies, he eliminated the order as a haven for those who wished to
become monks simply to escape military or other obligations, as well
as purged it as a sanctuary for political exiles and potential enemies.
Regardless of whether the kings of Burma who purified the Order

were motivated by political or by religious reasons, their actions had empirically observable political and economic consequences favorable to the state.

But successful confiscation without a *sāsana* reform was far more difficult to achieve. The Pagan king whose acts of confiscation failed miserably was the same king whose predecessor had lavishly patronized the *sangha,* namely Klacwā. His reign had to overcome the extravagance of King Nātonmyā, who himself was not entirely free from similar pressures. In A.D. 1211, the *mahāthera* of the "Painted Monastery" brought a case to court suing the king for taking glebe lands.[28] In 1235, King Klacwā confiscated lands "upstream and downstream," including those that belonged to a minister of his predecessor who had dedicated his fief to the *sangha.* The head monk of the monastery who had received the fief took the case to court, at which time the king appointed an investigative committee that included some of his relatives. In spite of this (or perhaps because they wanted to undermine his power), the committee found that Klacwā's predecessor had indeed given the land to his minister legally and the latter had in fact validly dedicated the lands to the monastery. The king had little choice but to accept the decision and reconfirm the donation's validity by performing the "act of pouring water."[29]

Confiscation of secular property, however, did not require much justification, and there were those in court more than eager to deprive political opponents of their economic resources. In 1265 an officer who "received the anger of the king" had his lands confiscated, and he subsequently fell from office.[30] In 1279, the "Great King took the 40 fields of *brahman mahādan"* (that is, a grant of land given to certain Brahmans for their services at court), and in 1299, one hundred *pay* (approx. 175 acres) of good land, originally given to a certain military corps, were confiscated.[31]

There was legal protection against this abuse, however. A statute in the law books stated that:

> (If) a person makes a gift to a monastery . . . (or) to a specified *rahan* . . . on the death of the donee (the *rahan*) the members of the Order shall not inherit such property, but it should revert to the donor.[32]

This meant that a person could choose a specific monk (normally a member of the family who had decided to enter the Order) to endow with lands and people, to build a monastery for, and to dedicate his holdings to.[33] When the monk died, the property would revert to the *donor*. It was a way to retain property in the family, receive merit, and avoid confiscation during politically unfavorable times. Thus in 1241, a woman dedicated one hundred fields to the king's preceptor, who "ate" them for eight years. When he died, she took the fields and rededicated them to another monk.[34] Donations of this type to specific monasteries usually meant that the monastery became known by the donor's name, such as the Anantasū Monastery, named after the donor Anantasū.[35] Another in 1242 was simply referred to as "our own personal monastery."[36] In 1271, an investigation over the ownership of *kywan* revealed another case to which this law applied: witnesses at the trial testified that the preceptor of a past king (Nātoṅmyā) had received certain commended workers from the king, and the subsequent decision by the court stated that because the monk had died, the property would remain in the deceased king's family.[37] In 1291, the grandson (or perhaps great grandson) of the queen "inherited all her property," which had been donated to the Order.[38]

Not only could laypersons retain property given to specific members of the Order, monks themselves could inherit secular property belonging to their lay relatives. In 1248, a dignitary by the name of Saṅkrammasu died leaving his lay property to one of his relatives who, having become "broke and poor," sold it to some Cakraw Karens. The ownership was then disputed by a grandson of Saṅkrammasu, Mahākassapa, who had become the head monk of the Jungle Monastery. The court eventually ruled in favor of the latter because, they declared, "there was a record on the register *(cā raṅ amhat)* that the king had indeed given the land to Saṅkrammasu, grandfather of Mahākassapa. . . ."[39]

While some people gave their property to particular members of the Order with the knowledge that it still belonged to them, others kept title to their lands but donated the services of their *kywan* and the produce of their lands. In this way it was possible to retain ownership of the land and labor while the revenue from the land and service of the workers were classified as tax exempt because they were being used for the religion. So that there might be no misunderstanding with regard to ownership, one donor stated: "Let not the masters Pañña (and) Tirit [monks] and their seven generations who live at the monastery own these *purā kywan;* (but) let only my children, grandchildren, and descendants own them."[40]

Of all the methods thus available to the king to control land and labor devolution to the *sangha,* none in fact worked well enough, for they all had countervailing forces built into them. True, permission had to be granted, but in cases where clear title could be proved the king could not (and did not) actually refuse to pour the water of consecration. Confiscation without *sāsana* reform worked occasionally but only on a small scale, and it could be avoided by endowing secular property to specified members of the Order. Purification had scriptural justification, was practiced by great Buddhist kings such as Aśoka and Parākramma Bāhu I, and appealed to pious members of the public as well as to some members of the *sangha* who wished to purge the Order of unorthodox and undisciplined elements. Better still, purification enabled the state to confiscate *sangha* land with approval of the *sangha* itself. Yet it was an involved affair that took years to complete.

The dilemma was that even if purification were successful, the king, whose legitimacy was in part defined by his religious function, could not thereafter simply stop donations to the *sangha.* He still had to build a larger and better work of merit than his predecessors', for political as much as for religious reasons. Neither could he halt the system of fiefs and rewards on which his power depended, even though *mahādan* often ended with the *sangha.* The irony was that on the one hand, the king was benefactor of the religion and on the other, he and the *sangha* were competing for the same "fixed" material resources of the society. Purification was a safe, though exhausting, method to temporarily stop or slow down the process of land and labor devolution—in effect to give the state a breathing spell. But invariably the process would begin again. It is in this way that Burmese institutional history was cyclic. As long as the economy remained embedded in religion and politics and one institution immersed in another, there was no escape from this cycle. Only if the church separated from the state, and the economy from society, could this cycle have conceivably been broken. The Burmese king, in short, was a prisoner of the institution of Burmese kingship.

It is not difficult to document the recurrence of this cycle in Burmese history, particularly during the reigns of Aniruddha and Kalancacsā in the eleventh century, Narapatisithu in the twelfth century, Dhammaceti in the fifteenth century, Thalun in the seventeenth, Bodawhpaya in the eighteenth and nineteenth centuries, and Mindon in the nineteenth.[41] But more importantly, it was probably a recurring process well before it emerged in Burma, possibly as old as Buddhism itself, as suggested by Aśoka's purification of the *sangha* that resulted in the Third Great Council, and particularly by Vijayabāhu and Parākramma Bāhu I of Śrī Laṅka. Even Buddhist literature hints of the socioeconomic consequences of an uncontrolled *sangha* and the need to purify. The *Māllālaṅkāra Vatthu* noted that

> The inhabitants of the Magatha country, seeing that so many persons chiefly belonging to the first families, were embracing the professions of Rahans, said amongst themselves: behold how the Rahan Gaudama, by his preaching, causes the depopulation of the country, and forces countless wives to the unwished for state of widowhood. . . . What will become of our country?[42]

In a word, the decline of royal power in Pagan, to be discussed in the Conclusion, can be attributed to the same cause as its development: the growth of the *sangha*.

The King and the Princes

Next to the king on the cone were his kin, the princes *(man sā)* of royal blood, usually composed of his sons and brothers. Because of concubinage, the category of prince proliferated, and anyone who was a son of the king could rightly claim the title "prince," for it literally meant "son of the king." Marriage into the royal family, particularly the taking as wives of the king's daughters, enlarged this group further. Because of the size of this category and the ambiguities in precise relationships, claims to descent were also vague. As a result, only the sons of the chief queen (and king) were eligible to the throne. The rest, if competent, were provided with technically inalienable fiefs, titles, and offices that provided a balance of power in the court between potential antagonists. Four chief princes were chosen to represent symbolically the Four Lokapālas and placed in the four apartments, arranged according to the cardinal points, that surrounded the king's residence.[43] They were the "Prince of the Eastern (Front) Palace," a prince of the Northern Palace, known

simply as the "Northern Prince," and a "Southern Prince," called
Dakhaṇa Im Sūkrī ("Headman of the Southern House").⁴⁴ (The contemporary epigraphs so far have failed to yield a "Western Prince.")

Throughout Burmese history, the heir apparent was formally
referred to as "Lord of the Eastern (Front) Palace" *(Im-Rhiy-Man)*.
In Pagan, he was also known as *Man Hla* ("The Handsome
Prince")⁴⁵ and sometimes as *Sū Nay Tō* ("The Young Highness")⁴⁶
in the way Prince Klacwā, the heir, was referred to in 1225 prior to
his accession. That the heir resided in the eastern quarter of the palace suggests that the order of succession moved in the auspicious
clockwise direction, making the Southern Prince next in line, followed by the Western Prince, and lastly by the Northern Prince.
(Moving counterclockwise would constitute *apradaksinā,* which was
performed usually at funerals and not very appropriate for auspicious occasions.)

There are some indications, as in the eighteenth century, that in
Pagan these four lines of princes with their retainers served sepa-
rately in times of war.⁴⁷ In the eleventh century, Aloncañsū, as a
prince in King Kalancacsā's court, held the office of *cac sūkrī* (commander-in-chief),⁴⁸ while King Nātonmyā, as a prince under Narapatisithu, also served as a general,⁴⁹ as did Uccanā, son of King
Klacwā, who served as *man sā cac sūkrī* ("Prince, commander-in-
chief").⁵⁰ It is conceivable that each prince served in the capacity of
a commander in charge of one of the four divisions of the army
(caturanga), symbolically protecting each cardinal direction. Perhaps
the Northern Prince did indeed lead the Northern Cavalry and the
Southern Prince, the Southern Cavalry, two units that were in fact
part of Pagan's military structure.

It is not certain but probable that each of these princely titles gave
its holder rights over landed estates as fiefs. Kalancacsā had the fief
of Hti-luin (as a result, the king was referred to as "Lord of Hti-
luin"). Aloncañsū, his grandson, may have held the same fief; if so,
it would place the Cañsū estate in Hti-luin, fairly close to the capital.
Moreover, King Aloncañsū made heavy donations in this area after
his successful career as a general, as if to reward his constituents for
supporting him.⁵¹ Pegu, a trade center with an undoubtedly handsome revenue, was given as a fief, as was Takon in the unpredictable
northeast frontier, to the prince with outstanding military abilities.
Yet both were far from the court. These fiefs seemed to have been
held temporarily while the recipient enjoyed the king's favor. Princes

of royal blood were apparently not given alienable, hereditary estates from crown lands. Only rights to them were given in exchange for administration. The king could and did strip princes of their rank and exile them, as King Aloṅcañsū was said to have done with his son, Maṅrhaṅco (Minshinsaw).[52]

Each *maṅ sā* was given a princely title *(rai ka sū, cañsū, pyaṁ khī, and thok rhū)*, which may have been retained by the family and its descendants as time passed.[53] Perhaps possession of these titles was indicative of eligibility to the throne. The inscriptions of Pagan reveal at least two of these four titles: *cañsū* (as in Aloṅcañsū) and *pyaṁ khī*.[54] Aloṅcañsū, Narapati Cañsū (Narapatisithu), and Narathihapade (also called *Cañsū*) may all have been of the Cañsū princely family. Befitting their titles and rank, princes dressed in robes "with the *tuyiṅ* skirt fastened beneath it, worthy to be worn by princes only."[55] Kalancacsā's palace inscription showed how dress and insignia—usually in the form of *pasos* (Burmese *sarong*), headdresses, swords, and other such symbols—were attached to persons of rank.[56] Apparently many such practices survived into the nineteenth century, particularly in those areas of Upper Burma associated with the preservation of the classical culture and where descendants of royalty were said to reside. There the *myo wun* or governor of Myingyan held the title Maha Mingaung Yaza, and his insignia consisted of a golden umbrella, gold cup, silver spittoon, and a sword laid on a stand with an ornamented sheath.[57] His subordinates were given similar but inferior insignia.

The prince's retainers must have included his relatives and others whose interests were similar. Artisans who had raised their socioeconomic status through temple building or military personnel who had acquired land for distinguished service sometimes married into princely families, hoping eventually to work their way closer to the throne. A close analysis of the genealogies of the Pagan kings shows at least several occurrences of this pattern, the best example represented by King Narathihapade, whose mother was "the daughter of a turner" (carver in wood or stone).[58]

Because princes of royal blood were always contenders for the throne, the critical ties between them and the king must have been personal; that is, they survived mainly at the "pleasure of the king." However, as some princely rights to property in time may have developed into heritable estates (even if illegally), institutional autonomy may have begun to evolve within the context of personal relations. Not all grants given by the king were revoked, neither were all grants temporary. The precise nature of the fief depended largely upon its location, the recipient, the circumstances, and the strength of the monarch.

The King and the Queens

The king had a countless number of concubines but only four queens, one of whom was of royal birth—the chief or "Southern Queen."[59] All four were known by the title *ami purā* ("consort of the king"), while concubines, unless raised to *ami purā* status, were called *moṅ ma*. Like the princes, each of the four queens possessed a directional appellation. The most important position, naturally, was that of chief queen, for it was through her that royal succession was determined. Only offspring of the chief queen had legal claims to the throne. The chief queen was usually a half-sister or close cousin of the king, and her degree of royalty was determined by her affinity to the chief queen before her.[60] Her primary political function was to provide the link between changing generations of royalty.

The king's eldest daughter by the chief queen was designated Tapaṅtuiṅ Princess, "Princess of the Solitary Post," the (unmarried) female counterpart to the heir apparent.[61] Her title in Pagan was *Maṅ Mi Krī Tuiṅ Sañ,* "Great Queen of the [Solitary] Post." The princess of the solitary post symbolized the legitimating criteria of the royal household; her union with a prince of the solar line would perpetuate the purity of the original dynasty and her role as guardian of the solitary post assured the royal family's proper descent. Since the legitimacy of new kings was in part dictated by union with this princess, (who then became the chief queen) she was thus a major component of legitimate succession. Her formal Sanskrit title was Tri Lokacandanā Mahādewī ("Queen, Moon of the Three Worlds"), while her Burmese title *Uiw Chok Pan,* derived from the term *u shyac pan,* meant "flower adorning the forefront [head]."[62] According to the directional associations among the queens, her place in the South Palace indicates her fertility role. She represented the regenerative, procreative (assuring stability), permanent, and continuous aspects of an ever-changing counterpart. Kalancacsā's mythical genealogy, wherein his father of the solar line (representing the changing, celestial element) married his mother of the *nagi* lineage (representing the stable, chthonic element), was symbolic of the chief queen's role.

The chief queen was called *maṅ nhama tō*, literally "king's royal younger sister." The term *nhama,* however, can also mean "cousin," and in extremely rare situations, even "wife." In normal usage, interchanging "cousin" for "younger sister" is quite acceptable, since they are terminological equivalents, that is, in Burmese kinship classification, generation and sex are the main determinants.[63] But the definition of "wife" for *nhama* suggests only royal usage, for ordinary persons would normally not call a wife *nhama,* while the word *tō* indicates its royal (or sacred) nature. In other words, the use of *nhama tō* to mean "wife" made sense only when used by royalty.

The significance of the brother-sister relationship (or its near equivalent) in royal marriage patterns is shown in a legend attributed to the period in Burmese history associated with the first royal family. In this legend, the king's queen, while trying to rescue her brother Mahāgiri who was being treacherously burned by the king, was also consumed by the flames. Their spirits became malevolent and would not rest until they were enshrined as *nat*s by the king. He placed images of each of them on either side of the main gate of Pagan, where they stand today. Shrines were erected also on Mount Popa, their "fief," where rites to them are performed yearly.[64] Called the Mahāgiri (in Sanskrit, "Great Mountain") Spirits, they became in effect guardians of the royal family and its descendants as well as of the capital and the throne. But more than that, they also occupy the top positions on the pantheon of Thirty-Seven Nats (second only to Sakka) and are both the "household guardians" or *einhsaung nat.* Significantly, Mahāgiri's sister is called *Nhama Tō Krī.*[65] The myth may well symbolize her role as a model for the chief queen, guardian of the throne and her title *(Nhama Tō Krī)* the "proper" relationship of the royal couple. Whether or not the brother-sister *nat* legend originated from royal marriage patterns is difficult to say, but there is little doubt of the symbolic role of brother and sister in protecting the integrity of the throne. The political function of royal endogamy in Burma, among other things, was quite clearly to provide continuity in political institutions such as succession where discontinuity was inevitable.

The rules of royal succession at Pagan have been reconstructed primarily from actual descent practices found in the contemporary sources, although examples from other periods in Burmese history have been used to help corroborate certain principles. Indeed, one finds that institutions such as royal descent tend to change little, particularly in societies where custom and tradition are significant determinants of legitimacy. Admittedly, there was much ambiguity in the process of deciding succession. Besides general rules, there were always other factors involved, such as the abilities of the princes, the nature of factional struggles in court, and the source and distribution of military power. In general, however, one principle seems to have been clear and paramount: succession was determined on the basis of the offspring of the chief queen.[66] If the chief queen had a son, there were no problems theoretically; if a daughter, then the daughter was designated Tapaṅtuiṅ Princess. Like the informal title given to the heir, *Maṅ Hla,* she had an equivalent one, *Cuiw Maṅ Hla,* "Sovereign of the *Maṅ Hla,*" expressing in no uncertain terms her role in deciding succession.[67] In this case, she would marry a half-brother if possible—of the same father but from a different mother.

The diagram in Figure 4, reconstructed from contemporary inscriptions only, substantiates the theoretical criteria of succession. It shows that the position of crown prince was in fact determined by his relationship to the chief queen. Four selected inscriptions were used to document the diagram because of the critical information they contain.[68] The diagram represents but a small section of a larger genealogy, which, however, we cannot reproduce here. It should be noted that several of the inscriptions used nicknames or abbreviations, which they assumed their contemporaries knew.

In very general terms, the diagram may be interpreted as follows: Chief Queen Phwā Jaw (Sumlūla), as an old woman, in 1271 erected an inscription in which she recalled "my husband *(laṅ)* the King, my son the King, and my grandson the King." Her grandson could obviously not have been king until her son and husband had died or, put another way, her grandson could not have been called the king in 1271 if either her husband or son were still reigning. In 1271 King Narathihapade was the ruling king. Working backward in unbroken succession (as her statement suggests), we have the three kings Narathihapade, Uccanā, and Klacwā.[69] Klacwā was her husband, Uccanā her "son," and Narathihapade her "grandson." The terms, "grandson," and "son," should actually be "grandson-in-law" and "son-in-law," but Burmese kingship terminology allows this inclusion of a classificatory sibling.[70]

FIGURE 4

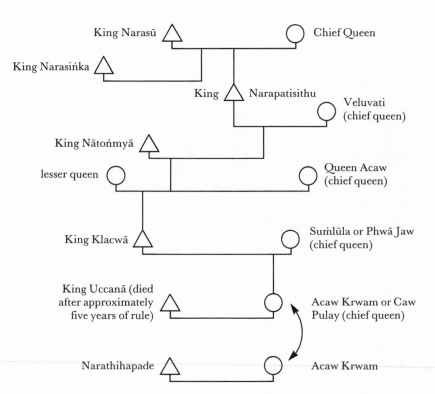

On Uccanā's death after a short reign of approximately five years, Narathihapade apparently married the chief queen, Acaw Krwam, securing royal credentials for himself and his descendants. Chief Queen Phwā Jaw referred to him as "grandson," it seems, because of his generational category in comparison to her "son," Uccanā. Furthermore, we know from Acaw Krwam's own inscriptions that she was the daughter of the Chief Queen Sumlūla by Klacwā. In one, she declared of her mother: "Chief Queen Sumlūla, Tri Loka-candranāma Mahādewī, Queen of the Southern Palace, her daughter Princess Acaw Krwam. . . ." In another, she said: "Princess Acaw Krwam, daughter of King Dhammarāja Jeyyasūra," that is, Klacwā. Finally, she stated that she was "Chief Queen of Uccanā, daughter of King Klacwā (and) of Queen Sumlūla."[71] She thus established the fact that she was not only the daughter of the chief queen by King Klacwā, but also the chief queen of King Uccanā,

Klacwā's successor, making Phwā Jaw's reference to Uccanā as "son" more likely "son-in-law."

Tracing this genealogy back a few more generations, we find that Klacwā was a son of King Nātoṅmyā and had been designated heir apparent.[72] But since the former had been a son of a lesser queen, he must have acquired the position of crown prince by virtue of his marriage to the daughter of the chief queen, a princess with the title *Cuiw Maṅ Hla*, who was none other than our Chief Queen Phwā Jaw.[73] As for King Nātoṅmyā, he was probably the son of the king and chief queen, but as the youngest of five brothers he needed something more than legitimate birth to secure his succession. Accordingly, the *Glass Palace Chronicle* tells the story that during an important session of councillors gathered to decide upon an heir, the royal umbrella by itself pointed to Nātoṅmyā, and he was given the epithet Htilominlo, "as the umbrella (willed it), so the king (he became)."[74] It is very probable that Nātoṅmyā became king by virtue of his military prowess, since he was a successful general under King Narapatisithu, which in part accounts for the symbolism of the umbrella's choice.[75] His subsequent marriage to one of King Narapatisithu's queens, Mrakan Sañ, moreover, suggests the existence of some doubts as to the legitimacy of his succession.[76] His father, King Narapatisithu, was a son of the king and chief queen, but Narapatisithu's elder brother Narasiṅkha had first priority to the throne and only after he died did the former acquire his status.

In theory, then, both the brothers of the king as well as the sons of the king by the chief queen were legitimate heirs: the brothers, by virtue of their mother, who had in the first place determined the status of their brother the king (unless, of course, he had succeeded through marriage to the Princess Designate, that is, the Tapaṅtuiṅ Princess); the sons, because of their mother, the contemporary chief queen. All indications are that the brother of the king normally succeeded first, if the king had been a son of the previous chief queen; but if the king had married the Tapaṅtuiṅ Princess, then his brothers would have had no claim. For at least four or five generations, consequently, the throne in Pagan passed to those who were either brothers or sons of the king and chief queen or those who married the daughters of the chief queen, making the independent variable the chief queen, the female side of the dynasty.

When succession worked in this manner, it was close to being ideal. In practice though, an obscure cousin could usurp the throne, a fact that can be detected by the usurper's subsequent marriage pattern. If he married his predecessor's chief queen (as Narathihapade did), it suggests that his status as legitimate successor was questionable, but it was also something he would want to do, not only for his own benefit but so that his offspring could have the advantage of being legitimate successors.[77] Thus when we find kings marrying their predecessor's chief queens, it usually, though not always, indicates some disruption in succession.

Throughout Burmese history, the primary source of political friction lay between brothers of the king and his sons, precisely because there was an added qualification to the succession rule: the king could, and did, appoint whom he desired as heir, though only from the legitimate pool of candidates. Tensions were especially acute if the sons of the king and his brothers were relatively of the same generation. If the king's sons by the chief queen were too young to rule by the time the king died and if the king himself had been a son of the previous chief queen—making his brother also a legitimate heir—the latter would find little opposition. In these cases, he might marry his brother's chief queen, although he was not a usurper. However, the problem arose when he himelf acquired male offspring, for although the chief queen's sons by her first husband had priority, the king could decide in favor of his own sons rather than his brother's. If he had daughters (or if she had daughters), they would marry each other and still avoid the apparently universal incest taboo, because they had different fathers. Indeed, it would seem that the latter case was ideal for succession and stability.

If the king's choice of an heir transgressed the rules of succession by a significant degree (say, for instance, he was the son of a minor queen or even a concubine), then marriage to the chief queen's daughter or another close equivalent would be arranged so that his claims to the throne could be more secure. In such cases, the court was ripe for factional struggle, and here the ministers played a significant role, especially since in many cases they were related to one or the other of the contenders and often it was they who tipped the scale in favor of whom they wanted. In Pagan, it appears that the two most frequent factions to conflict consisted of those around the heir and those around one of the sons of a lesser queen or, as we have seen, an uncle-nephew struggle.[78] The record of succession in Burmese history shows that, in general, the throne passed from father to son more often than from brother to brother.[79]

We noted in an earlier chapter how chief queens who survived their husbands were excluded from a group of royal ancestors preserved in gold statuettes. The idea that the chief queen could not be considered a royal ancestor if she survived union with the king places a great deal of significance upon her position as chief queen only in the context of such a union. The ideal of a male ancestor uniting with a female ancestress in order to determine her status is confirmed by Princess Acaw Krwam's statement claiming that she was chief queen of King Uccanā while her mother, the previous chief queen, still lived, though her father had died. This means that on the occasion of succession, both designates to the throne emerged as a united couple, and the previous chief queen had to step down. Thus what determined the royal status of the chief queen was more than royal birth—she had to be united with a male prince before she could be queen, the importance being placed upon her as progenitor of the dynasty.

There were thus three essential criteria that helped decide succession: birth, appointment, and marriage. But a legitimate successor could always be cast aside if another prince should show exceptional ability, even if he were not a son of the chief queen. There was always the fear that one of the half-brothers of the heir would prove himself to be an able general and thereby obtain the favor of the king and his ministers; so, even before appointment, rivalry must have existed. Moreover, the king's relatives could maneuver to arrange their son's marriage with the chief queen's daughter whenever the occasion might arise, as it did with Uccanā and Narathihapade.[80] The atmosphere created by these three criteria, often contradictory, enabled only the most gifted political and military leader to survive, further emphasizing the political reality that at this level, and for certain occasions, personalities qualified institutions.

The King and His Ministers

Although in rank, princes and ministers differed, in several cases, the chief princes filled the most important ministerial positions. These chief ministers were collectively referred to as "guardians of the kingdom," the *mantalaptiy,* with the suggestion that the kingdom was a *maṇḍala,* a symbolic replica of the universe.[81] We know that in 1276, at least, there were four chief ministers who served the king, and in 1291, a minister "on the east" was mentioned.[82] It is not certain, however, whether these four chief ministers were always comprised of the four chief princes; yet, that the former were royalty there seems to be little doubt. Nor can we be certain that the offices of the four chief ministers were distinct from those held by the four chief princes; they may have been the same portfolios but referred to on different occasions by different titles. For example, King Aloñcañsū as a prince held the office of commander-in-chief *(cac sūkrī)*, a ministerial position, calling himself "the right and left hand" of the king.[83] King Nātoñmyā as a prince also held the same post, referring to himself as the "left hand" of the king who won the Takoñ (Tagaung) War.[84] In another instance, the *cac sūkrī* was a prince who "led all the ministers and troops."[85] At the same time, Aloñcañsū as a prince was referred to as an *amat* (minister), and an uncle of King Nātoñmyā was the *mahāsaman* (minister of land records), while another uncle of King Klacwā filled a ministerial post.[86] Notwithstanding, there were distinctions in dress and insignia that separated ministers of princely rank from those without it.[87] In the seventeenth century, it was even made a criminal offense to transgress these dress codes.[88]

If the court structure in Pagan had anything to do with setting the norm for later Burmese institutions (and all indications are that it did), there may have been four chief ministers who together filled the highest administrative positions in the court, four "internal" ministers who were in charge of all palace affairs (as suggested by the positions of the prince-minister entitled *Dakhana Ìm Sūkrī*, "Headman of the Southern Apartment [or] House"), and four subordinates for each of these groups, equivalent to the nineteenth-century pattern of four *wungyi*, four *atwinwun*, and eight *wundauk*.[89] In practice, the number of chief ministers may have varied from time to time and—if the number of high-ranking secular dignitaries present at each royal dedication was indicative of those closest to the king— we can suggest with caution that at least four, and no more than eight, chief ministers functioned at any one time.[90] In general, the main division of function seems to have lain between external and internal (palace) affairs, the former probably, though not necessarily, outranking the latter. All ministers were *amat* or *amatayā*, a term that specified office and implied rank. To it were added additional titles, some of which revealed function while others did not. The two most important ministers were the *mahāsaman* and *mahāsenāpati*, the highest counterparts of *asañ* and *kywan-tō,* respectively, though, of course, neither was born into either group and was at least part of the court if not the royal family.

In nineteenth-century Burma, the office of the commander-in-chief *(mahāsenāpati)* was automatically reserved for the heir apparent.[91] In Pagan, on the contrary, the throne was apparently acquired by the *mahāsenāpati* because of his control of the military. Most of the records support the contention that the *de jure* successor was not always the *mahāsenāpati* or, conversely, that the *de facto* successor had not necessarily been designated as heir. King Kalancacsā, for example, a probable usurper, was King Aniruddha's commander-in-chief and later became king; Aloñcañsū, as we have stated, occupied the position of *mahāsenāpati* without being designated heir apparent; King Narapatisithu was general under Narasū, while the former's brother, Narasiṅkha, was heir; Nātoṅmyā, though fifth in line for the throne, was also apparently the commander-in-chief;[92] Klacwā was probably designated heir apparent, but his military exploits are completely unknown, and he is recalled in Burmese history as "the philosopher king" who tried to rule by *dhamma.* His son, Uccanā, seemed to be the only one who was both heir apparent *de jure* as well as commander-in-chief.[93] The latter's case may have been the origin for the heir apparent's ex-officio status of *mahāsenāpati.* Klacwā, the final *de jure* heir of the Pagan dynasty before its demise, was not commander-in-chief either. Indeed, giving the post of *mahāsenāpati* to the heir apparent only subsequently may have been one of the solutions to the problem of usurpation in Burmese history, thereby assuring, with military support, the integrity of the heir's office.

The *mahāsaman* was a scribe *(cā khī)* by profession and exercised authority over the administration of non-service land or labor, their use, their transfer, or their tax status.[94] He was the royal registrar of records. In 1183, when King Narapatisithu dedicated a temple, the *mahāsaman*'s presence was necessary to witness the act of legally releasing the donation from the secular to the religious sphere.[95] In 1229, the "person who measured and erected markers" for a land transaction was the *mahāsaman.*[96] In 1235, we find that ownership of land was recorded and confirmed by lists kept by the *mahāsaman.*[97] Even when the king gave some land as a gift to one of his queens (while they were frolicking on the river), the transfer of property had to be immediately reported to the *mahāsaman,* who subsequently recorded it.[98] In 1271, King Narathihapade transferred some of his property to his son Uccanā, and the *mahāsaman* supervised the transfer.[99] In 1278, another dedication and its official record was carried to the *mahāsaman*.[100] Even after the demise of the Pagan dynasty, a person with the title of *mahāsaman* can be found performing the same function.[101] All of the information collected by the *mahāsaman* was recorded in land registers called *cā raṅ* or *mōkwan*, which he kept in a long, low shed.[102] The title *mahāsaman* was appropriate for the most powerful civil official in the kingdom below the king, for it was probably derived from the Sanskrit *mahāsāmanta*, "the great vassal," who, according to historian A. L. Basham, often "acted as a minister of his suzerain." In Burma, the status of vassal was merged with that of minister.[103]

In addition to these two ministers, there were others who held the office of *amatayā*, most of whom served under either the *mahāsaman* or the *mahāsenāpati*. Under the *mahāsenāpati* were four commanders called *buih sūkrī* or "headmen of the troops," sometimes also called *senāpati*, who were in control of the four different military corps; cavalry (which was the most important), infantry, elephantry, and the fleet (rather than the chariots, the classical fourth corps in the Indian model). The *buih sūkrī* of cavalry had under him, as far as can be ascertained, three levels of officers: the *mraṅ mhū* (majors?), the *mraṅ ciy* (captains?), and *mraṅ khoṅ* (sergeants?). Each of these officers was a leader of his own group of cavalry, and he in turn gave his allegiance to the officer of whose cell he was a part. Thus the *mraṅ koṅ* led a group of cavalry troops, the *mraṅ ciy* officered a group of *mraṅ ciy*, the *mraṅ mhū* headed a group of *mraṅ ciy*, and the *buih sūkrī* of cavalry had under him a group of *mraṅ mhū*. This chain of command would proceed upward and end with the king, who received allegiance from the *mahāsenāpati*, the cell leader of the four *buih sūkrī*.[104]

Although little evidence exists with regard to the infantry, elephantry, or the fleet, enough is mentioned, including several ranks of officers, to suggest a structure similar to the cavalry. Under the *buih sūkrī* of the infantry, an officer called *naga buih* ("officer of the *naga* or dragon corps") was found, chief of a unit of the armor-bearers.[105] His rank may have been equivalent to the *mraṅ mhū* of the cavalry, and he could have been called *tat mhū* (the *mhū* indicating rank and *tat*, corps), the latter a term, however, taken from seventeenth-century infantry organization. We do find in Pagan the title of the officer under the rank of the *tat mhū*, the *khi sañ khoṅ* ("head of the foot soldiers"), equivalent to the cavalry's *mraṅ khoṅ swe sok* ("head of cavalry, blood drinker," i.e., a leader to whom allegiance was given by the ritual of drawing blood and drinking the mixture). Under them were the foot soldiers, called *sū ray* or "braves."[106]

The elephantry and the fleet must have been similarly organized with a hierarchy of officers under their *buih sūkrī*. Officers of the elephantry had the word *chan* (elephant) attached to their ranks, as the word *lhe* or *lhwokā* (war boat) was part of the title given to fleet officers.[107] The primary function of the fleet was not to fight but to transport troops and therefore would not include a special corps of soldiers but those who serviced and handled war boats.

The *Yüan Shih,* a Chinese account, mentioned a Burmese army of 40,000 to 50,000 men in the late thirteenth century, of which there were 800 elephants and 10,000 horses.[108] This number is similar to those given for the Burmese army between the sixteenth and nineteenth centuries in a variety of sources.[109] An inscription of King Narapatisithu, moreover, described him as lord of 17,645 soldiers, referring, in all likelihood, to the "standing army," composed largely of cavalry—as distinguished from the "conscript army"—altogether amounting to approximately 30,000 "riders."[110]

In contrast to the *mahāsenāpati,* the *mahāsaman* supervised groups not legally in crown service. Under him were scribes and other officials concerned with *asañ* affairs as well as those dealing with the land and labor of the *sangha.* The *vatthupicañ* was a minister most likely in charge of property rights and records of the *sangha* (*vatthu* meant *sanghika* property; *picañ* seems to be a scribal title).[111] He may have been what one inscription referred to as the "ecclesiastical commissioner," with authority over legal disputes between *sangha* and laypersons.[112] *Asañ* judges would have been responsible ultimately to the *mahāsaman,* and those who excelled in their duties received the title *manu* or *mano raja,*[113] after Manu, the primordial lawgiver of ancient India, whose name in Burma was synonymous with things legal and with law itself. This was the court's formal recognition of those who excelled in judicial matters. As chief justice, the *mahāsaman* held that title.[114] Those who did not hold such elaborate titles were simply referred to as "the law" *(taryā)* or *samphama* (judges) or their combination.

The King and His Advisors

Advisors to the king were responsible for the correctness of and officiated at auspicious and important events and ceremonies.[115] Consisting of monks and former monks, advisors were also responsible for the education of the princes and were often called *man saryā,* or "king's *guru.*"[116] Although part of their title indicates their status as monks *(sikhan),* their formal courtly title seems to have been *sukhamin* (literally, "wise men").[117] Some were clearly laypersons, who perhaps at the request of the king had shed the saffron robe to become ministers. One such person was the famous emissary of King Narathihapade by the name of Sikhan Disāprāmok, the *mahādhammarājāpandita,* who, on the king's request in the late thirteenth century, went as an ambassador of the Pagan court to negotiate with the Mongol leader at Peking, then contemplating an attack upon Pagan.[118] In addition to their function as advisors to the king, these *sukhamin* provided continuity and stability that helped reduce disequilibrium between reigns. As religious personages, most of them would have been immune to court intrigue and as apolitical elements would have tended to retain their positions despite kingly vicissitudes. Their longevity in court is demonstrated by Disāprāmok, who was advisor to four kings.

This entire court structure was linked to the people via the governors, the *samben-kalan* or *kalan-samben,* whose responsibilities were to the *mahāsaman* and the *mahāsenāpati,* in charge of *asañ* and *kywan-tō,* respectively. Although governors were probably not part of the court, they may have become so on occasion, for instance, when their political assets pleased the king.

In summary, the structure of the court was founded upon the Hindu-Buddhist principle of four cardinal points protecting a center. The princes, queens, and ministers were divided into east, south, west, and north points of the compass, surrounding the throne, ideally set in the center. The king who sat on this throne may have represented Sakka who ruled in Tāvatimsa, but ideology aside, these cosmological divisions provided the king with a mechanism for the separation of powers among his followers. These divisions, however, were also focal points around which political factions could be organized, requiring that the king perform in a manner consistent with his *kamma* and personally bring unity to the various components of the political *mandala.* He did this with rewards, titles, and punishment and by classifying people into royal and non-royal, ministerial and subordinate, court and countryside, independent and bonded, private and government, religious and secular.

Hierarchy as a vertical progression is a point of view of the detached observer. But one who was an integral part of Burmese culture might view the hierarchical structure in another dimension, as reflected in the Burmese system of classifiers, ingeniously developed by Alton Becker, who wrote:

> animate beings are ordered according to distance from Buddhahood. . . . If we conceive of a Buddha (and his words, relics, and images) as the center, then all animate beings can be located in the network radiating out from the center. Furthest away are animals, ghosts, and base, depraved people. Closer are ordinary humans. Then come people with some spiritual status, and closest of all are saints, monks, precious things, and members of royalty. Spiritual progression is movement from animality to Buddhahood.[119]

Put into political-secular terms, the king (instead of the Buddha in Becker's paradigm) would occupy the center and everyone would be ranked relative to this center. Sociopolitical progression, then, was movement from commonality to kingship, as spiritual progression was from animality to Buddhahood. If we combine the two dimensions of perceiving the court (vertical and horizontal), the result is a cone, formulated in the aesthetic consciousness of the people and represented by the ubiquitous Burmese Buddhist stupa, architecturally symbolizing the concept.

PART III

The Effects of Beliefs and Institutions on Events

8

The Economic Implications
of the Merit-Path to Salvation

LIKE ITS CONTEMPORARIES and near-contemporaries of Angkor, Suk-hodaya, and the island kingdoms, the Burmese kingdom of Pagan clearly benefited from Hindu-Buddhist culture. But more important, specific beliefs and ideas from Theravāda Buddhism primarily, in both a doctrinal and cognitive manner, combined with an economy of redistribution to stimulate economic development (hence, contributing to state formation) and institutionalized this relationship between religious ideology and the economy. More precisely, the desire for and the attempts to acquire merit were the motivating factors for the peoples' behavior in doing "good deeds," that is, practicing *danā* or "gift-giving" to the *saṅgha*. In return, the donor received social recognition and spiritual benefits. The procedure for acquiring merit integrated religion and economic growth: building temples and monasteries and endowing them with land and labor not only distributed goods and services, created jobs, and stimulated industry, it was the means to attain salvation. There exists no better testimonial to the relationship between the desire for merit and its quantitative material consequences than the estimated three to four thousand temples that once filled the 25 square miles of the capital city, Pagan, of which about twenty-five hundred still stand today. But even more significant were the consequences that temple building had on the kingdom's entire economy, the result ultimately of paid not forced labor used in Pagan's monumental architectural projects.

Heretofore, it was assumed that skilled labor was provided on a corvée or otherwise involuntary basis, and monumental architecture was therefore viewed as the "megalomania of royalty," which alleg-edly placed unproductive burdens on the populace, eventually exhausting labor supplies that could have been used for the maintenance of the state. Money and human resources were thus said to have been "wasted" on economically useless monuments, while people had emigrated from this "despotism," all of which then ushered the decline of Southeast Asia's ancient kingdoms. This pattern, it was argued, was particularly characteristic of Angkor.[1]

On the contrary, Pagan stands as an example of religious endowments and temple building that acted as stimulants to agricultural production and a variety of related "industries"; people were attracted into the kingdom where the religion flourished, the culture was exquisite, and festivities and work were plentiful. It was only after several hundred years of searching for merit and salvation that these tax-exempt endowments of land and labor became a drain on government resources; and it is only then that the decline of the state can be related to temple building—even then not so much to building per se but to the perpetual tax-exempt status of temple lands and their labor. In short, although temple building was in large part responsible for the formation of the unified state beyond the level of regional and localized political groups, it also subsequently helped destroy it, but not for the reasons that have been conventionally given.

Merit-Seeking and the Economy

As we have already observed in past chapters, the desire for a better rebirth through the accumulation of merit was the stated reason that inspired people to give much of their wealth to the *sangha;* less often, it was fear of the various hells in Buddhism and their clearly frightening descriptions that compelled people to do good. What is not stated, however, is that the produce of lands and service of workers given to the *sangha* were tax exempt, and the returns on such investments—given the regularity with which conspicuously abundant secular property was confiscated by government on a variety of pretexts—were extremely good. As Melford Spiro wrote of twentieth-century Burma:

> although these returns cannot be cashed in, so to speak, until some future existence, their accumulation builds up large reserves in the form of merit. . . . Like Weber's Puritans, many Burmese keep a merit account book in which all expenditures on merit production are

entered [in Pagan, the inscription did precisely that], and the units of merit thus achieved can be compared with the units of demerit attendant upon violation of the Buddhist precepts.[2]

Burmese therefore choose religious spending over economic saving, since the former is a "highly profitable investment for the future, as well as a source of pleasure in the present. Economic saving, on the other hand, is not only a risky, if not an unprofitable, investment for the future; it also precludes the enjoyment of those few pleasures available in the present. In the Burmese behavioral environment, religious spending is by far the more rational decision to make. . . ."[3] These observations of twentieth-century Burmese behavior are valid for the eleventh, twelfth, and thirteenth centuries, as this chapter will show. What is important to note here is that beliefs—cognitive or otherwise—were transformed into action by an economy of redistribution.

Without pursuing the many issues involved in the debate on ancient economic systems it should suffice to say that Pagan's economy possessed those fundamental features of what Karl Polanyi has called "redistribution," a type of economy characteristic of several well-known agrarian civilizations in world history. These economies differ as much in structure from the modern, self-regulating market systems as they do in principle. They are, for example, not simply miniatures or primitive models of modern systems but different in nature. More important, such economies are thoroughly "embedded" in noneconomic institutions, rituals, and behavior: few distinctions can be detected between what is "economic" and what is "religious"; the "just price" is derived from noneconomic concerns of philia such as kinship and community standards of good will; the exchange of goods is often an exchange of services; trade is for self-sufficiency, not gain; and figures showing equivalencies (or prices) are not necessarily the result solely of the supply-demand price mechanism but are administered by the state, often upholding social custom. Redistribution, moreover, implies the presence of a storage system, which is the material foundation for political organization as well as centricity.[4] In such systems, market economies were not nonexistent; rather they were dispersed and localized pockets operating on the geographical (and moral) extremities of what was considered the center of the culture.

This conceptual world resembles a number of concentric circles, the inner ones representing village, city, or kingdom; movement from the center outward reflects degrees of diminishing morality.[5] The innermost circle defines the morality of daily (in this case, economic) life. Within this inner core, gift-giving, exchange, and similar activities are governed or constrained by a myriad of social factors such as kinship bonds, family ties, and clan affinities. Here, concepts such as the "maximum allocation of resources" or "minimizing of costs" are absent, and it is here that individuals "paid as much as they could afford rather than as little as they could haggle for."[6] Beyond the inner circle, exchange is less constrained by social and familial bonds, though the people with whom one deals here may still be part of one's moral world. Here, exchange is perhaps more "equal." But at the outside circle—that is, on the border of one's moral world—strangers are encountered, and it is there that one tries, in economic jargon, to "maximize profits" and "minimize costs." There are few social constraints here and it is at this geographical (and moral) area that a self-regulating market with prices based almost solely on supply and demand can be found. For the Kingdom of Pagan, this moral world was defined by religious, social, political, and to a lesser extent, ethnic criteria, and religion, law, and conceptions of the state and man were as important in the structure and functioning of its economy as were money institutions.

Temple Construction, Redistribution, and Economic Development

There were essentially two methods by which the power of the court and higher officialdom was distributed in Pagan society: one was by a secular fief system—a subject already discussed in a previous chapter—and the other by temple construction and religious endowments, along with the revenues they generated. This activity further served to enhance the social, economic, and, ultimately, the political life of the kingdom. The returns for the king and other wealthy donors were in the form of both long-term spiritual benefits and immediate social recognition highly favorable to their political images. It was in this way that the economy was embedded in two noneconomic institutions—political organization and religion.

The following temple inscription—one of many—demonstrates how the desire for merit was related to the redistribution of wealth.

It was chosen for its explicit statements concerning payment to workers and to show the amount of wealth involved in just one donation.

In the country called Arimaddanapūra, which softens the heart, the king was a noble king of the Law. The minister of that king was named Asavat. He was a minister of the register (?). His wife, out of piety, made the *kū* in that minister's burial ground. By the benefit of the work of merit done by that wife, may all creatures reach *nirapān*. The wife of Asavat . . . gave as *purā kywan* . . . (names followed). Fields: 3½ in the area of . . . ; 7½ in the area of Riy Krañ ("clear water"), 50 in the area of Riy Tañ Pucwan Khywaṁ ["prawn fisheries"?]. In all, 61 fields. May they get water channels. Also 5 cows. As for these fields I have offered, may the masters of the *sangha* beginning with the *Purhā* [Buddha], have all they need (from these fields, in terms of) the requirements and medicines. Should my child, grandchild, (or) relatives in time to come seize these fields, *kywan,* and cows offered by me, may he (they) go to hell. . . . And may he (they) not behold the Buddha [Metteyya] for many dispensations. . . . Bricks for building the wall . . . [broken, but apparently of the temple-monastery complex]. Cartage fee: 78 *klyap* [one *klyap* equalled approximately a half ounce of silver]; building the *kū* . . . ; cartage fee . . . ; building the *kū* . . . fee . . . ; 4 *klyap* given to the blacksmith; 7 *klyap* given to the painter who painted the *kū,* 120 given to the painter who painted the monastery. Seven for the purchase of *rañay* [honey?]; 30 had to be given the carvers; 20 given to the image-makers; 2 given for plastering the wall; 2 *klyap* of gold for painting the throne; 10, the price of wood for the lean-to; 3½ *klyap,* the price of stones for the wall; 13 of silver, 3 *klyap* of *khwak,* the price of mortar for the *kū* and monastery gates; 20 silver for 5 cows; 5 *klyap* for toddy-juice; 5 *klyap* of silver for the trays; 77 *klyap* of silver, the price for 62 *tanak* of [honey?]. Twenty-five *klyap* of silver, the price of 248 *tanak* of milk. Three hundred and twenty *padi,* the price of plaster; 30 of *padi* as provisions for 300 stone bricks; 120 of *padi* given to the pounders for grinding mortar; 140 of *padi* as provisions for the masons; 54 *tan* [approximately equal to as many bushels] of *padi* as provisions for the painters; 20 of *padi* as provisions for the *tacañ sañ* [adze men?] and carvers. The price of *padi* . . . (was) 1 *klyap* . . . for 4 *tan;* in terms of silver, these were 38 *klyap.* Three *klyap* of silver for 1½ *viss* [approximately 3 lbs. 5 oz. per *viss*] of copper for the spire of the *kū;* 12 *klyap* of silver for 1½ gold [leaf? for gilding] the spire; 2 *klyap* of silver for 3 *klyap* of *mercury;* 10 of silver given for the work on the spire of the *kū;* 10 of silver for the price of iron; 20 of silver given for cartage for hauling the wood; 50 of silver for the price of all ornaments, vermilion, lime, . . . lac . . . ; 10 of silver given to the image-makers for ten standing Buddhas; 20 of silver given to the painters; 1 lower garment and waist-cloth given to (each of) the mercury men; 1 piece of fine black cloth to (each of) the painters; 30 lower garments and waist-cloths given to the 30 carpenters; 4 lower garments and waist-cloths given to the masons; 1 horse to the image-makers; 1 horse to the masons and carpenters; 1 lower garment and 1 waist-cloth each to the carpenters. There were 2 kilns (?) for the bricks with which the *caṅkama* [plinth] and brick monastery were constructed; 60 [*klyap*] of silver the price of bricks; 22 *klyap* the cartage charge; 6 *klyap* the cartage charge for hauling wood for the *caṅkama;* 10 of silver, wages given to the adze men (?). One *klyap* of silver for making the gate of the brick monastery; 1¼ of silver for 1 block of stone for the threshold [arch] of the door; 3½ as wages for the masons who constructed the brick monastery; 2 *klyap* of silver for 1 *klyap* of *khwak* [each?] cartage charges. Two *klyap* for 1,350 betel nuts. Two *klyap* for 4 *taṅ* of *padi*. One *klyap* for 1 white cloth. Five *klyap* of silver for 20 stones for threshold doors.[7]

In this one inscription alone, the payment to craftsmen and artisans for the construction of the temple—without calculating the value of the endowed land, fields, and temple servants—came to a minimum of 961 *klyap* of silver for wages and materiel. Of all the donations made during the eleventh to the thirteenth centuries, about 20 percent were made by royalty, at an average estimated cost of 20,000 *klyap* of silver per temple.[8] The non-royal elite (perhaps we could call them the officialdom for this purpose) contributed approximately 55 percent of the total wealth donated, at an average estimate of 900 *klyap* of silver per temple. Commoners gave the remaining 25 percent, at an approximate cost of 400 *klyap* of silver per temple. Pagan apparently built approximately 4,000 temples during its zenith.[9] Twenty percent or 16 million *klyap* would have been the contribution of royalty (20 percent of 4,000 times 20,000 *klyap*); 55 percent or 1.98 million *klyap* would have come from the higher officialdom (55 percent of 4,000 times 900 *klyap*); and 25 percent or 400,000 *klyap* from commoners (25 percent of 4,000 times 400 *klyap*). All this was accomplished over the period of approximately 100 to 150 years, A.D. 1100–1250, when most of the temples were built. Although it is a cumulative figure, it does not, on the other hand, include repairs or additions made to the temples, the value of the annual yield from endowed lands, the value of the indentured labor, and the amount of per capita tax the bonded laborers ordinarily would have had to pay had they not been exempt. It represents only the obvious costs involved in building the complexes initially, and only in terms of wages and materiel. Wealth, harnessed to the kingdom-at-large by the requirements of taxation, was being channelled back to lower (and other) segments of society in a manner characteristic of economic redistribution—by means of noneconomic (religious) institutions and rituals. Moreover, labor used in monumental architecture was paid, and no corvée, to my knowledge, was used for this purpose. Payment was made also in highly prized commodities, if not in silver and gold.[10] Indeed, as one donor stated, "with my endowment, I gave them jobs and food."[11]

In addition to immediate economic benefits for artisans and craftsmen, temple construction had far-reaching effects on many others. Each temple was supported by an endowment of land and labor, the annual yield of which was divided rather precisely. Portions were allotted to pay craftsmen or artisans to repair and maintain the buildings; cooks, firewood suppliers, musicians, and dancers who provided their services;[12] clerks or scribes *(cā khī)* who copied damaged and worn religious manuscripts;[13] lay accountants and brokers who managed the endowment funds;[14] and *kappiyaka-raka* or trustees of monastic property who supervised all of the above.[15]

Endowments of land and hereditary labor made in perpetuity implied stability in these institutions as well as longevity for the consequences. It meant that year after year, jobs for persons on temporary or permanent service tenure were secure, the produce of the land was predictable—for irrigation networks based on reservoirs and other nonseasonal sources of water such as perennial rivers were often part of a donor's contribution[16]—and social benefits were consistent. The latter included education, as schools were invariably a part of a temple-monastery complex: One donor built twenty schools "within the first wall," another built ten, and a third five.[17] Students received instruction, room, board, and books. "Let the 40 *pay* of *padi* land offered . . . (be) for the maintenance of the students at the monastery . . . " stated one donor;[18] "let the students 'eat' of this land," recorded another.[19] Daily public sermons were given in *dhammasala* or preaching halls, a normal part of a donation.[20] When boys were ordained as novices—an occasion every good Buddhist mother wished her son to experience—the public was invited to partake of the food and enjoy the music and other festive treats offered during such ceremonies.[21] Prestigious complexes boasted at least one main temple, a monastery, schools, a library, resthouses for pilgrims, and several latrines.[22]

Building a temple was thus an "investment," beneficial to a particular locality as well as to areas distant. Once built, the temple became a "field-of-merit" and pilgrims throughout the kingdom would continually patronize it long after the initial money was spent. (Even today Burma receives precious foreign exchange from tourists—pilgrims of sorts—who visit temples built centuries ago.) Many donations included provisions for reclaiming old land as well as claiming new land and constructing new and repairing old irrigation works. In the same way that today's endowments to universities stimulate economic growth and sociocultural development in their communities, the Kingdom of Pagan benefited. Places distant from the capital were also affected favorably by temple construction.[23] Towns and villages whose industries included the production of raw and finished materiel—such as stone, marble, ivory, gold, silver, cloth, bricks—used in construction and decoration were assured a stable demand. Temple construction in the city of Pagan sustained the economic life of villages such as Maṅbū, where *parabuik* (material on which to write) was produced; Ñoṅ Ui (Nyaung-U) where lacquerware was made (used for many household and monastic items, such as monks' alms bowls, betel-nut boxes); Pakokku, whose teak industry supplied the material for wooden monasteries; Cakuiṅ, the home of goldsmiths, blacksmiths, coppersmiths, masons, stone- and wood carvers, painters, and carpenters;[24] and Muchipuiw, where the sugar palm, salt, coal, limestone, gold, petroleum, and gypsum industries were located. (Sugar-palm juice, boiled down into jaggery, was an invariable part of the daily food offerings made to the monks. Limestone was burned to make lime, used not only in packets of betel nut for chewing but for the whitewash of temples. Gypsum or plaster of paris was used for sculpture molds and plastering of temple walls. Crystallized limestone or marble was used for making Buddha images.)[25]

If, as is being argued here, temple construction and the economic development of the kingdom in its formative years are intimately related, then the period in which the greatest number of temples was built and the one in which the most money was spent should coincide with the era in which the kingdom reached its height in military and political power. The greatest period of expansion occurred during King Narapatisithu's reign (1173–1210), even if the foundations for this success were laid by his predecessors. The Kingdom of Pagan remained in its grandeur at least through King Nātoṅmyā's reign, which ended around 1234, and perhaps even partly through King Klacwā's reign to 1240. The curve began in the mid-eleventh century, reached a peak at the end of the twelfth century, and started to decline toward the middle of the thirteenth century.

The most important inscription to support this claim, together with the totality of the data compiled and analyzed, is the Dhammarājaka Pagoda Inscription of 1196 of King Narapatisithu.[26] The information in this inscription, corroborated by various other inscriptions and votive tablets, reveals the extent of the Pagan empire in this monarch's reign, a period of noticeable military organization and territorial expansion. Places that had been hitherto considered frontier areas were being cleared, cultivated, and settled. Parts of Lower Burma near Pusim (Bassein) and Tala were also being settled, places that had been once considered foreign. Prior to this time, the kingdom consisted largely of central Burma, and although raids and military expeditions had been carried out by previous kings to parts of Lower Burma, virtually no evidence existed of settlements or the clearing and cultivating of land under central auspices in areas outside of the central dry zone. It is only in the second half of the twelfth century that such expansion was noticeable. Indeed, not until the Dhammarājaka Inscription was erected were the other two economic centers of central Burma (Maṅbū and Toṅpluṅ) even mentioned.[27] Thus the most extensive growth in Pagan's history occurred between 1150 and 1250. As Marc Bloch said of medieval Europe, "if the population had not been more numerous than before and the cultivated areas more extensive; if the fields . . . had not become capable of yielding bigger and more frequent harvests, how could so many . . . [goldsmiths, masons, sculptors] have been brought together in the towns and provided with a livelihood?"[28]

Approximately sixty-five temples of Pagan have been set apart by the Archaeological Department of Burma because of their condition, accessibility to tourists, and aesthetic and art-historical significance. They have been clearly identified by name and are thus a convenient sample to use in determining whether there was a relationship between the period of growth of the kingdom and the quantitative

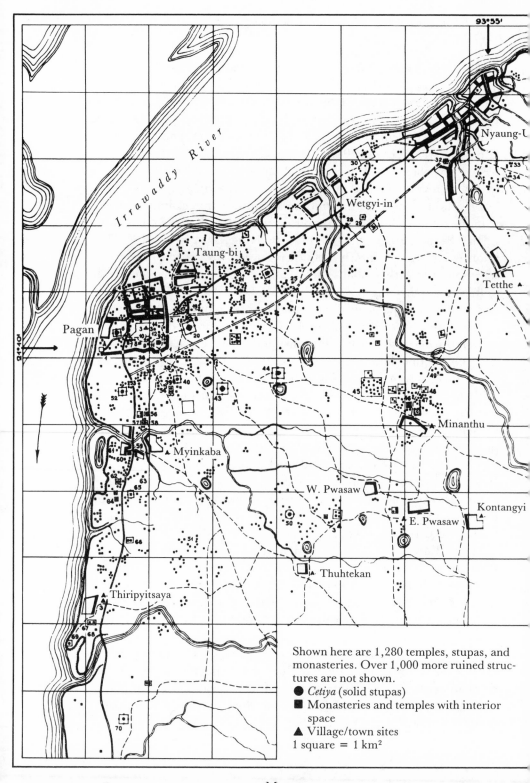

Shown here are 1,280 temples, stupas, and
monasteries. Over 1,000 more ruined structures are not shown.
● *Cetiya* (solid stupas)
■ Monasteries and temples with interior
  space
▲ Village/town sites
1 square = 1 km²

MAP 4
Location of Pagan Temples

data on temple building. Of these sixty-five representative temples, only eleven were built in the latter half of the thirteenth century.[29] Thirty-six of them (over 50 percent) were constructed in the twelfth century and the early part of the thirteenth, and the rest in the eleventh century. The greatest burst of agricultural, military, and economic activity coincides therefore with the period in which the greatest percentage of these temples was built (see Map 4 for these and other temples). The total number of donations to the *saṅgha* also coincides with this period of economic expansion, as we shall observe in the next chapter.

This period, during which Buddhism was heavily patronized by royalty, when monasteries and temples were abundant and well endowed, when the public enthusiastically supported the Order—in other words, a time of economic opportunity and cultural excite-

---

1. city walls
2. Tharaba gate
3. Location of royal palaces
4. Bu Paya
5. Pebin-gyaung
6. Gawdawpallin
7. Mimalaung Kyaung
8. Pahtothamya
9. Nat-hlaung-gyaung
10. Nga-kywe-nadaung
11. Thatbyinnyu
12. Thandawgya
13. Shwegu-gyi
14. Pitakattaik
15. Mahabodhi
16. library building of 19th century(?)
17. Tainggyut
18. Ananda monastery
19. Min-o-chantha group
20. Ananda
21. Nga Myet-nha
22. monastery
23. Upali Thein
24. Htilominlo
25. Hlaingshe (1)
26. Alopyi
27. Hlaingshe (2)
28. Kubyauk-nge Wetkyi-in
29. Kubyauk-gyi Wetkyi-in
30. Shwezigon
31. Kyanzittha Onhmin
32. Sapada
33. Myatha Onhmin
34. Thami-whet Onhmin
35. Kyaukku Onhmin (not shown)
36. Myinpyagu
37. Penantha
38. Loka-hteikpan
39. Shinbin Thalyaung
40. Shwe-hsan-daw
41. Nga Myet-hna
42. Myebontha
43. Dhammayan-gyi
44. Sulamani
45. Hsinbyushin monastery
46. Le Myet-nha (temple and monastery)
47. Payathonzu group
48. Thambula (temple and monastery)
49. Nandamannya
50. Dhammayazika
51. Tamani Asu monastery
52. Mingalazedi
53. Nga Myet-hna and Hsinpyagu (or Pasada)
54. Loka-okshaung
55. Thayambu
56. Kubyauk-nge Myinkaba
57. Kubyauk-gyi Myinkaba
58. Myazedi
59. Manuha
60. Nanpaya
61. Hpyatsa Shwegu group
62. Abeyadana
63. Kyazin
64. Somingyi (temple and monastery)
65. Nagayon
66. Seinnyet group
67. Hpetleik and Atwin-zigon groups
68. Kyauk-sagagyi
69. Lokananda
70. Sittana-gyi

Adapted from U Kan Hla, "Pagan: Development and Town Planning," *Journal of the Society of Architectural Historians* 36, 1 (March 1977): 15–29.

ment—attracted skilled workers, religious figures, pilgrims, and scholars from adjacent areas and abroad. Pagan at this time was renowned for its cultural milieu; Indians, Mons, Shan, Arakanese, Chinese, and even one "white foreigner" (probably a light-skinned Indian) worked and resided there.[30] Pagan's literary activity reached such a level of sophistication that even in the international Buddhist world, the Pali literature of Burma was considered exemplary.[31] It was a place to which students were sent and from which scholars came. In the Burmese version of the *Māllālankāra Vatthu,* a treatise on Gautama's life, Kassapa's assessment of Rājagaha, the capital of Magadha, as a suitable city to hold the First Great Buddhist Council could have applied equally well to Pagan: "The city and its suburbs were very populous; the people lived in affluent circumstances; alms could easily be procured, even for a large Assembly, during any period of time; monasteries about the city were both numerous and of great extent. . . ."[32] Indeed, the description by a contemporary Singhalese monk who had visited Pagan was not unlike Kassapa's characterization of Rājagaha:

> Arimaddana . . . is rich in the presence of treasures, courts, and great families. . . . In this (city) there shines a circle of firm, lofty, and spacious bulwarks skillfully adorned, which is like the mass . . . of the monarch's glory. . . . The monarch's chief abode, a palace white as the peak of a snowy mountain, crowned by the presence of balconies accumulated by the succession of storeys, and displaying long lines of gold, cries shame everyday upon Devendra's elephant Airavata for sporting in the Nandana peak that delights the gods.[33]

With such impressions of Pagan, people must have flocked to the kingdom, especially to the capital city and its splendors.

But a positive relationship between religious endowments and a healthy economy continued only as long as royal patronage remained viable, as demonstrated by an incident involving the Shwesandaw Pagoda of Prome in nineteenth-century Burma. This temple-complex, built in the eleventh century, had enjoyed yearly revenues of 5,000 rupees from its endowments during the pre-Annexation period of British rule which included Prome. But in 1882, its rents were appropriated by the British government. As a result, the temple almost immediately fell into ruin and disrepair. More important, the social and economic life of that whole area, which had depended upon these religious endowments, decayed as well. People moved away to find jobs elsewhere, industry and commercial activity declined significantly, and the entire area became desolate.[34] Similarly, when King Thalun in 1635 moved his capital back to Ava from Pegu in Lower Burma (previously thriving with economic activity), the latter became desolate and stagnant. By his action, the king not only removed the political but also the economic and social center of gravity, to a large degree dependent upon religious institutions.

When Thohanbwa, the Shan chief of Mohnyin, destroyed the Burmese dynasty at Ava in the early sixteenth century and persecuted Buddhism, he was said to have stated that "the pagodas are the spiritual and material banks of the Burmans, and should be despoiled of their treasures."[35] He was correct not only in that the relic chambers of most Buddhist temples were filled with gold, silver, rubies, and other precious stones and valuable items, but that there was as well a sensitive structural relationship between the economy of the country and the pagodas. The temples were more than simple depositories of a kingdom's wealth: they directly and indirectly stimulated economic and demographic growth and hence prosperity. By removing the riches that were stored in the various temples, one might say Thohanbwa "killed the goose that laid the golden egg": for people, the basis of wealth in early Southeast Asia, moved away from areas where the religion was not patronized. Thus we find in the early sixteenth century an exodus of people from the Ava region to Toungoo (farther south and east), where descendants of the defunct Ava dynasty had formed a new Burman capital whose rulers once again patronized the religion in the traditional manner.[36] People connected economically to religious institutions, such as craftsmen and scribes; those intellectually related, such as scholars and monks; and those whose salvation depended upon supporting the latter all flocked to the new capital. Once it began to flourish, others followed suit. (Toungoo in fact became the nucleus for the next capital of a unified Burma.) The Burmans did not move away from Ava because (as it has been argued) there was no affinity between the Shans who ruled Ava and Burmans but because their religion and their livelihood were no longer in Ava.

When in early Southeast Asia, conquering kings made a conscious effort to remove the symbols of their victims' autonomy and power—be it the *liṅga* in Champa, the Tipiṭakas in Thaton, the tooth-relic in Śrī Kṣetra, the Mahāmuni image in Arakan—they destroyed not merely the religious and political center of their enemies but their source of economic survival as well.

In summary, the institution of religious endowments in general and temple construction in particular *attracted* manpower to Pagan and stimulated the social and economic development of the kingdom in its early years. From a small fortified village to the capital city of a kingdom roughly equivalent in size to any Burma would thenceforth build, Pagan grew when the quest for legitimacy and salvation were realized by economic action, which in turn significantly increased the demographic and material basis of the state. But the same forces that created Pagan would eventually destroy it—as we shall observe in the next chapter.

9

The Decline of Pagan

HISTORIANS have long analyzed major events, such as the "fall" of a kingdom, by combining two types of causes. The first consists of what we refer to as "remote origins," broad trends and patterns that develop slowly over long periods of time, piling up as combustible material, so to speak, until the second type of cause—what we call "immediate origins," events and individuals—finally ignites the smoldering material—and brings to completion the broader patterns and trends. To someone influenced by anthropologists, however, the historians' "remote origins" could be interpreted to mean not so much events per se but *institutional relationships,* which do in fact establish patterns and trends and in whose contexts only do the "immediate origins" or causes make sense. The most important institutional relationship in Pagan was that between state and church, a relationship where the focus of economic resources had shifted significantly by the second half of the thirteenth century, upsetting the domestic balance of ideological and political power, which in turn weakened the state and invited internal as well as external forces to bring to completion a process that had been occurring for close to two hundred and fifty years. It is largely with this process and secondarily with the immediate events of the last several years of the Pagan dynasty that this chapter is concerned.

Institutional Factors: Remote Origins

A shift in the focus of political power, according to Edmund Leach, is social (structural) change, for society is to be defined not by ethnic groups but by political relations.[1] We are familiar with the political relations that existed in Pagan: between royalty and non-royalty, between higher and lower officialdom, between independent and bonded commoners, but most important, between *sangha* and government. A shift in the focus of power among any of these groups meant structural change.

In the mid-ninth century, when Pagan rose to become the capital of a large kingdom, it was the result of a shift in the focus of political power from Kyaukse to Pagan and from a decentralized, local elite in the former, to a centralized, military, and court elite in the latter. With the integration of Buddhism, the focus of power—at first spiritual and economic—moved to the *sangha* and the groups that benefited from its growth. The material growth of the *sangha* had also enabled those directly associated with its development (artisans and *kappiyakaraka* as well as other trustees of glebe property) to slowly improve their own economic status. (A good example of this was King Narathihapade, whose family origins went back to the artisans.) The more money that was bestowed upon the *sangha,* the more jobs and demand for materials there would be. With an increase in their living standards, artisans and craftsmen bought (or acquired as payment) land and property. Although hereditary occupation hindered economic mobility for bonded groups, it secured a better economic status for those in the "right" jobs. And with the legal right to inherit, their descendants in time also became landowners. However, as the accumulation of wealth did not gain them the social recognition or spiritual status they desired, a large segment of their wealth flowed back to the *sangha* in the form of endowments. And as we discussed in chapter 7, title to property could legally remain with one's descendants, while the revenue from land and the service of one's servants, instead of being taxed or otherwise utilized by the state, were exempt.

As the *sangha* as a whole grew wealthier, it became more sectarian —for its parts had become economically independent with self-sustaining endowments of land and labor—and also less dependent materially upon the state and ideologically more independent from the *mahāsangharāja* who headed the established branch. Sectarian conflicts that arose were normally resolved by the arbiter, the king. But unlike earlier kings, the thirteenth-century leaders were not as successful in uniting the *sangha* under one head. Part of the reason stemmed from unsuccessful purification. For it to succeed, the support of important segments of the population was needed, and that support in the thirteenth century was lacking because the material and social interests of the artisans, as well as those whose lands and livelihood were protected as religious endowments, conflicted with the political and economic implications of purification.

The institution of granting fiefs for subordinates "to eat" exacerbated the problem and helped create further centrifugal tendencies. Personal ties that had enabled the unification of Kyaukse from nineteen villages into a kingdom were disintegrating with the development of institutions such as inheritance. Heritable property destroyed the dependence of society built on personal ties, to be replaced by one built on institutions. Fiefs that were once given "at the royal pleasure," rather than reverting to the king on the death of the holder became heritable and were instead bequeathed to the fief holder's descendants or to the church. Each alienable award of royal land to the king's followers reduced the state's real holdings; and every time an "eater" of a fief donated his share to the religion—which invariably happened—another source of revenue for political patronage was forever lost. As rights to that revenue shifted to the *sangha*, temple trustees gradually "inherited" the right to collect the taxes once due the state. A shift in disposal rights—there was no need for grain to move physically from one locality to the next—was in essence a shift in political power; in this case, from the king and royalty to the *sangha* and its "employees." The relgious sector was, in effect, usurping the political and economic role of government as the temple monastery complex became a granary and a treasury; yet it did not provide the military and administrative services required of secular fief recipients in return.

Understandably, the *sangha* came to be viewed increasingly as the source of material well-being, and in time the perception of temple-monasteries as the actual source of patronage for a large segment of society began to erode the government's ability to function in that same role. As the *kammarāja* became less able to retain his economic (and ideological) monopoly over the redistribution of wealth (and merit), his power diminished while at the same time his image corresponded less with society's expectations of legitimate kings. No longer was he perceived as having that limitless reservoir of *kutho* (merit) and *phun* (glory) around which the politically ambitious gathered, nor was he any longer able to generate that quality that had convinced others (and possibly himself) of his role as intermediary between heaven and earth. The awe with which his followers had once regarded him also dissipated. It was therefore not surprising to find King Narathihapade, in the latter part of whose reign the state showed the most obvious signs of decentralism, attempting to recapture those symbols of kingship, to such an extent that their artificiality was obvious even to his contemporaries.

In other words, what had once been assets became liabilities. The *sangha* that once had a positive effect upon political expansion and economic growth, initially supplying "culture," ideology, and the framework for a "universal" belief system, had, by the end of the thirteenth century, seriously depleted the state's economic resources, and the focus of power in the Pagan kingdom moved to the *sangha* and its wealthy patrons. In short, the processes and institutions that had originally created imperial Pagan were the same ones ultimately responsible for the kingdom's decline.

The Flow of Wealth to the *Sangha*

That the shift in the focus of political power was primarily caused by the shift in the focus of economic resources can be seen in Table 1. Although further research is undoubtedly needed to determine the total acreage of cultivated, especially *padi,* land there may have been at the height of the Pagan kingdom, estimates based on the information available at present show approximately 500,000 to 600,000 cultivated acres, most of them probably in *padi* (see Table 2). This means that about 63 percent of *padi* (or productive land nevertheless, as well as a significant labor force to work it) once owned or controlled by the crown were eventually acquired by the *sangha*.

Since the sources for the period before 1050 are spotty at best and only after the latter half of the eleventh century was there a yearly record of donations, Table 1 represents approximately 250 years of donations to the *sangha,* mostly of land and labor but in some cases also of cash. Moreover, not all known inscriptions of Pagan that have been found to date are represented in the table, because we have no access to another volume yet to be published, although some of the inscriptions to be included in that volume are available in other publications that have been used.[2] Furthermore, unreliable or illegible inscriptions (as well as those lost, of course) were not used, reducing the full impact of the estimates. The dates given in the table are arranged according to twenty-five and fifty-year periods, in order to provide a relationship between political and economic fac-

TABLE I
Donations to the *Sangha* During the Pagan Dynasty

Inscriptions	*Padi* Land (in *pay*)	Labor	Silver (in *kylap*)[a]
In 25-Year Periods			
Before 1050	300		
1050–1075	6,055		2,000
1075–1100	108.5	323	
1100–1125	666.5		
1125–1150	1,073	423	
1150–1175	1,339	307	
1175–1200	34,941.5	2,733	
1200–1225	39,065.5	2,534	54,127
1225–1250	67,296.5	7,784	37,176.5
1250–1275	35,426	5,939	22,834
1275–1300	20,940	1,597	2,130.75
Undated[b]	1,011	343	842
TOTALS[c]	208,222.5[d]	21,983	119,110.25
In 50-Year Periods			
Before 1050	300		
1050–1100	6,183.5	323	2,000
1100–1150	1,739.5	423	
1150–1200	36,280.5	3,040	
1200–1250	106,362	10,318	91,303.5
1250–1300	56,366	7,536	24,964.75
Undated[2]	1,011	343	842
TOTALS[c]	208,222.5[d]	21,983	119,110.25

[a] One *kylap* equals .566 ounce of silver
[b] These undated inscriptions are clearly of the Pagan period, as their orthography, content, style, and references to specific kings attest.
[c] These totals are not definitive by any means, and as more inscriptions are found, they will undoubtedly increase. But they do represent the present state of knowledge.
[d] One ordinary *pay* equals 1.75 acres; one royal *pay* equals 3.50 acres. Using the smaller unit, this comes to a total of 364,389.375 acres; using the larger, it amounts to 728,778.75 acres.

tors. Thus, two aspects of the process of decline may be seen in this record: the total *padi* acreage (364,389) and the total number of people (21,983) that went to the *sangha,* as well as their steady increase through the centuries, reaching a peak in the mid-thirteenth century, until the final years of the dynasty when they began to decline.[3]

Most of the land given outright or as endowments to the *sangha*—perhaps a good 95 percent—was productive, revenue-yielding *padi*

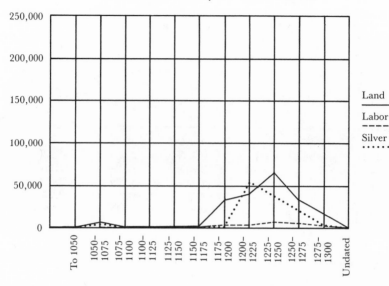

FIGURE 5
Donations in Twenty-Five-Year Periods

Land
Labor
Silver

Donations in Fifty-Year Periods

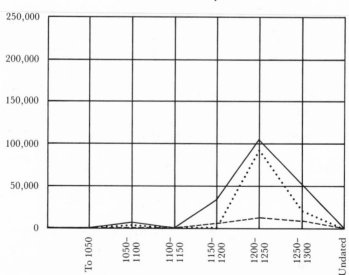

FIGURE 5 (CONT.)
Cumulative Donations in Twenty-Five-Year Periods

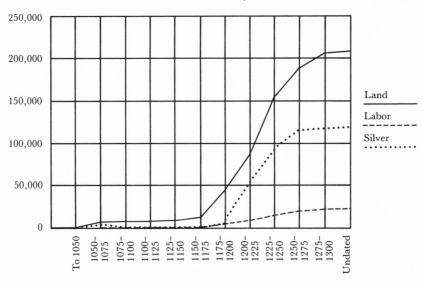

Cumulative Donations in Fifty-Year Periods

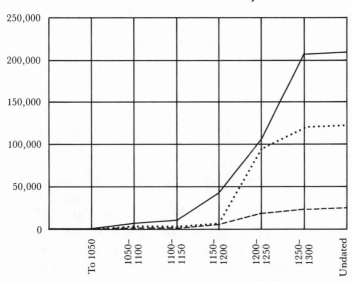

land, called *lay*.[4] Other types of land were also given to the *sangha*:
kaing, land cultivated during monsoons (unirrigated); *yā*, cultivated
land in general; and *uran*, garden land, which in most cases was even
more valuable than *padi* land. The value of these different types of
lands, of course, differed, but they were all nevertheless productive.
Rarely—I know of only a very few cases in two hundred years—was
waste land or "wild land" *(mle ruin)* ever donated to the *sangha*.
(After all, merit is equivalent to the gift given to the church, and a
gift of waste land simply would not acquire much merit for the
donor.) And in cases where potentially productive but undeveloped
land was given, people to work it were usually donated along with it,
thereby assuring its productivity in a few years. The issue then is not
how much total cultivable acreage there was in Upper Burma, but
how much irrigated land still belonged to the government by the end
of the thirteenth century, since invariably, irrigated land meant
crown land.

The maximum total irrigated *padi* acreage in the part of Upper
Burma under Pagan's control was, according to the best estimates,
about 570,465 acres. Table 2 gives the major irrigation works known
to have been built in "Burmese times" and the probable acreage
they commanded.[5] Because we do not have information on productive acreage as it changed over time—as it must have since not all
irrigation works were likely to have been operating at full capacity
all the time—our sources dictate that we compare similar categories:
total *padi* acreage donated to total *padi* (or productive) acreage available, under normal circumstances. If 570,465 acres is an accurate
estimate of the total irrigated (mainly *padi*) land in Upper Burma at
the time (indeed, it is the only reliable estimate) and the 364,389
acres of donated land represent mostly irrigated *padi* land, approximately 63 percent of all such land or rights to them had moved to the
exempt sector (legally or disguised as such) by the end of the Pagan
dynasty, from which the crown could no longer extract revenue. The
same would apply to the services of the people who had become *purā
kywan*. (This entire analysis has actually minimized *sangha* holdings
while maximizing total productive acreage, as a deliberate counter
to my own argument.) In any case, *padi* land in the amount of
364,398 acres for a thirteenth-century Southeast Asian kingdom is
in itself significant, regardless of the percentage of the total productive acreage it represents. Compare for example the total number of
acres that Angkor's western *baray* irrigated: only 32,500, yet it was
highly important to that kingdom.

TABLE 2
Major Irrigation Works

Location	No. of Acres of *padi*	Period Built
Meiktila Lake	18,000	pre-11th century
Kyaukse Lake	5,000	prehistoric
Yamethin Lake	5,000	prehistoric
Nanda Lake	?	prehistoric
Maungma Lake	?	Aloñcañsū's reign (1113–1167)
Sagaing District	68,000	Pagan
Mu Canals	300,000	Narapatisithu's reign (1173–1210)
Mandalay District	20,000	Pagan
Man Canals	15,000	prehistoric
Salin Canals	20,000	prehistoric
Kyaukse Kharuin	119,465	pre-Pagan and Pagan
TOTAL	570,465	

The period in which most of these donations occurred is also of importance. Of those whose records survived, the bulk was made in the period 1200–1250. Of that, approximately half can be designated to the reigns following that of King Nātoṅmyā, who had much to squander after his father's immense program of expansion. Note, for example, the sizeable increase in the years immediately following King Narapatisithu's reign (the years 1200–1225 in Table 1), approximately the reign of King Nātoṅmyā. The reigns of Klacwā, Uccanā, and Narathihapade, toward the end of the thirteenth century, saw continued patronage, which suggests that they too were living off their predecessors' efforts. In certain cases, furthermore, the amount that a person from the commoner class donated to the *saṅgha* in the thirteenth century was sometimes equal to or in a few cases even larger than that donated by a prince in the eleventh and early twelfth centuries. Yet the price of labor and land (of the same quality) remained virtually the same.[6] In fact, the ratio of non-royal to royal donations in the thirteenth century increased considerably, although during this same period royal donations as a group and in terms of total value still surpassed by far donations from those of non-royal status. The same could be said of labor donations. In the last hundred years of the dynasty, a total of 17,854 persons, again a rather conservative estimate, were donated to the *saṅgha*, without accounting for births or deaths. The record of donations in Table 1 moreover excludes much of the expenses incurred in the actual construction of the temples themselves—paid mostly in cash—which would considerably increase the costs involved. (The amounts given in silver, however, sometimes represent those expenses.) In any case, the amount of wealth, both in terms of cash and especially in terms of land and labor—the latter, a nonstatic expenditure of perpetually productive value—that changed ownership in the last hundred years of the Pagan dynasty was clearly significant enough to disrupt the economic foundations upon which the power of the state was built. Quantitative change in the economic structure had shifted the focus of political power from the government to the *sangha* and its clients.

Although this transfer of wealth was a process that had been operating for two and a half centuries, as long as there had been land and labor to replenish the loss and effective leaders to exert their influence on the *sangha*, the government had no serious problems. With much of the wealth that had made Pagan sequestered in the tax-exempt sector by the end of the thirteenth century, however, the state could no longer maintain its armies at the same level it once enjoyed nor the loyalty of its officialdom, while its control of the manpower resources of the kingdom had become ineffectual. At the same time, the *sangha* could not compensate for this loss, especially in military terms, without losing its raison d'être as a religious institution. The decline of Pagan was actually a shift in the focus of political and economic power.

The consequences of a wealthy *sangha* were also of serious ideological significance to the material weakening of the state. A *sangha* concerned with the affairs of this world, large and conspicuous for its material consumption, was considered "impure," but it operated in the interest of artisans and similar groups, who were provided with continuous employment. In contrast, a truly austere and ascetic *sangha*, controlled by the king's primate, expounding strict adherence to the *Vinaya*, renouncing this world as it should, small, and nonconsuming (or conceptually "pure") ran counter to the economic interests of these same groups. Michael Mendelson has argued that "whenever Buddhism was strong, the *nat* cult weakened . . . (and) throughout Burmese history, 'pure' Buddhism and a strong king go together, while 'Animism' coincides with the triumph of the forces of locality and rebellion."[7]

The "purity" of Buddhism and a strong king are ideologically related, precisely because, I would argue, it was also structurally related: An economically and politically weak *sangha* was necessarily also austere, ascetic, concerned with other-worldly pursuits, with relatively few material possessions—the result of successful purification, in turn indicative of a strong king. On the other hand, "impurity" of Buddhism (or as Mendelson suggested, animism's triumph) and a weak king are also ideologically related for the same reason: An economically and politically strong *sangha* was necessarily large, disunited, and wealthy, concerned with this world and its material wealth—the result of monastic landlordism and a depleted government treasury—all at the expense of the king. In other words, the *conception* of purity and impurity of the church and religion were *structurally* related to the constantly changing economic and political balance between government and *sangha*. Thus under kings Aloñcañsū and Narapatisithu, known for their leadership and military prowess, the *sangha* was relatively orthodox; but under kings Klacwā and Narathihapade, whose reigns showed signs of weakness and instability, the *sangha* was materially rich, politically powerful, and relatively unorthodox, with animism and related folk beliefs re-emerging openly.

No able leader came forward to meet the challenge this institutional problem posed for Pagan in the late thirteenth century. Although the eleventh- and twelfth-century rulers had been successful within the same ideological parameters that faced later leaders, by the late thirteenth century the economic conditions had changed, creating over the years contradictions in the structure and conceptual system that they as individuals did not or could not resolve. Even able leaders would have been caught in a contradiction that was far larger than they were, since often the only choice open was between practical reform and changing the very nature of Pagan society, including the basis of their own legitimacy.

The problem began to manifest itself during King Nātoṅmyā's reign, though it was not conspicuous to Pagan leaders at the time because Narapatisithu had left a bulging treasury. Nātoṅmyā lavishly endowed the *sangha* with wealth obtained from his father's conquests and expansion. Indulgence was the character of his reign, displayed by elaborate court ceremonies, growth of court language and protocol, increase in ostentatious display of titles and insignia, all of which were enjoyed by a new glorified royal family of queens, princes, princesses, and concubines. Evidence of all the trappings of luxury and wealth, excellence in art and architecture, and patronage of royal followers were found most conspicuously in the court of Nātoṅmyā. His name itself epitomized this extravagance: "King with many earrings [*nā toṅ myā*]."

But such high living had serious effects on his successors' reigns. King Klacwā in vain attempted to recapture some of the wealth of the government by "confiscating lands upstream and downstream," as one inscription noted. He met stiff opposition from the rich and powerful monasteries, by then gorged with the riches of conquests, in all likelihood supported by the rising artisan "class," which depended upon the status quo of the *saṅgha*'s position for its own material well-being. Klacwā even tried moral persuasion, emulating King Aśoka, by erecting stone pillars around the capital extolling the virtues of moral living. The kingdom was by this time in trouble structurally, as its economic resources had gotten dangerously out of control and heavily committed to the religious sector. Yet Klacwā, like other Burmese kings caught in their own legitimating ideology, was compelled to patronize and promote the religion. His works of merit, although less imposing when compared to those of this wealthier and more extravagant predecessors, were nevertheless grand, despite the growing deficit.

Narathihapade ascended the throne in 1254 to fulfill the need for reinvigorating the kingdom, after Klacwa's successor Uccanā had failed to accomplish it in his short reign of five years between 1249 and 1254. Narathihapade's reign witnessed renewed efforts at consolidating the wealth of the empire, but most of these efforts were symbolic. Unlike Kalancacsā's reign, which had a genuine need for symbols, Narathihapade's reign needed substantive structural and material reform: namely, to reconstruct the economic relationship between church and government, to retrieve lost land, and to curb spending on the religion—in other words, to regain some of the state's economic resources. But he made matters worse by continuing the monumental building tradition, being interested in showing the public that his reign was legitimate and grand and perhaps to minimize his plebian background. His need for legitimacy inspired the origins of the ceremony of representing, in gold statuettes, one's royal ancestors, as if to say, "these kings of Pagan were *my* ancestors." Narathihapade also claimed to be lord of the thirty-five white elephants and (inappropriately during this period of economically hard times), boasted of "consuming 300 dishes of curry daily."

Despite these less than practical measures of renewing the vitality of the kingdom, the earlier part of his reign did provide some security, perhaps the lull before the storm. It is in such an institutional context that the "immediate causes" of Pagan's decline should be viewed; events that accelerated and brought to fruition the "remote causes"—the process that I have been describing.

Political Events in the Late Thirteenth Century: Immediate Causes

Toward the end of Narathihapade's reign, the Mongols had begun to establish their influence over the region: from Central Asia to Japan and from Burma to Vietnam. In 1271, they sent envoys to Pagan to affirm its tributary relationship with China, but neither the tribute nor the envoys returned to Peking. Perhaps sensing the tension between Pagan and its northeast borders, the Mons of Lower Burma broke out in rebellion in 1273 under the leadership of Wareru (Wagaru). Since the northeast had always been more important to the Burmans, however, Pagan concentrated its forces in that direction. The two most important towns that defended the central plains from northern attacks, Ñachoṅkhyaṁ and Koṅcaṅ (Ngasaunggyan and Kaungsin), held off the subsequent Mongol attacks, presumably in retaliation for the disappearance of their envoys. But in 1283, a larger Mongol force—consisting of Yunnanese and other local troops—was sent. On December 3, 1283, Ñachoṅkyhaṁ fell, along with Koṅcaṅ a few days later. By February, Takoṅ (Tagaung), further south and on the route to Pagan, had fallen to the Mongols, and its Burman governor was deposed. But by May 10 of the same year, Pagan had recaptured Takoṅ, which had been left to regional powers, probably the Shans, after the Mongols decided to withdraw from the heat of the plains.

Knowing full well that relations with Peking were essential to the interests of Pagan, King Narathihapade sent Disāprāmok, a minister to four Pagan kings, to China in December of 1284 on a diplomatic mission. He reached Peking in 1286, and according to the inscription that he subsequently erected to commemorate the feat, he convinced the "Chinese king" that "small" Pagan was not in the interest of Peking's grander designs and that Pagan's glory derived less from military power than from religion.[8] But Kublai Khan had already sent troops to Burma, which were now ordered to halt at its northern border. King Narathihapade meanwhile, apparently not realizing that Disāpramok's negotiations were successful, retreated to Lower Burma—hence his name Tarokpliy Man, "King who fled from the Chinese"—and in 1287 was killed by one of his sons, Sihasū (Thihathu), then governor of Prome. Overstepping their orders, the Mongol troops decided to attack, and by 1288 may have in fact reached Pagan, although the sources are not clear on this event.

A year later on May 30, 1289, after the Mongols had departed, Klawcwā (Kyawswa), a legitimate heir, recaptured the throne with the support of the so-called "Three Shan Brothers," who were important in the political events of these years.[9] By 1293, Pagan had reasserted its control over Lower Burma by taking Tala (Dalla), an important city there which had fallen to the Mon rebellion. In 1297, Klawcwā once more attempted negotiation and sent his son-in-law Kumārakassapa to Peking to reestablish friendly relations. The following year, however, the Three Brothers revolted, took Pagan, perhaps in June of 1298, and in the following year executed the king and two of his sons, placing a third, sixteen-year-old Caw Nac (Sawnit) on the throne. Kumārakassapa returned and with Mongol help captured Mrancuin (Myinzaing), the capital from which Asankharā (Athinkhaya), one of the Three Brothers, ruled and probably reached Pagan in 1301. But the Three Brothers allegedly bribed the Mongol officers, who then left Burma along with Kumārakassapa, who had no other choice.

From then on, the Three Brothers divided central Burma among themselves, ruling it from their capitals of Panya (Pinya), Mrancuin, and Cakuin (Sagaing), while Pagan became more a symbol of the past and a center for legitimacy. None of the Three Brothers was strong enough to unite the area until in 1309, when Sihasū, the youngest, was crowned king at Pagan, adopting the grandiose titles of early Pagan kings. By 1310, Asankharā had died, and we are uncertain what happened to the other brother, Rajāsankhram (Yazathingyan). In 1312, approximately, Sihasū built a new capital at Panya and attempted to link his genealogy to the earlier kings of Pagan and took as queens Narathihapade's daughter and Klawcwā's widow. In 1364 a new capital (Ava) and dynasty were founded by Sihasū's descendants. It was not until 1426 that Mohnyin Mintaya, a contender to the throne, broke with Sihasū's line, though links with earlier Pagan monarchs continued to be made. In fact, well into the fifteenth and sixteenth centuries—and indeed into the eighteenth and nineteenth—the kings of the Toungoo dynasty, particularly Minkyinyo and Tabinshwehti, continued to trace their genealogy to the kings of Pagan, Pañya, and Ava, the latter in 1546 even crowning himself at Pagan.

To summarize, the emergence of autonomous centers of power in the central plains under the Three Shan Brothers; the reemergence of the Mon power in parts of Lower Burma with Wareru; the defeats by the Mongols; as well as other events such as the success of Sukhodaya in the latter half of the thirteenth century in supporting Chiengmai, once under Pagan's hegemony; and the threat of hill tribes, especially the Sak-Kantu around one of Pagan's important irrigated provinces near Manbū—all were symptomatic of Pagan's internal weakness and were the *immediate* causes that accelerated the process of institutional decentralization of that kingdom. In 1398, Mingyi Swasawke with clear hindsight remarked in an inscription that the "Burmese empire [had] disintegrated because of internal strife."[10]

But as a legitimating tradition as well as a city, Pagan survived well into the fourteenth and fifteenth centuries, as Paul Bennett has shown.[11] The traditions of Pagan continued precisely because the cultural institution par excellence that could (and did) perpetuate them—the *sangha*—had the economic means to do so. As a city, Pagan remained the cultural center, the "museum" of the "high tradition" in Burma, preserving in the dry climate the architectural splendors that verified the civilization's achievements and glory, while Pañya, Cakuiṅ, and Mrañcuiṅ in turn took the status of political and economic capital, until Ava emerged to create a new dynasty that unified central Burma for approximately a hundred and fifty years.

That the civilization of Pagan survived so long politically testified to the ability of each generation of leaders to adapt to new socioeconomic needs and circumstances, created in part by their predecessors. These leaders supplied the wherewithal to survive, while the institutional and material environment furnished them with a context in which to do so effectively. But the institutional dilemma that confronted the kings in the late thirteenth century was too difficult to resolve: the *sangha* represented the very essence that had made

Pagan more than a simple military kingdom, although it had just as effectively drained the economic base that had created the civilization in the first place. Yet the government could not survive unless it virtually eliminated the *sangha*'s role in the economic and social life of the society and took back its sources of wealth, which it was unwilling and unable to do. As a result, the Buddhist *sangha* survived beyond the kingdom that had nurtured it to become the stabilizing pillar of continuity, as well as, paradoxically, the major causal factor of periodic discontinuity in the institutional history of Burma.

This cycle of consolidation and dispersal—of patronage to the *sangha* to glorify beginnings, leading eventually to loss of wealth; of allegiance based on personal ties subsequently undermined by allegiance based on heritable property; of a pure, austere, and ascetic *sangha* becoming impure, wealthy, and sectarian; in short, a movement from the creative forces of a society to those same forces that over time became destructive ones—was to repeat at least three more times in the history of precolonial Burma.[12] Admittedly, the recurrence of such phenomena would never follow exactly its predecessor's path; there would be adaptations, changes, new factors and actors. But the circumscribing pattern, the institutions that allowed this cycle to repeat—namely, the merit-path to salvation, the ideology of the king as supreme benefactor of the religion, and the "fixed" or limited land and labor resources of an inland, agrarian society—did not change substantively or permanently.[13] And because the principles and material environment upon which the society were founded remained the same (or substantively similar), each generation and dynasty suffered the same (or substantively similar) consequences. The longevity of each dynasty in Burmese history hinged upon the abilities of its leaders to successfully meet this institutional challenge. The Pagan dynasty lasted approximately three and a half centuries; the Ava dynasty, one and a half; the Toungoo dynasty, two centuries; and the Konbaung dynasty, one and a quarter centuries. The story of *how* they handled what was essentially an institutional "given," is the narrative history of precolonial Burma.

CONCLUSION

The Significance of Pagan to Burmese and Southeast Asian History

Continuity of the Classical System

THE ORIGINS OF THE STATE has been a subject of intense study by anthropologists and historians for several decades. The origins of the state in Burma, however, is a topic that has received very little attention, theoretically or empirically. Yet the emergence in the past two decades of a fair amount of usable archaeological, epigraphic, and literary evidence has allowed us to reconstruct a picture not only of the way in which the first Burmese state emerged but, once it was formed, of the *types* of action that occurred between individuals and groups and the *forms* of political, economic, and social interaction that predominated—the major concerns of this study. What still needs to be articulated (and perhaps equally important) is Pagan's significance to Burmese society and history, a topic that this concluding chapter addresses. In fact, the title of this work, *Pagan: The Origins of Modern Burma,* was chosen to express these very same concerns; namely, that at Pagan were laid the institutional foundations of the modern Burmese state and society. This implies continuity beyond the destruction of Pagan as a viable state, suggesting that the classical system itself—though perhaps not the state—continued beyond the dynasty that created it to become the guiding framework of Burmese society at least until the British conquest in 1886. Indeed, that many of its principles continue today is an argument worth considering.[1]

This classical system consisted of five fundamental components: Theravāda Buddhism, intermingled in various ways and to different intensities with other "Great" and "Little Traditions" but primarily involved with the merit-path to salvation (kammatic Buddhism); an economy of redistribution embedded primarily in religion, but also in politics, social status, and law; an administration based on an agrarian environment, juxtaposed to and affected by a limited (and continuously low) supply of labor; a cellular and hierarchic social organization consisting of both patron-client ties on the one hand and horizontal classes on the other; codified law, whose principles reflected the values inherent in these institutions, founded upon the concept of hierarchy and communalism, which upheld, supported, and articulated the essence of Burmese conceptions of justice; and a polity based on the *kammarāja* form of kingship, with a structure that supported (and also contradicted) it, rituals that justified it, and symbols that simplified it. All these components were as significant in the Kingdom of Pagan as they were in Konbaung Mandalay.[2]

With the political demise of the Pagan dynasty in the late thirteenth century, subsequent dynasties did not *fundamentally* alter Pagan institutions. Indeed, in Burmese history, the reverse was often true: *because* of dynastic change, succeeding rulers actively promoted the retention and resurrection of traditional forms to insure their own legitimacy. Ultimately, the underlying cause is the concept and value of change.

Even a preliminary study of Burmese historiography in particular and its conceptual system in general tells us that the perceptions of and value attributed to change were substantively different from those of the West.[3] In Western historical writing, societies are invariable perceived as constantly changing, often significantly, while change itself is equated with progress, and progress is, of course, highly valued. Originality and newness therefore become important goals. In contrast, although change is indeed viewed as inevitable in Burma—especially in Buddhist thought where everything is impermanent—it is seldom if at all associated with progress as we understand it. Innovation and newness, as a result, are not goals feverishly sought after; rather, custom and tradition of the "purer past" are the models to emulate. The entire precolonial, monarchical era should thus be viewed as one entity in which "classical" beliefs, structures, and relationships were recreated, elaborated upon, refined, embellished, and—most important—preserved through periodic resurrection.

That is not to say, of course, that nothing changed or that society was static, only that the real issue becomes one of the degree of change—of these critical institutions. It would be entirely misleading to suggest that significant and permanent transformations of institutions occurred between the origins and the demise of monarchical Burma simply because a great deal of time had elapsed or because there had been political and dynastic upheavals. On the contrary, dynastic cycles arguably reflect institutional continuity. Because the same assumptions and beliefs concerning man, salvation, time, order and disorder, justice, authority, and legitimacy persisted along with the structures that necessarily upheld those beliefs, each new dynasty was forced to face the same (or in effect the same) institutional challenges that its predecessors had to face. And unless each new dynasty was willing and able to transform radically the beliefs and assumptions upon which its own rise to power was based, which it was not, or the material environment changed significantly, altering political and social behavior as well as the economic system, which it did not except once, temporarily, the "classical system" had to remain intact.

But none of the histories of Burma so far published argues for this continuity. Instead, Burmese history has usually been depicted as if it were in a state of continual upheaval. The main reason for this appears to have been the reliance of historians on narrative sources of history, mainly the chronicles. Not that these types of sources are useless, but, intrinsically, they suggest change rather than continuity, for they are concerned largely with events, and each event, by nature, is different from the next. In the hands of historians who viewed history as linear and progressive, Burmese history became a series of major upheavals, the result of the invariable transformations thought to occur because one "period"—essentially a collection of events—had passed on to another. Consequently, not only is there an unwillingness to use the information derived from one arbitrarily defined period for another, but when continuities transgress these sacred boundaries we call them "atavisms" or "anachronisms." We become bound by our own creations—the periods in history—made essentially for heuristic purposes, forgetting that they are artificial in the first place. Placed in their proper perspective—within the framework of institutions—events become the "contents" of a form, details that operate within a continuous institutional framework without substantively altering that larger form. It is the strength of this "classical" form, both structural and ideological, that kept men from outstripping events and events from overriding institutions. Thus we need to view classicism as a continuous entity, as society itself, and not subject to artificially created boundaries between "periods." Only evidence of *institutional* change, and then to a significant degree (what is "significant" will always be problematic), should determine whether or not the "classical" system ended when the Pagan dynasty in which it had its birth also came to a political end at the close of the thirteenth century. The "classical Burmese state" was a recurring phenomenon that persisted throughout precolonial Burma until the British eliminated one of its critical components—the monarchy.

Because institutions, and the principles upon which they stood, as well as the material environment remained relatively the same, post-Pagan Burmese history was affected in much the same way it was in Pagan. This was particularly true with regard to the relationship between the state and *sangha* and the effect it had on certain historical patterns.[4] More precisely, the merit-path to salvation and the criteria for political and social legitimation in a society with finite agrarian resources continued to create the economic problems of exempt revenues found in monastic landlordism. The problem was exacerbated in subsequent centuries, for gifts of land and labor to the *sangha,* made in perpetuity, meant all new donations were added to those already extant, thereby creating a continual and cumulative rather than new or particularistic kind of problem. That donations of this kind to the *sangha* continued at a relatively constant level in the First Ava period, immediately following the Pagan period, is certainly clear. In the next period, the Toungoo, donations of land per se may have declined somewhat, but added to the already large amounts of exempt land in Upper Burma it was a total increase and could only exacerbate the burden of the state. Since this period (the sixteenth century) saw increased commercial activity, the state may have donated less land during that time in any case, because it had more cash and less land. Indeed, one of the reasons Toungoo kings shifted their center of power from an agricultural setting to a commercial one in Pegu may well have been the pressure exerted by the increasing loss of productive lands in Upper Burma to the *sangha.* Certainly relative state expenditure on the religion (relative to its total wealth) remained significantly consistent well into the late nineteenth and even twentieth centuries.

It is true that with the destruction of each dynasty, in the absence of law and order some religious land with unclear title may well have been illegally taken. In other cases, religious land might also have been sold or mortgaged illegally by the *sangha*'s lay caretakers. But even in these cases, the official files, should they survive, would continue to show their religious and therefore tax-exempt status, still useless for state purposes. Despite these occasional and for the most part quantitatively miniscule reversals, the totality of donations already made and those continually being made would always have been an increasing rather than a decreasing burden on the state.[5] This was all the more critical because the economic mainstay of most of Burma's dynasties lay in agriculture, whose productivity was fixed or stable relative to labor, for labor was a highly scarce commodity at least until after the second half of the nineteenth century. What all this means is that at the beginning of each new dynasty, its budget would have been already heavily committed to the religion.

There was only one viable solution to the problem that legitimacy-seeking Pagan kings could use—*sāsana* reform or purification of the Order. A wealthy *saṅgha* implied that the monks were violating *Vinaya* rules; therefore, reform was ideologically justifiable. Materially, *sāsana* reform should have reduced the size of the *saṅgha* (and therefore its holdings as well), making it easier to control, and allowed the state to regain both productive land and services of people heretofore exempt. Politically, purging the Order eliminated sanctuaries for rebel leaders, contenders for the throne, and other opponents of the king. The entire process, if successful, should have tipped the ideological, economic, and political balance back in the favor of the king, thereby giving his reign a new lease on life.

However, once the *saṅgha* was purified, it once more attracted public patronage, in fact even more vigorously, for the quality of one's merit was contingent on the purity of the monks one supported. The *saṅgha* would again incur royal favor, especially from those kings with questionable legitimacy, since doctrine held the king to be protector and perpetuator of the religion. Eventually, public and royal patronage would recreate the problems of monastic landlordism, forcing subsequent rulers to reform the *saṅgha*. In other words, the effects of purification, even if successful, in the long term were temporary, for parts of legitimation ideology recreated the problems that other parts of it sought to resolve. That was the reason, despite his purification of the *saṅgha* in the late twelfth century, King Narapatisithu subsequently built the monumental Dhammarājaka Pagoda, at a cost of over 40,000 *klyap* of silver in addition to the endowed labor and land; that King Thalun, after his *sāsana* reform, which included forbidding people to become monks, never-

theless built the grand Rajāmaniculā Pagoda; that King Bodawhpaya built the huge Mingun Pagoda after countrywide administrative reforms and revenue inquests concerning the *bona fides* and
extent of tax-exempt religious lands; and that King Mindon, after
holding the Fifth Great Buddhist Synod as well as purification of the
Buddhist texts and the Order, was still known for his generosity with
the *sangha*.

The crux of the problem was this: as long as the society's beliefs
and the legitimating system encouraged the growth of monastic
landlordism and as long as there was a structural contradiction—
between the king as benefactor and patron of the religion on the one
hand and competitor for the finite resources of the kingdom on the
other—the economic and political problems would remain to plague
each new dynasty. And given the ideological, material, and institutional boundaries within which Burmese monarchs could operate
successfully, their responses would be (and were) remarkably similar
to those of the Pagan monarchs, with similar results. In short,
monastic landlordism and *sāsana* reform persisted in post-Pagan
Burmese history in much the same way and for much the same reasons. The manifestation of this continuity of structural contradictions was the dynastic cycle in Burma.

The Dynastic Cycle: Manifestations of a Structural Contradiction

Four dynasties (or five, depending upon one's interpretation)
reigned in Burma from the mid-ninth to the late nineteenth century,
and the patterns surrounding their rise and decline were remarkably
similar. At the beginning of each cycle, one finds a decentralized
structure, with political and economic resources dispersed among
regional and local units of authority. This was normally followed by
the appearance of a *min laung*, a "savior king" in effect, a charismatic leader endowed with exceptional military abilities who, with a
band of loyal followers, forged a centralized polity, complete with a
royal family, a palace, a court, and a capital, out of the political frag-
ments. The "savior king" would then harness various cultural paraphernalia to legitimize his claim to kingship, especially patronage of
the *sangha* and building of a royal temple, along with genealogical
links with the Buddha's tribe, heroes of past dynasties, and with

mythical ancestors important to those he was attempting to unite. As the state grew, so did the *saṅgha,* and at the apex of the cycle the state would be unified politically and administratively, while the monarch would be in control of the kingdom's revenues. The inclusion of the *saṅgha* in the unification process was absolutely necessary, for it acknowledged the state's success, glorified its conquests, legitimized its king, and provided a source of merit for the salvation of the society. The *saṅgha* would be considered pure, unified under the king's appointee, the *mahāsaṅgharāja.* A few generations after the zenith of each cycle, however, we would find a wealthy and sectarian *saṅgha,* a depleted treasury, a faction-ridden court, and a state politically and economically weakened, with neighboring tributary chiefs and kingdoms ready to declare their independence. *Sāsana* reform at this crucial juncture might avert the premature destruction of the state, but if it were unsuccessful the center's weakness would invite internal dissension and external invasion and, invariably in Burmese history, destruction of the dynasty by one of its neighbors. The forces of localism would once more dominate the political scene, while the people waited for the *min laung* to reappear and begin a new cycle.

Thus, the Kingdom of Pagan in the ninth century was united under its founder Pyuminthi (Pyusawhti). By at latest the eleventh century the *saṅgha* needed purification, and so King Aniruddha, with monks from Lower Burma, proceeded to purify the Order and "persecute the heretics." King Kalancacsā continued this process with his own reform of the scriptures. In the mid-twelfth century, King Narapatisithu purified the Order again. In the mid-thirteenth century, King Klacwā faced a strong and wealthy *saṅgha,* which he attempted to reduce in size and power. His failure subsequently brought the Pagan dynasty to an end. The Upper Burma that was divided into armed camps following the demise of the Pagan kingdom was, in the 1360s, reunited in typical *min laung* fashion by Thado Minbya, who went on to create the First Ava dynasty. By 1438, Mohnyin Thado had to once more purify the Order. In characteristic *min laung* fashion, Tabinshwehti of the Toungoo dynasty once more reunified Burma after the Shans had destroyed Ava in 1527 because, their chief declared, the pagodas were the "material and spiritual depositories of the Burmans and should be despoiled of their treasures." Tabinshwehti subsequently established the foundations for a Burmese state that expanded well beyond its traditional boundaries into Laos on the east and Arakan on the west. Once again, many of the resources derived from such growth and expansion shifted to the *sangha*. The Toungoo rulers, apparently sensitive to the temporary nature of revenues derived from conquest and of the growing scarcity of taxable agricultural sources in Upper Burma, moved their capital to Pegu, thus tapping the lucrative sixteenth-century commercial revenues of Lower Burma. King Bayinnaung in fact was compared to "the great Turk" by foreign travellers, who, however, noted the "excess of gold" spent on pagodas.

But this attempt to harness more and a different source of wealth was short-lived, for the dynasty's hold on the commerce of Lower Burma was broken by the Thais. Consequently, King Thalun in the early 1630s moved his capital back to Upper Burma. By this action, his major economic resources once more reverted to land and labor that were "fixed," as it had always been. In order for the dynasty to survive, society had to be restructured according to the demands of the dry zone's socioeconomic and geopolitical conditions. And the only legitimate model that Thalun and his successors had was the Pagan model, so to it they returned. Subsequently, he purified the Order, prohibited movement of crown people to the religious sector, and in general tightened his administration. The organization of people and land therefore reverted to old and familiar forms, which in any case had been preserved in central Burma, the cradle of Burmese civilization.

Thalun's reforms did not produce something substantively new and different, rather they restored traditional institutions. (Indeed, the concept of reform in Burmese history had always meant a return to a purer past rather than change to an unknown future.)[6] Subsequently, the old, familiar problems reemerged. Reaping the fruits of Thalun's purification, his successors enjoyed the benefit of a fuller treasury to heap largesse on the *sangha*. By the 1750s, the state had grown weak once more. When the resulting factionalism destabilized the court, the Mons from the south moved up to central Burma and destroyed the dynasty. (The drain of central wealth to secular sources, as Victor Lieberman has suggested, does not contradict the argument; in fact, it may have helped exacerbate the problem.)[7] Out of the ashes rose the *min laung* Alaunghpaya, who reunited the forces of decentralism shortly thereafter. His subsequent reconstruction of the polity naturally included patronage of the *sangha,* which was continued by his successors, until his grandson, Bodawhpaya, once

more had to reform the Order. He instituted a most extensive revenue inquest in the late eighteenth and early nineteenth centuries,
which reassessed the relative wealth of the religious sector. By these
measures, his treasury began to bulge again.[8] But again, Bodawhpaya's successors eventually depleted that restored wealth by lavish
donations to the *sangha*. The first steps of decline were already beginning to surface in the first quarter of the nineteenth century, when
the British took all of Lower Burma in the 1850s. Despite being
land-locked and pressured from all sides (and perhaps because of
perceiving an impending doom), King Mindon continued to treat
the *sangha* in the traditional manner. He held the Fifth Great Synod
and purified the Order. It may have given his successor, Thibaw, a
respite, but it was too late. Even though the latter continued to
patronize the *sangha,* by 1886 the dynasty had once more collapsed
when in the usual manner, an outside power, this time the British,
conquered it.

Unlike the other conquerors of the Burmese state, the Shans of the
thirteenth and fourteenth centuries and the Mons of the eighteenth,
the British had totally different assumptions concerning their role in
the modern world and abolished the institution of kingship itself,
which the previous conquerors had never done. By so doing, they
eliminated not only the major source of patronage for the *sangha* but
also one of the major components of the classical system. Thus the
cycle had to end.

Economic Implications of Religious Behavior
in Other Theravāda Societies

It is highly unlikely that the relationship between universal Theravāda doctrines such as the merit-path to salvation and its political and
economic implications were unique to Burma. Although there is no
space to document in detail here the amounts of land and labor held
by the *sangha* in other Theravāda Buddhist countries, the hints of
similar processes at work in these places are worth mentioning. Was
Aśoka's Third Buddhist Council prior to the decline of the Mauryas
a reflection of a similar problem? Had the *sangha*'s holdings grown to
such an extent that it hindered the state's ability to keep its wealth?
Buddhist literature such as the *Māllālankāra Vatthu* stated that the religion in Magadha had taken most of the able-bodied men into the

sangha, causing the state great concern. Did the Third Council of Aśoka, therefore, attempt to reduce the size and diversity of the Order so that the Order and its wealth could be better controlled? Were the Muslim incursions into Buddhist India, especially in the eleventh century, a result in part of a weak state and a wealthy *sangha,* a tempting target for neighboring states?

Similarly, did the rhythmic Chola raids on Śrī Laṅka's ancient capitals coincide with the material growth of the *sangha* there, particularly since the Chola empire was fed and sustained by plunder, as George Spencer has argued?[9] Contemporary inscriptions of Śrī Laṅka as well as its chronicles mention numerous attempts at *dhammasaṅgiti* ("conference in order to purify the *sāsana*") by Kumara Dhatusena in the sixth century A.D. and Dala Mugalan and Salamevan in the seventh century A.D. The Galvihāra Rock Inscription, the Jetavanārāma Sanskrit Inscription, and the Mihintale Tablets of Mahinda IV (tenth century) are very explicit about the economic implications of religious purification. The dynastic vicissitudes in Śrī Laṅka (Anuradhapura, Polonnaruva, Kandy), the persistence of the merit-path to salvation as a significant part of its belief system, and the abundant evidence of temple-monastic complexes there suggest a situation similar to Burma's.

In Thailand, labor losses of the monarchy to its princes and nobles have been well documented. Akin Rabibhadana, for example, showed that the strengths and weaknesses of the monarchy depended to a large extent on the movement of corvéeable labor from the state to its subordinates.[10] People lost to the *sangha* would have certainly exacerbated the problem, for even the foreigner Constant Phaulkon, during his brief tenure as chief minister, was said to have purified the Order and forced monks to leave the *sangha* to serve the crown. In 1722, a royal edict ordered noble patrons whose clients had become monks to make certain that these clients were eventually restored to their original corvée groups. We also hear of tax-exempt *sangha* lands even in distant provinces such as Nagara Sri Dharrmaraja being subject to meticulous scrutiny by officials at the capital. Even in the remote interior of what is now Thailand-Laos, the merit-path to salvation produced monastic wealth, as the *That Phanom Chronicle* shows. In 1842, a Presbyterian missionary, W. P. Buell, wrote home from Bangkok that there were "difficulties" between church and state, that "people have fled to the priesthood to escape the army and assignment to the Cochin-China front"; and that the king, as a result, had issued orders for an examination of the monasteries.[11]

Thus in these three Theravāda Buddhist countries, patterns of historical, institutional, and ideological relationships very similar to those found in Burma seem to have been present: the persistence of the merit-path to salvation as a major feature of its belief system producing a wealthy church; the recurrence of *sāsana* reform or religious purification with clear economic implications to deal with the problem in a socially acceptable manner; and the frequent rise and decline of dynasties, whose strengths and weaknesses seemed to have been related to the problem of "monastic landlordism."[12] There is also clear evidence of monastic landlordism in China and Japan. But in both T'ang China and Oda Nobunaga's Japan, the solution was not *sāsana* reform, but outright military destruction of the church and confiscation of its property.

The Issue in Modern Burma

When Burmans once more assumed self-rule after 1948, elements of the pattern recurred because the traditional criteria for political legitimation remained intact. The concern with the *sangha* today, however, is less economic and more political and is less obvious in Ne Win's regime than it was under U Nu's. It is nonetheless a serious and deeply rooted concern. Ne Win's regime favors, as in the past and for similar reasons, the austere, fundamentalist sects. In fact, their appeal was sought during anti-Communist campaigns called "Buddhism in Danger" *(dhammantaraya)* that allied these monks with the military. In 1965, Ne Win convened at Hmawbi an All-Sangha, All-Sect convention to purify ritually the Buddhist hierarchy. It was a symbolic act as well as a political necessity. Through purification, he demonstrated his responsibility as head of the *sangha* —or more accurately, as the head of the head of the *sangha*. Politically, he may have used this to displace concentrations of political power within the *sangha* that had developed during U Nu's premiership, and he was able to force through a limited successful registration of monks. Subsequently, his government (Ministry of Home and Religious Affairs) has periodically administered exams for advancement in the *saṅgha* hierarchy. Thus he has not allowed the *saṅgha* to develop the same political position as it had during U Nu's regime.

As in traditional times, strong leaders went hand in hand with a unified and austere monkhood. In 1965, and again in 1969 and 1974, Ne Win confronted the *saṅgha* over demonstrations and cracked down on its political proselytizing activities. As in traditional times, too, he currently patronizes or asks the advice of one sect over another, thereby giving his "blessing" (and credence) to that particular sect by favoring it in public. Such patronage has the effect of swaying the public toward a particular sect while weakening the other, more political, ones. Kings often did this, patronizing the austere groups over the more powerful and wealthy ones, pointing to the former's greater purity, and consequently reducing the influence of the more powerful ones. In the case of Ne Win, he turned for guidance to the Shwegyin Sect in Amarapura, which is enjoying one of its greatest revivals.

After consultations with leading abbots in December of 1979 and January of 1980, Ne Win convened a second All-Saṅgha, All-Sect convention in May of 1980. Purification was carried out here. Furthermore, in his address to the BSPP (Burma Socialist Program Party) Central Committee in December 1979, he had indicated that he wanted to make certain the monkhood was registered on a national basis. In June of 1980, the Ministry of Home and Religious Affairs began to form ecclesiastical courts to weed out undesirables from the *saṅgha,* and like Mindon before him, Ne Win concluded the convention with a proclamation of general amnesty (for which he received much merit) and the release of some 14,000 prisoners. Almost all his political opponents were freed, and those who had fled the country, like U Nu, were invited to return.[13] We should note again, that the issue is not the success of the purification in terms of numbers purified but the attempt to do it as well as its promulgation, for the necessity of such action by the state confirms the continuity of the relationship between state and church, along with the criteria for their being and the methods that articulate that relationship. In other words, the traditional conceptual system and the rituals that reveal its principles must have been intact.

In short, although both U Nu and Ne Win carried out *sāsana* reforms, admittedly the relationship of the *saṅgha* to the state was now more political than it was economic. Without a monarchy and royalty as the primary patron of the religion, the *saṅgha* did not regain its traditional share of the national wealth, and as a result, monastic landlordism ceased to be as critical to government as it once had been. Moreover, the economic effects of the merit-path would not be as significant to twentieth-century Burma with the emergence of a more modern economy (at least one that was partially linked to the world market system), as it would have been to a state once dependent almost entirely on a limited amount of irrigated land and scarce labor. But as long as the merit-path to salvation does remain a major concern of the Burmese, wealth will continue to flow into the religious sector. That the *saṅgha* still holds considerable wealth is no secret, but how much, and how much of it is directly related to revenue otherwise usable by the state, is unknown. The extent to which Burma will eventually become the type of secular society that we know of in the modern world—not that it should— depends upon substantive change of this intimate relationship between religious belief and economic action or elimination of the belief entirely.

Abbreviations

ASB	Archaeological Survey of Burma
BEFEO	*Bulletin l'École Française d'Extrême-Orient*
BODAW	*Inscriptions Copied from the Stones Collected by King Bodawpaya and placed near the Arakan Pagoda, Mandalay.* Burma Home Department.
BSOAS	*Bulletin of the School of Oriental and African Studies*
EB	*Epigraphia Birmanica.* Archaeological Survey of Burma.
PPA	*Inscriptions of Pagan, Pinya, and Ava (in the Burmese text as) deciphered from the ink impressions found among the papers of the late Dr. E. Forchhammer (and edited by Taw Sein Ko).* Burma Home Department.
JAS	*Journal of Asian Studies*
JBRS	*Journal of the Burma Research Society*
JRAS	*Journal of the Royal Asiatic Society*
JSEAH	*Journal of Southeast Asian History*
JSEAS	*Journal of Southeast Asian Studies*
JSS	*Journal of the Siam Society*
OI	*Original Inscriptions Collected by King Bodawpaya in Upper Burma and now placed near the Patodawgyi Pagoda, Amarapura.* Burma Home Department.
SIP	G. H. Luce and Pe Maung Tin, *Selections from the Inscriptions of Pagan.*
SMK	*She Haung Myanma Kyauksa Mya* [Ancient Burmese inscriptions]. Archaeological Survey of Burma.
EM	E. Maung, *Pagan Kyauksa Let Ywei Sin* [Selected Pagan inscriptions].
SGP	Superintendent of Government Printing

See Bibliography for works not cited in full in Notes.

Notes

Introduction

1. By "the state" I mean the total unit, the whole polity including the government, economy, social and religious structure, legal system, and administration.

2. The term "Burmese" refers to the national, cultural, and political category, the term "Burman," to the ethnolinguistic group.

3. Victor B. Lieberman, *Burmese Administrative Cycles: Anarchy and Conquest, c. 1580-1760.* Frank N. Trager and William J. Koenig, *Burmese Sit-tàns 1764-1826,* The Association for Asian Studies Monograph no. 36 (Tucson: University of Arizona Press, 1979).

4. John R. W. Smail, "On the Possibility of an Autonomous History of Modern Southeast Asia," *JSEAH* 2, 2 (1961): 72-102.

5. Karl Polanyi, C. M. Arensberg, and H. W. Pearson, *Trade and Market in the Early Empires.*

6. Edmund R. Leach, "Hydraulic Society in Ceylon," *Past and Present* 15 (1959): 2-25.

7. Paul Wheatley, "*Presidential Address:* India Beyond the Ganges—Desultory Reflections on the Origins of Civilization in Southeast Asia," *JAS* 42, 1 (November 1982): 13-28.

8. Marc Bloch, *Feudal Society,* trans. L. A. Manyon, 1:59.

9. O. W. Wolters, *History, Culture and Region in Southeast Asian Perspectives* (Singapore: Institute of Southeast Asian Studies, 1982).

10. Paul Wheatley, *Nāgara and Commandery: Origins of the Southeast Asian Urban Traditions.*

11. Burton Stein, "The Economic Function of a Medieval South Indian Temple," *JAS* 19, 2 (1960): 163-176; George Spencer, "Temple Money-Lending and Livestock Redistribution in Early Tanjore," *Indian Economic and Historical Review* 5, 3 (1968): 277-293.

12. M. C. Ricklefs, "Land and the Law in the Epigraphy of 10th Century Cambodia," *JAS* 26, 3 (1967): 411-420.

13. George Coedès, *Angkor: An Introduction* (New York: Oxford University Press, 1963), and Lawrence Palmer Briggs, "The Ancient Khmer Empire," *Transactions of the American Philosophical Society,* n.s., 41 (February 1951).

14. Chas. Duroiselle, Introduction to Burma Home Department, *OI.*

15. What a word or phrase means in Burmese, especially Old Burmese, depends considerably on its reading and its context. There is very little disagreement on the reading, though there is some on the meaning of terms. One therefore needs to be familiar with several occurrences of a word or phrase in similar contexts before reaching a conclusion on its meaning. The interpretation of Old Burmese inscriptions in this book rests on such familiarity, mainly with their published versions, but as well with the works of other scholars on Pagan, most notably the late G. H. Luce, the late Pe Maung Tin, Than Tun of Mandalay University, and U Bokay, resident archaeologist at Pagan. As stated in the acknowledgments, John Okell of the School of Oriental and African Studies, the University of London, and his help in my initial reading of Old Burmese was absolutely indispensable but he is not to be held responsible for mistakes made in this book.

16. *The Glass Palace Chronicle,* trans. Pe Maung Tin and G. H. Luce, p. ix.

17. Michael Aung-Thwin, "Prophecies, Omens, and Dialogue: Tools of the Trade in Burmese Historiography," in *Moral Order and the Question of Change: Essays on Southeast Asian Thought,* ed. Alexander Woodside and David K. Wyatt, pp. 78–103.

Chapter 1

1. For a summary and analysis of the issues, data, and problems dealing with prehistory in Southeast Asia, see Donn Bayard, "The Roots of Indochinese Civilization: Recent Developments in the Prehistory of Southeast Asia," *Pacific Affairs* 53 (Spring 1980–1981): 89–114; see also Karl Hutterer's explanation of the coexistence of prehistoric and historic elements in Southeast Asia in *Current Anthropology* 17, 2 (June 1976): 221–242.

2. A variety of published and unpublished, mainly Burmese sources have been used to reconstruct this early period. See my article on this subject in *Asian Perspectives* (forthcoming) for a tentative reconstruction of this period. I have deliberately, perhaps unfortunately, left out Arakan's place in the formation of the Burmese state. The best and most recent account of early Arakan is Pamela Gutman's dissertation "Ancient Arakan: With Special Reference to Its Cultural History Between the 5th and 11th Centuries," The Australian National University, 1976. For urbanization in the entire region, see Paul Wheatley's recent work on the formation of cities in early Southeast Asia entitled *Nāgara and Commandery: Origins of the Southeast Asian Urban Traditions,* University of Chicago, Department of Geography Research Papers, nos. 207–208 (Chicago, 1983), chap. 4.

3. Robert Wicks, who completed a doctoral degree in art history at Cornell University, has studied the dispersion of coins in early Southeast Asia. Some of the information on these coins in my study is derived from personal communication with Mr. Wicks. For an example of his work on numismatic methods to aid in the reconstruction of early Southeast Asian history, see his "Bull/Trisula Coin Issues of the Fifth to the Eighth Century From Arakan, Assam and

Bengal: A Revised Typology and Chronology," *American Numismatic Society Museum Notes* 25 (1980): 109–133.

4. Fan Ch'o, *Man-shu*, trans. G. H. Luce, Cornell Southeast Asian Studies Data Paper no. 44 (Ithaca, 1961), p. 91. See also Charles Backus, *The Nan-Chao Kingdom and T'ang China's Southwestern Frontier* (Cambridge: Cambridge Univ. Press, 1981), especially chap. 5.

5. Gordon H. Luce, *Old Burma–Early Pagán*, 1:3–8.

6. G. H. Luce and Pe Maung Tin, *SIP*, pp. 1–2.

7. For a detailed narrative of the last several years of the Pagan dynasty, see Paul J. Bennett, "The 'Fall of Pagan': Continuity and Change in 14th Century Burma," *Conference Under the Tamarind Tree: Three Essays in Burmese History*, Yale University Southeast Asia Studies Monograph Series, no. 15, pp. 4–11; G. H. Luce's "The Early *Syäm* in Burma's History," *JSS* 36 (1958): 123–214; and Edouard Huber's "La Fin de la dynastie Pagan," *BEFEO* 9 (1909): 633–680.

8. Michael Aung-Thwin, "The Nature of State and Society in Pagan: An Institutional History of 12th and 13th Century Burma," Ph.D. diss. University of Michigan, 1976. See also "The Role of *Sasana* Reform in Burmese History: Economic Dimensions of a Religious Purification," *JAS* 38, 4 (August 1979): 671–688.

Chapter 2

1. Sir Richard Temple, *The Thirty-Seven Nats: A Phase of Spirit-Worship Prevailing in Burma* (London: W. Griggs, 1906), pp. 28–36. See also *Judson's Burmese-English Dictionary*, rev. and enlarged by Robert C. Stevenson and F. H. Eveleth (Rangoon: Baptist Board of Publications, 1966), pp. 480, 559, 1075, 1079, 1087.

2. Archaeological Survey of Burma, *SMK*, no. 139, p. 225 (A.D. 1231); no. 143, p. 242 (A.D. 1233); and no. 159, p. 266 (A.D. 1235). Unfortunately, the first inscription is worn precisely at the place that gave the number of deities under Sakka. The readers of this inscription have tentatively agreed that the number should be 44. In Burmese, however, the numbers could easily be 33, the 3 being far more similar to the 4 than it is in English. Moreover, it is already well established that Sakka heads not only the gods of Tāvatiṁsa but was also (in Burma) head of the Thirty-Seven Nats. The thirty-three, plus the Four Lokapālas, usually referred to as *nat*s, account for the thirty-seven. See also *SMK*, no. 135, p. 219 (A.D. 1231).

3. *Judson's Burmese-English Dictionary*, p. 1075; *SMK*, no. 139, p. 225.

4. *EM*, no. 1, p. 1.

5. Paul Ambrose Bigandet, *The Life, or Legend, of Gaudama, the Buddha of the Burmese, with Annotations: The Ways to Neibban, and Notice of the Phongyis, or Burmese Monks*, p. 71; G. H. Luce and Pe Maung Tin, *SIP*, no. 43, p. 112 (A.D. 1265).

6. Bigandet, *Life, or Legend, of Gaudama*, p. 208.

7. Other than Richard Temple's *Thirty-Seven Nats* mentioned above, the best modern account is Melford E. Spiro, ed., *Burmese Supernaturalism* (Englewood Cliffs, N.J.: Prentice-Hall, 1967).

8. *Judson's Burmese-English Dictionary,* p. 558.

9. H. L. Shorto, "The *dewatau sotāpan:* A Mon Prototype of the 37 nats," *BSOAS* 30 (1967): 138–139.

10. Archaeological Survey of Burma. *List of Inscriptions Found in Burma,* p. 40; Gordon H. Luce, *Old Burma–Early Pagán,* 1:286–288.

11. *SIP,* no. 17, p. 31. The reading can mean that the person being dedicated had been condemned to death but was pardoned by the monks to become a pagoda "slave." There is serious doubt that such obviously unorthodox practices, to say the least, would have been mentioned in Buddhist donations.

12. Thus most inscriptions call those who "heard," "saw," or "knew" of these dedications *sak siy,* witnesses.

13. *SMK,* no. 22, p. 44; Burma Home Department, *OI,* no. 28, p. 36.

14. Archaeological Survey of Burma, *Report of the Director,* 1916, p. 26.

15. Temple, *Thirty-Seven Nats,* p. 9.

16. *SIP,* no. 53, p. 149.

17. *The Glass Palace Chronicle,* trans. Pe Maung Tin and G. H. Luce, p. 81.

18. G. H. Luce's account of the variety of religious influences in vol. 1 of *Old Burma–Early Pagán* is clearly the most scholarly and by far the best. See also U Mya, *Apayratnanā Luiṅ Kū Phurā* (Rangoon: The Archaeological Survey of Burma, n.d.), pp. 59–66, as well as Nihar-Ranjan Ray, *Brahmanical Gods in Burma* (Calcutta: Calcutta University, 1932), and his *Sanskrit Buddhism in Burma* (Amsterdam: H. J. Paris, 1936).

19. U Aung Thaw, ed., *Reports on the Excavations at Beikthano* (Rangoon: Ministry of Union Culture, 1968), p. 5.

20. ASB, *Report of Director,* 1902–1903, p. 7.

21. Luce, *Old Burma–Early Pagán,* 1:201–227.

22. Archaeological Survey of Burma, *Pictorial Guide to Pagan,* ed. U Aung Thaw, p. 32.

23. ASB, *Report of Director,* 1913, p. 23.

24. *SIP,* no. 1, p. 1. See also H. L. Shorto's work entitled "The Gavampati tradition in Burma," in *Dr. R. C. Majumdar Felicitation Volume,* ed. Himansu Bhusan Sarkar (Calcutta: Firma K. L. Mukhopadhyay, 1970), pp. 15–30.

25. G. H. Luce believes that the Nanpaya actually glorified the Buddha and theorizes that perhaps the original icon of the latter had not survived; see *Old Burma–Early Pagán,* 1:286. Other "one-faced" temples not cruciform in ground plan or Hindu are the Rhuykū (Shwegu), Sabbaññu (Thatbyinnyu), and Pahtothamya, among many others.

26. Archaeological Survey of Burma, *EB,* 3:4. A. L. Basham, *The Wonder that was India* (New York: Grove Press, 1959), p. 298.

27. *EB,* 3:35–36.

28. Wm. Theodore de Bary, ed., *Sources of Indian Tradition* (New York, 1970), 1:20. He cites the *Śatapatha Brāhmana,* 2.1.1, pp. 1–14.

29. See Ray, *Sanskrit Buddhism,* pp. 40–61, and Luce, *Old Burma–Early Pagán,* 1:184–200.

30. Edward Conze, *Buddhism: Its Essence and Development* (New York: Harper Torchbooks, 1959), p. 147.

31. Ibid., p. 176.

32. U Mya, *Apayratnanā Luiṅ Kū Phurā,* pp. 59–66; G. H. Luce, "Old

Kyaukse and the Coming of the Burmans," *JBRS* 42, 1 (1959): 102–104; and U Tin, "Mahayanism in Pagan [Burmese text]," *JBRS* 19 (1929): 37–38. See also ASB, *Pictorial Guide,* pp. 54–59, and G. H. Luce's "Aspects of Pagan History —Later Period," in *In Memoriam Phya Anuman Rajadhon,* ed. Tej Bunag and M. Smithies (Bangkok: The Siam Society, 1970), pp. 139–146.

33. ASB, *Pictorial Guide,* pp. 56–59.

34. Ray, *Sanskrit Buddhism,* pp. 40–61; ASB, *Report of Director,* 1916, p. 12, and Than Tun, "Mahākassapa and His Tradition," *JBRS* 42 (1959): pp. 99–118.

35. *EB,* 3:144.

36. *EM,* no. 3, p. 4.

37. Conze, *Buddhism,* pp. 124, 137.

38. Ibid., pp. 116–117.

39. *EM,* no. 3, p. 4.

40. *EM,* no. 12, p. 25; *SIP,* no. 43, p. 112.

41. Conze, *Buddhism,* pp. 120–135.

42. Ibid., p. 138.

43. *SIP,* no. 11, p. 19.

44. *EM,* no. 6, pp. 11–12.

45. *EM,* no. 8, p. 13.

46. *EM,* no. 15, pp. 29–30.

47. *SIP,* no. 19, p. 35; *EM,* no. 31, p. 59; *SMK,* no. 97, p. 152.

48. See the discussion by Melford E. Spiro in *Buddhism and Society: A Great Tradition and Its Burmese Vicissitudes,* chap. 2.

49. Bigandet, *Life, or Legend, of Gaudama,* pp. 232, 409.

50. *SIP,* no. 40, pp. 103–104.

51. *SIP,* no. 26, p. 55.

52. This is a paraphrase of many such statements.

53. *SIP,* no. 38, p. 93.

54. *SIP,* no. 21, p. 42.

55. *SIP,* no. 32, p. 75; no. 49, p. 132.

56. *EM,* no. 46, p. 122.

57. Tun Nyein, trans., *Inscriptions of Pagan, Pinya, and Ava,* p. 119.

58. *EM,* no. 2, p. 2.

59. *SIP,* no. 43, p. 112.

60. *EM,* no. 47, p. 129.

61. Tun Nyein, *Inscriptions,* p. 51.

62. *EB,* 1:166.

63. Conze, *Buddhism,* pp. 125–126. For some Theravādins, however, the idea of grace was acceptable, as illustrated by one donor who felt that his request for long life was solely dependent on "the *will* [emphasis added] of the most excellent Buddha Master . . ." (*EM,* no. 10, p. 18), while another believed that the Bodhisatta . . . , shall verily become a Buddha that saves (and) redeems all beings . . ." (*EB,* 1:146).

64. Melford E. Spiro, "Buddhism and Economic Action in Burma," *American Anthropologist* 68 (October 1966): 1163–1173.

65. Edmund R. Leach, *Political Systems of Highland Burma: A Study of Kachin Social Structure,* p. 149.

Chapter 3

1. These concepts are presented here not so much in their canonical or textual sense necessarily but in their Burmese usage. Therefore, the textual version of a *cakkavattī* is less relevant than the Burmese perception and use of it. One should also note that the term *devarāja*, although it seldom if at all appears as such in indigenous sources, is used here because the implicit associations between *deva* and man encourages me to do so. We should not confuse *devarājika* elements with the *devarāja* itself, especially as it was used in Cambodia. For the latest work on the *devarāja*, see Hermann Kulke, *The Devaraja Cult*, Cornell Southeast Asia Program Data Paper, no. 108 (Ithaca: Cornell Univ. Press, 1978). Similarly, *kammarāja* is an analytical term. The term *dhammarāja* is used in Burmese sources but normally as part of a larger royal title.

2. Archaeological Survey of Burma, *EB*, 1:146.

3. Gordon H. Luce, *Old Burma–Early Pagán*, 1:88.

4. *EM*, p. 130.

5. *EB*, 1:112–115.

6. George P. Malalasekera, *Dictionary of Pali Proper Names* (London: John Murray, 1938), 2:957–965.

7. Ibid., 1:178, 832, 833; this was technically the *cakkavattī*'s *cakkaratna*, the *arindama*.

8. *EB*, 1:128, no. 2.

9. *EB*, 1:120.

10. *EB*, 3:58.

11. Burma Home Department, *BODAW*, 1:270–271; U Kala, *Mahayazawindaw Gyi* [The great royal chronicle], 3:212–217.

12. Pamela Gutman, "Ancient Arakan: With Special Reference to its Cultural History between the 5th and 11th Centuries," Ph.D. diss., The Australian National University, 1976, pp. 296–310, gives a detailed description of the plaque. Although the relationship of the plaque to the royal city is my own interpretation, I nevertheless owe the initial stimulation to her work.

13. J. George Scott and J. P. Hardiman, eds., *Gazetteer of Upper Burma and the Shan States*, vol. 1, pt. 2, p. 154.

14. *BODAW*, 1:270–273.

15. The walls today have more *pyathat* than the original thirty-seven when it was first built; see n. 16.

16. Michael Aung-Thwin, "Sacred Space, Sacred Time, and Sacred Energy: Dimensions of the Exemplary Center," in *The City as a Ceremonial Complex*, ed. Bardwell Smith (forthcoming). See also John Spellman, "The Symbolic Significance of the Number Twelve in Ancient India," *JAS* 22 (1962–1963): 79–88.

17. G. E. Harvey, *History of Burma*, pp. 327–328. For a slightly different version, see Richard Temple, *The Thirty-Seven Nats: A Phase of Spirit-Worship Prevailing in Burma* (London: W. Griggs, 1906), p. 10.

18. There are many different reasons for propitiating the Thirty-Seven Nats today, and the stories that surround their origins as told today differ in some

respects from those found in older texts. Moreover, the Thirty-Seven Nats discussed here are the terrestrial ones, whose model, though not content, derives from the thirty-seven celestial deities (i.e., the combination of the thirty-three *deva*s of Tāvatiṁsa and the Four Lokapālas). Furthermore, I am more concerned here with the relationship of these thirty-seven to conceptions of kingship than with the sociological category in which they might fit today. As for the manipulation of the number thirty-seven, King Tabinshwehti's case illustrates the point. In 1485, an inscription made explicit reference to Sakka and the Thirty-Six Lords (see *BODAW,* 1:246). Yet we know that after Tabinshwehti's death in 1550, he was given a place on the pantheon of Thirty-Seven Nats, whose number remained unchanged. Hence, one of the earlier members of the thirty-seven had to make room for a more recent and better known figure. It was usually accommodated by making the latter a reincarnation of one of the former ones.

19. Personal communication: F. K. Lehman. See also Craig Reynolds, "Buddhist Cosmography in Thai History, with Special References to Nineteenth-Century Change," *JAS* 35, 2 (February 1976): 203–220.

20. Melford E. Spiro, ed., *Burmese Supernaturalism* (Englewood Cliffs, N.J.: Prentice-Hall, 1967), p. 92.

21. H. L. Shorto, "The *dewatau sotāpan:* A Mon Prototype of the 37 Nats," *BSOAS* 30 (1967): 132–133.

22. *EB,* 1:151, 167; Scott and Hardiman, *Gazetteer of Upper Burma,* vol. 2, pt. 2, p. 126.

23. *"Slapat Rājawaṅ Datow Smin Roṅ"* [A history of kings], trans. R. Halliday, *JBRS* 13, 1 (1923): 48; also G. H. Luce and Pe Maung Tin, *SIP,* no. 47, p. 128, mentioned the phrase "to spread the Religion" in a clearly military context.

24. *The Glass Palace Chronicle,* trans. Pe Maung Tin and G. H. Luce, p. 77.

25. Archaeological Survey of Burma, *Report of the Director,* 1918, p. 12–13.

26. *BODAW,* 2:627, 633, 937.

27. Archaeological Survey of Ceylon, *Epigraphia Zeylanica* (Colombo, 1912–1927), 2:242–255.

28. Tun Nyein, trans., *Inscriptions of Pagan, Pinya, and Ava,* p. 8.

29. Michael Aung-Thwin, "The Role of *Sasana* Reform in Burmese History: Economic Dimensions of a Religious Purification," *JAS* 38, 4 (August 1979): 671–688. Objections to this article can be found in Victor Lieberman, "The Political Significance of Religious Wealth in Burmese History: Some Further Thoughts," *JAS* 39, 4 (August 1980): 753–769, to which a rebuttal was made in Aung-Thwin, "A Reply to Lieberman," *JAS* 40, 1 (November 1980): 87–90.

30. C. O. Blagden and Pe Maung Tin, "Talaing Inscription on a bell cast by Anauppet-lun Min," *JBRS* 18, 1 (1928): 33.

31. Archaeological Survey of Burma, *SMK,* 2:104–139.

32. *SIP,* no. 20, p. 41, and no. 38, p. 94.

33. *EB,* 1:126 no. 2.

34. Stanley Tambiah, *World Conqueror and World Renouncer.*

35. Michael Aung-Thwin, "The Nature of State and Society in Pagan: An Institutional History of 12th and 13th Century Burma," Ph.D. diss., University of Michigan, 1976, p. 212.

36. *SMK,* no. 96, p. 143.

37. *SMK,* no. 205, p. 347.

38. *Alaungmin Taya Ameindaw Mya* [The royal edicts of Alaungmin Taya], ed. Hkin Hkin Sein (Rangoon: Burma Research Commission, 1964), p. 21.

39. *BODAW,* 1:288.

40. *EM,* p. 1.

41. *EM,* p. 184.

42. *EB,* 1:117.

43. *Judson's Burmese-English Dictionary,* rev. and enlarged edition, comp. Robert C. Stevenson and F. H. Eveleth (Rangoon: Baptist Board of Publications, 1966), p. 732.

44. Twinthintaikwun Mahasithu, *Twinthin Myanma Yazawin Thit* [Twinthin's new royal chronicle of Burma], 1:270.

45. U Kala, *Mahayazawindaw Gyi,* 2:164.

46. Twinthintaikwun, *Yazawin Thit,* p. 261.

47. *Glass Palace Chronicle,* p. 60.

48. Ibid., p. 65.

49. Ibid., p. 62.

50. Ibid., p. 64.

51. Melford E. Spiro, *Buddhism and Society: A Great Tradition and Its Burmese Vicissitudes,* pp. 283, 410.

52. Dankwart A. Rustow, ed., *Philosophers and Kings: Studies in Leadership* (New York: George Braziller, 1970), pp. 1–32, and Ann Ruth Willner's work on charismatic leadership, *The Spellbinders: Charismatic Political Leadership* (New Haven: Yale Univ. Press, 1984).

53. See Michael Aung-Thwin, "Divinity, Spirit, and Human: Conceptions of Classical Burmese Kingship," in *Centers, Symbols, and Hierarchies: Essays on the Classical States of Southeast Asia,* ed. Lorraine Gesick, pp. 45–86.

54. Michael Aung-Thwin, "Hierarchy and Order in Pre-Colonial Burma," *JSEAS* 15, 2 (September 1984): 224–232. The contrast between the concerns for tyranny and anarchy was very nicely analyzed by Robbins Burling in his *The Passage of Power: Studies in Political Succession* (New York: Academic Press, 1974).

Chapter 4

1. See G. E. Harvey, *A History of Burma.*

2. Eric Wolf, "Kingship, Friendship, and Patron-Client Relations in Complex Societies," in *Friends, Followers, and Factions: A Reader in Political Clientelism,* ed. Steffen W. Schmidt et al., pp. 174–175, is my source for the definition of patron-client ties.

3. I owe the original insight to Louis Dumont's inspiring *Homo Hierarchicus: The Caste System and Its Implications,* trans. Mark Sainsbury, Louis Dumont, and Basia Gulati.

4. Emil Forchhammer, ed. and trans., *King Wagaru's Manu Dhammasattham: Text, Translation, and Notes,* p. 32, mentions *akyan ci so sū* ("one who is under obligation"?).

5. A statement in the inscriptions (G. H. Luce and Pe Maung Tin, *SIP,* no.

21, p. 42, and no. 32, p. 77) makes such a contrast: *"ciy tō mū sō kywan cut lhwat tō mū sō kywan . . ."*

6. *EM,* no. 58, p. 169.

7. Carl H. Lande, "The Dyadic Basis of Clientelism," in *Friends, Followers, and Factions,* ed. Steffen W. Schmidt et al., pp. xiii–xxxvii.

8. See *SIP,* no. 26, p. 56; no. 24, pp. 49–52; no. 44, p. 119; *EM,* no. 46, pp. 124–125.

9. Akin Rabibhadana, *The Organization of Thai Society in the Early Period, 1782–1873,* Cornell University Southeast Asia Program Data Paper no. 74 (Ithaca, 1970). Akin deals only with Thailand, but others have extrapolated to other parts of Southeast Asia.

10. Michael Aung-Thwin, "The Nature of State and Society in Pagan: An Institutional History of 12th and 13th Century Burma," Ph.D. diss., University of Michigan, 1976, p. 122.

11. Archaeological Survey of Burma, *SMK,* no. 41, p. 66; no. 97, p. 158; no. 138, p. 223; no. 146, p. 247; and passim. For an article in English that deals with these various occupations, see Than Tun, "Social Life in Burma, A.D. 1044–1287," *JBRS* 41 (1958): 37–47; also G. H. Luce, "Economic Life of the Early Burman," *JBRS* 30 (1940): 283–335.

12. *SMK,* no. 207, p. 352, mentioned a carpenter (?) under crown service.

13. For the Toungoo period, see Victor B. Lieberman, "Southeast Asian Administrative Cycles: The Burmese Pattern, c. 1570–1760," Ph.D. diss., University of London, 1976, chap. 2 (revised and published as *Burmese Administrative Cycles: Anarchy and Conquest c. 1580–1760*). See also J. S. Furnivall and Pe Maung Tin, eds., *Zambudipa Okhasaung Kyan* [Treatise on the crown of Jambudipa], pp. 19, 30, 39, 101, 102. For the Konbaung period, see U Tin, *Myanma Min Okchokpon Sadan* [Administrative records of Burma's kings], 5 vols. (Rangoon: SGP, 1931–1933), 4:4; also Burma Home Department, *BODAW,* 1:211–212, 224.

14. As G. H. Luce in "Old Kyaukse and the Coming of the Burmans," *JBRS* 42, 1 (1959): 97, has shown, the term *asañ* was "strikingly absent from Kyaukse inscriptions"; Kyaukse was that well-irrigated section of the kingdom where the choice royal lands were located and to which only crown bondsmen were given rights.

15. Personal communication: Gordon H. Luce, Jersey, England, 1974.

16. Hla Pe, "Some Cognate Words in Burmese and Other Tibeto-Burman Languages. 1. Maru," *JBRS* 43 (1970): 9.

17. Archaeological Survey of Burma, *She Haung Mon Kyauksa Paung Chok* [Collection of ancient Mon inscriptions], no. 67, p. 100.

18. *SIP,* p. 78.

19. Marc Bloch, *Feudal Society,* 1:68.

20. *SIP,* p. 143; Tun Nyein, trans., *Inscriptions of Pagan, Pinya, and Ava,* pp. 100–101, 138.

21. *SMK,* pp. 176–177; *EM,* p. 66.

22. *SIP,* pp. 29–30; *EM,* p. 144.

23. Forchhammer, *Wagaru Manu Dhammasattham,* p. 3.

24. *SIP,* p. 92; *SMK,* p. 21.

25. Forchhammer, *Wagaru Manu Dhammasattham,* p. 3.

26. *EM,* p. 86.

27. Ibid.

28. *SMK,* p. 176.

29. *SIP,* p. 101.

30. *SMK,* pp. 155, 178.

31. *EM,* p. 1.

32. The word *ciy* ("to contract"? "to oblige"?) is often used with the word *ṅhā* ("to hire"), as in *ciy ṅhā,* leading one to relate bondage or obligation with employment or contract. See *SIP,* p. 20.

33. *EM,* no. 31, pp. 87–88.

34. We certainly do not consider today's professional athletes slaves, even though their "owners" constantly "buy," "sell," and "trade" them. In fact, I feel that today's professional athletics is a good example of a situation where one's obligations are equivalent to one's body and may be precisely the reason for retaining bondage terminology.

35. *SIP,* no. 11, pp. 19–20.

36. Tun Nyein, *Inscriptions,* p. 65; *EM,* no. 15, p. 31; *SIP,* no. 32, p. 78.

37. *EM,* pp. 133, 135, 139, 140, 171.

38. *EM,* p. 118.

39. *SIP,* no. 11, p. 20; no. 34, p. 84. *SIP,* no. 25, p. 53 and no. 32, p. 78, showed that *kywan* were given in perpetuity. For the seventeenth century, see Than Tun, "Administration Under King Thalun (1629–1648)," *JBRS* 51, 2 (1968): 179.

40. *SMK,* no. 194, p. 329.

41. *SIP,* no. 26, pp. 55–59.

42. Archaeological Survey of Burma, *Report of the Director,* 1965, p. 31; Burma Home Department, *OI,* p. 170; Tun Nyein, *Inscriptions,* p. 65; *SIP,* p. 78.

43. The term *kywan-tō* in twentieth-century Burma is used to refer to oneself (the personal pronoun "I") when speaking to a superior or equal in polite contexts. A variation of *kywan-tō* was used in this same way as early as the twelfth century in the term *atuiw kywan,* "we thy servants." In contrast, in areas of Burma where royal authority had been minimal or nonexistent, hierarchic terminology had little effect on the polite "I" *(kywan-tō)* and *ṅgā* was used regardless of superiority or inferiority in age and status. Today *ṅgā* is used as the impolite "I" or with those clearly lower in age or status from oneself. Thus the word *kywan-tō* changed from a narrow legal, political, and economic definition to a more general and social one, where everyone, relative to everyone else, was in fact a *kywan-tō,* "thy royal servant." The change reflects a transformation from a hierarchy with a monarchy to a modern, democratic republic of equals where hierarchic terminology, though used, no longer makes sense.

44. *SMK,* no. 36, p. 58 (A.D. 1197), showed that the word *amhu* probably applied to a list of government officials. Other inscriptions (*SIP,* no. 27, p. 62; no. 37, p. 91; *EM,* no. 49, p. 139) indicate that those who owed service had the words *ahmu ra, ahmu ma ra,* "one who has duty" and "one who does not have duty," prefixed to their names.

45. U Kyaw Dun, in his edition of *Myaxma Sa Nyunbaung Kyan* [Anthology of Burmese literature], 1:40, quotes the edict of 1367 which showed that *ahmudan* were already present and functioning by then.

46. Furnivall and Pe Maung Tin, *Zambudipa Okhasaung Kyan*, pp. 60–62. *SIP*, no. 28, p. 65 and no. 42, p. 110, showed that *mahādan* ("the great gift," i.e., of the king) lands were being worked by *kywan-tō*. In *SIP*, no. 4, p. 5, King Aloñcañsū dedicated laborers who were *kywan-tō* to the *sangha*. In *SMK*, no. 194, p. 320, as we have seen above, three ministers with apparent military portfolios (as suggested by their titles) were referred to as *kywan-tō*. *SIP*, no. 9, p. 17, recorded that *kywan-tō* were working on *mle tō*, royal lands.

47. Than Tun, "Administration Under King Thalun," pp. 183–184. For a recent study of this period in Burmese history, see Lieberman, *Burmese Administrative Cycles*.

48. *EM*, no. 56, p. 153.

49. Forchhammer, *Wagaru Manu Dhammasattham*, p. 23.

50. Indeed, virtually everyone dedicated as *purā kywan* during the two hundred years of this study, with the exception of those who dedicated themselves and those donated by poor people, at one time had belonged to the crown.

51. *EM*, no. 19, pp. 38–40; no. 31, p. 73; no. 37, p. 91; no. 53, p. 149; Tun Nyein, *Inscriptions*, p. 100.

52. Archaeological Survey of Burma, *EB*, 3:46, 51–52.

53. Than Tun, "Administration Under King Thalun," pp. 180–183.

54. Aung-Thwin, "Nature of State and Society in Pagan," p. 189, nn. 50 and 51. There were instances in which favorites of the king gave their *mahādan* to their descendants as Mra Kan Sañ did to her grandchild. See *EM*, no. 52, pp. 146–147.

55. Edmund R. Leach, "Hydraulic Society in Ceylon," *Past and Present* 15 (1959): 2–25. The term "cellular" used by Leach is not applicable in every way but represents a situation that I feel is close enough to the Burmese case.

56. Aung-Thwin, "Nature of State and Society in Pagan," pp. 187–188. See also Than Tun's "Social Life in Burma," and G. H. Luce's "Geography of Burma Under the Pagan Dynasty," *JBRS* 42 (1959): 40.

57. G. E. Harvey, *History of Burma*, pp. 351–352.

58. Ibid., p. 348; *SIP*, no. 31, p. 72, shows a similar pattern in Pagan.

59. Aung-Thwin, "Nature of State and Society in Pagan," p. 186–187.

60. Shin Samantapāsādika Silavaṁsa, *Jatatawbon Yazawin* [History of royal horoscopes], ed. U Hla Tin, pp. 90, 95. Of these towns, three, including Lhuiñtak and Toñtwañ, both significant centers during Pagan times, had to supply 1,000 men each; while Prome, also important during the Pagan period, sent 800; Ramañsañ, 700; and Calañ, 600 men. Twenty-two towns, most of which were located in areas that surrounded the capital, each sent 400 men. Three towns provided 300 men each; thirteen, 200 men each; eight, 100 men each; seven, 80 men each; twenty-five, 70 men each; seven, 40 men each; nineteen, 30 men each; two, 20 men each; and fifteen had been deemed *lhwat*, that is, released from their obligation, probably for previous service of an outstanding nature or loyalty shown during a struggle for the crown. Identification with

these towns and their prestigious military traditions among people of Upper Burma was still strong in the nineteenth century.

61. *EM,* no. 11, p. 20.

62. Tun Nyein, *Inscriptions,* p. 111 and *EM,* no. 41, p. 137, show groups of people responsible to an overseer appointed by their patron. *EM,* no. 43, p. 116, makes it even more explicit: "and I left instructions with Tan Mhwaṁ, the foreman [*sūkrī*] of the *kywan* of the Cūḷāmaṇi Pagoda."

63. G. H. Luce, "The Early *Syāṁ* in Burma's History," *JSS* 46 (1958): 124, and "Mons of the Pagan Dynasty," *JBRS* 36, 1 (1953): 1–19; Paññacāmi, *Sāsanavaṁsa* [History of the religion], trans. Bimala Churn Law, p. 82.

64. *EM,* no. 23, p. 44.

65. *SIP,* no. 22, p. 45; *SMK,* no. 101, p. 268.

66. *SMK,* no. 121, pp. 193–200.

67. *EB,* 3:51–52. In Burma, only crown soldiers were entitled to carry weapons and publicly display them.

68. Ba Shin, *Lokahteikpan* (Rangoon: Burma Historical Commission, 1962), p. 23.

69. *SIP,* no. 28, p. 65 *(mliy khuin samphaṅ); SMK,* no. 172, p. 295; *SIP,* no. 14, p. 26; *EM,* no. 5, pp. 9–10; *SIP,* no. 6, p. 12.

70. *SIP,* no. 29, p. 68.

71. See *EM,* no. 31, pp. 58–89, for an example of the *saṅgha* acting as a vehicle for upward mobility.

72. See Harvey, *History of Burma,* pp. 351–352; Than Tun, "Administration Under King Thalun." Victor Lieberman's well thought out analysis in his *Burmese Administrative Cycles,* pp. 20–21, gives a good assessment of population growth and patterns in precolonial Burma.

73. Harvey, *History of Burma,* p. 333. See also Charles O. Hucker, *China to 1850* (Stanford: Stanford Univ. Press, 1978), p. 140.

Chapter 5

1. G. H. Luce and Pe Maung Tin, *SIP,* no. 24, p. 49; p. 129; p. 140; Archaeological Survey of Burma, *SMK,* no. 40, pp. 64–66. Tin Hla Thaw's "History of Burma: A.D. 1400–1500," *JBRS* 42, 2 (December 1959): 135–151, shows how the word *praṅ* was used in the sense of "country" or "kingdom."

2. G. H. Luce, "Old Kyaukse and the Coming of the Burmans," *JBRS* 42, 1 (1959): 75–109.

3. *SIP,* no. 27, p. 61.

4. *SIP,* no. 43, p. 113. *Arap* were mentioned in various inscriptions: *SIP,* no. 44, p. 119, mentioned Sacmatī Arap; no. 29, p. 69, had Ṅhak Pac Toṅ Arap; and no. 49, p. 133, had Toṅ Twaṅ Arap. *Arap* had other meanings, however, and must therefore be interpreted in context.

5. Luce, "Old Kyaukse," p. 97; ibid., p. 85.

6. Michael Aung-Thwin, "The Nature of State and Society in Pagan: An Institutional History of 12th and 13th Century Burma," Ph.D. diss., Univ. of Michigan, 1976, p. 192, nn. 97, 100; also see *SIP,* no. 29, pp. 68–69.

There is at present no complete study designed to calculate the acreage of irrigated *padi* land in central Burma during this period. Attempts have been made in chapter 9 to provide at least a tentative answer (see Table 2). Based on that, a conservative estimate of *padi* land excluding all other crops as well as excluding Lower Burma's Delta, which had not yet been drained, it appears that about 600,000 acres may have been under cultivation most of the time. Not dependent on rain, which was in any case meager (about 45 inches a year), and based on perennial streams, yields were consistent and were perceived to have been consistent. One donor expected 12,000 *taṅ* (one Burmese *taṅ* was equal to approximately 156 lbs.) of *padi* out of approximately 6,637 acres of irrigated *padi* land per crop, of which there were normally two and sometimes three (see Tun Nyein, trans., *Inscriptions of Pagan, Pinya, and Ava,* p. 137). I consider this a low yield for a traditional rice-growing society. I am in the process of conducting more precise studies on population and agriculture of precolonial Burma and at present the figures are by no means final. In any case, on 600,000 acres, at worst one million eighty thousand *taṅ* of *padi* per crop could be produced, double that for two crops and triple that for three crops. All this excludes sesamum, chillies, maize, oil, betel nuts, and a host of other valuable products. I am aware of the fact that chillies and maize are considered New World crops and were not supposed to have arrived in Asia until the Spanish and Portuguese brought them there. However, there is a growing body of literature on corn in Asia before the Spanish and Portuguese. See for instance M. D. W. Jeffrey's "Pre-Columbian Maize in Asia," in *Man Across the Sea: Problems of Pre-Columbian Contacts,* ed. Carroll L. Riley et al. (Austin: University of Texas Press, 1971). In Pagan itself, a donation of A.D. 1248 mentions a basket of chillies (see *SMK* 2: 99–103). There were several other such cases. G. H. Luce's "The Geography of Burma Under the Pagan Dynasty," *JBRS* 42 (1959): 32–59, mentions both chillies and maize, but he assumes the New World argument to be correct. The term for maize or corn, *pyoṅ,* if it stands alone, can mean other things, but if attached to another word *bhū* means corn on the cob.

7. *SMK,* no. 41, pp. 65–69.

8. Gordon H. Luce, *Old Burma–Early Pagán,* 1:34–38.

9. Luce, "Geography of Burma Under the Pagan Dynasty," p. 49.

10. *EM,* no. 9, p. 17 (A.D. 1192), and *SIP,* no. 49, p. 133 (A.D. 1290).

11. *SIP,* p. 103. However, Hla Pe, in "A Tentative List of Mon Loanwords in Burmese," *JBRS* 50 (1967): 79, offers the suggestion that *nuiṅṅaṁ* may have come from *nigama,* "market town," to which F. K. Lehman and others object.

12. *SMK,* no. 41, pp. 65–69.

13. Ibid. See also Karl Polanyi, C. M. Arensberg, and H. W. Pearson, *Trade and Market in the Early Empires.* Contact with the Cholas began as early as Kalancacsā's reign; his inscriptions mentioned how the "Coḷi Prince" was "converted" to Buddhism by the king. Moreover, most of the names of Indians found at Pagan were of south Indian origin, and art and architectural influence at Pagan point to both Andhra and east Bengal. In addition, seals of Aniruddha and Co Lu (Sawlu) found in the Isthmus of Kra region and *The Glass Palace Chronicle*'s accounts of Aloṅcañsū's exploits in the same region show Pagan's interests in that area.

14. Burma Home Department, *BODAW,* 2:627.

15. Ba Shin, *Lokahteikpan* (Rangoon: Burma Historical Commission, 1962), noted that Kalancacsā appointed governors to the area. Coastal towns in Lower Burma, particularly Tala (opposite modern Rangoon) and Pegu, were apparently lucrative ports of trade over which the king appointed princes, far from the capital and court intrigue. Kings Klawcwā and Klacwā were known, respectively, as "the King who died at Tala" and "the Lord of Pegu."

16. *SIP,* no. 38, p. 95 (A.D. 1266); no. 49, p. 137 (A.D. 1291).

17. *SMK,* no. 84, p. 130.

18. *SIP,* no. 43, p. 114; no. 49, p. 137; no. 43, p. 116.

19. *EM,* no. 56, p. 158, mentions the "Pakuiw Maṅ Krī, Klacwā"; see Luce, *Old Burma–Early Pagán,* vol. 2, supplement entitled "List of Kings," for Klawcwā's title; Luce, "Pagan Dynasty," (typescript) II.10 stated that Co Lu, Aniruddha's son, erected five Pali inscriptions that were found at Mergui.

20. Ba Shin, *Lokahteikpan,* p. 23.

21. *SIP,* no. 4, p. 7; no. 46, p. 125; G. H. Luce, in "The Early *Syāṁ* in Burma's History," *JSS* 46 (1958): 136, wrote that Anantapicañ in 1278 was commander of these three *mriuw* while Minister Koñcaṅ, who "ate" Koñcaṅ, had had the same job earlier.

22. *SIP,* no. 44, p. 119; no. 6, p. 12.

23. *SMK,* no. 64, p. 101 (A.D. 1212), line 23.

24. Ibid.; *SIP,* no. 18, pp. 32–33; no. 29, p. 68; *SMK,* pp. 179, 365.

25. *Judson's Burmese-English Dictionary,* rev. and enlarged by Robert C. Stevenson and F. H. Eveleth (Rangoon: Baptist Board of Publications, 1966), p. 796.

26. *SMK,* p. 66.

27. Tun Nyein, *Inscriptions,* pp. 31–32; Archaeological Survey of Burma, *Report of the Director,* 1917, p. 38; *SIP,* no. 4, p. 7, records Narapatisithu giving his generals fiefs to "eat" in northern Burma. See also *SIP,* nos. 46–47, pp. 125–130.

28. *SIP,* no. 12, p. 21; no. 23, p. 48; no. 30, pp. 70–71; no. 40, p. 106; *SMK,* no. 154, p. 258; no. 205, pp. 347–349; no. 212, p. 361; and Tun Nyein, *Inscriptions,* p. 55.

29. Tun Nyein, *Inscriptions,* p. 52.

30. Ibid., pp. 32, 33, 35.

31. *SIP,* no. 28, p. 65; no. 24, p. 50, in which the ratio of silver to gold was given as one to ten, with one exception, when it was one to twelve.

32. *SIP,* no. 44, p. 121.

33. *SIP,* no. 44, p. 120.

34. Aung-Thwin, "Nature of State and Society," pp. 187, 188, n. 25.

35. *SIP,* no. 29, pp. 68–69 (A.D. 1246) records the names of these officials. Acalaphira, for example, was related to the royal family, companion of the Heir Apparent Uccanā, Klacwā's son, who was in charge of Mlacsā, the seat of government for the Eleven Kharuin of Kyaukse.

36. Tun Nyein, *Inscriptions,* pp. 32, 35, 138.

37. Ibid., p. 36.

38. *SIP,* no. 52, p. 145.

39. Tun Nyein, *Inscriptions,* p. 35.

40. *SIP,* no. 40, p. 103 (A.D. 1271). See Clarence Maloney, "Origins of Civilization in South India," *JAS* 29 (1970): 603–616.

41. Aung-Thwin, "Nature of State and Society," p. 64.

42. *SMK,* no. 142, p. 230; J. George Scott and J. P. Hardiman, eds., *Gazetteer of Upper Burma and the Shan States,* vol. 1, no. 1, p. 447, vol. 2, no. 2, p. 152.

43. Aung-Thwin, "Nature of State and Society," p. 64.

44. G. H. Luce, "Economic Life of the Early Burman," *JBRS* 30 (1940): 336.

45. Scott and Hardiman, *Upper Burma Gazetteer,* vol. 2, no. 2, p. 51 and passim. Also see Luce, "Economic Life of the Early Burman."

46. Marc Bloch, *Feudal Society,* trans. L. A. Manyon, 1:67.

Chapter 6

1. E. Maung's difficult to find *Expansion of Burmese Law* and the even more difficult to acquire volumes by Emil Forchhammer, *The Jardine Prize Essay,* and Sir John Jardine, *Notes on Buddhist Law,* are the few available works. The latter two were published nearly a century ago. Even they did not deal with the origins or development of Burmese law based on the earliest lithographs; rather, they touch on various aspects of legal problems found in Burmese law. There are also some articles, such as U Hla Aung's works in the *JBRS* and Than Tun's work called "Law in Pagan," the latter virtually unavailable, as it was published in *The Rangoon Teacher Review.* R. Lingat's short work on Burma's legal institutions, "Evolution of the Conception of Law in Burma and Siam," *JSS* 38, 1 (1950): 9–31, should be mentioned, but here too it was not the result of research in original and primary sources, least of all Old Burmese. This is an untouched field for those interested in the subject. There are many references to law and several occasions of civil suits recorded in the inscriptions, from which a genuine legal study could be made. The seventeenth century is less difficult to deal with, the sources becoming more prolific, and by the nineteenth century, there are many more materials to work with. In fact, about half of the legal codes of premodern Burma that are extant were compiled then.

2. M. B. Hooker, "The Indian-Derived Law Texts of Southeast Asia," *JAS* 37, 2 (February 1978): 201–219.

3. Emil Forchhammer, *The Jardine Prize: An Essay on the Sources and Development of Burmese Law,* 8 vols. (Rangoon: SGP, 1885), passim.

4. Much of this information can be found in the nineteenth-century Burmese bibliography compiled by Atwinwun Maingkaing Myosa, *Piṭakat Thamaing Sadan* [A history of literature], p. 185.

5. G. H. Luce, "Aspects of Pagan History—Later Period," in *In Memoriam Phya Anuman Rajadhon,* ed. Tej Bunnag and Michael Smithies (Bangkok: The Siam Society, 1970), p. 137.

6. Jardine, *Notes on Buddhist Law,* 4:5 and 7:9. Also see the compilation by U Gaung, *A Digest of the Burmese Buddhist Law concerning Inheritance and Marriage; being a collection of texts from thirty-six Dhammathats, composed and arranged under the supervision of the Hon'able U Gaung, C.S.I. ex-Kinwun Mingyi,* 2:4.

7. Mabel Haynes Bode, *The Pali Literature of Burma,* p. 87.

8. Jardine, *Notes on Buddhist Law,* p. 19.

9. Vincentius Sangermano, *A Description of the Burmese Empire, compiled chiefly from Burmese documents,* trans. William Tandy.

10. U Gaung, *Digest,* passim.

11. Bode, *Pali Literature of Burma,* pp. 31–34; Paññacāmi, *Sāsanavaṁsa* [History of the religion], trans. Bimila Churn Law, pp. 72–74; Archaeological Survey of Burma, *EB,* 3:137–184.

12. Archaeological Survey of Burma, *SMK,* no. 26, pp. 46–47.

13. *EM,* no. 16, p. 33; G. H. Luce and Pe Maung Tin, *SIP,* no. 16, p. 29; Burma Home Department, *Inscriptions Collected in Upper Burma,* 1:176; and *SMK,* no. 31, p. 94.

14. *SMK,* no. 137, p. 221; no. 186, p. 319.

15. L. D. Barnett, "The Manavulu-Sandesaya," *JRAS* 9 (April 1905): 267.

16. *EB,* 3:121. Ānandathera was one of the four monks whom Chapada, a monk from Pagan who went to Śrī Laṅka to study and be ordained in the Mahāvihāra tradition there, brought back with him from Śrī Laṅka to Pagan in order to form a valid Order. Of these four monks who returned, three of them, Sivali, Ānanda, and Tamalinda, are mentioned in contemporary Pagan inscriptions. See *SIP,* no. 45, p. 121, and *EM,* no. 45, p. 120 where Tamalinda and Sivali are respectively mentioned.

17. U Kyaw Dun, ed. and comp. *Myanma Sa Nyunbaung Kyan* [Anthology of Burmese literature] 1: 255–256, 331.

18. *EM,* no. 58, pp. 168–169.

19. *EM,* no. 58, p. 166.

20. *EM,* p. 171.

21. British Library, Oriental mss. 3447, A and B.

22. U Hla Aung, "The Burmese Concept of Law," *JBRS* 53, 2 (1969): 27–41. He quotes from E. Maung, *Expansion of Burmese Law,* who had apparently used the original edicts. See also Than Tun, "Administration Under King Thalun (1629–1648)," *JBRS* 51, 2 (1968): 181, for information on legal matters in these edicts. Sangermano, *Description of the Burmese Empire,* chap. 24, has additional information.

23. British Library, Or. 3475, A and B.

24. Emil Forchhammer, ed. and trans., *King Wagaru's Manu Dhammasattham: Text, Translation, and Notes,* chap. 12, no. 99, p. 35.

25. Ibid., chap. 15, no. 146, p. 53.

26. *SIP,* no. 41, pp. 106–110.

27. Tun Nyein, trans., *Inscriptions of Pagan, Pinya, and Ava,* pp. 130–133.

28. Forchhammer, *Wagaru Manu Dhammasattham,* chap. 14, no. 116, pp. 23–24.

29. Sangermano, *Description of the Burmese Empire,* p. 276.

30. *SIP,* no. 41, p. 108; *EM,* no. 31, p. 66.

31. *EM,* no. 31, pp. 58–90.

32. Sangermano, *Description of the Burmese Empire,* p. 226.

33. Ibid.

34. Ibid., pp. 263–264.

35. Ibid., p. 261.

36. *SIP,* no. 21, pp. 43–44.

37. *SIP,* no. 41, pp. 107–110, no. 21, p. 44 (Sū Chañ Ratanākuṁthaṁ, "barrister Ratanākuṁthaṁ," was referred to as the counsel for Anantasū); *EM,* no. 24, p. 47, lines 3–4; *SMK,* no. 146, p. 248.

38. *EM,* no. 31, pp. 58–90; no. 21, p. 43; no. 22, p. 44; no. 59, p. 170; *SIP,* no. 36, p. 89; *SMK,* no. 146, pp. 246–248; Than Tun, *Khit Haung Myanma Yazawin* [History of ancient Burma], pp. 162–163.

39. Sangermano, *Description of the Burmese Empire,* p. 224.

40. *EM,* no. 22, p. 44, lines 4–5; *SMK,* no. 105, p. 173, nos. 112–113, pp. 185–186.

41. *EM,* no. 21, p. 43; *SIP,* no. 36, pp. 88–89.

42. *SMK,* no. 73, p. 117 (A.D. 1261), and Than Tun, *Khit Haung,* p. 171. The description of the judicial structure as given by the *Shwe Myañ Dhammathat* in Sangermano is virtually the same as what I have reconstructed for Pagan from the inscriptions—two levels of justice, the village or town level and the appellate level. The *Shwe Myañ Dhammathat* states that "after the chiefs of the villages or the governor of towns, have given their judgement in any case, if the parties are dissatisfied with the decision, they may have recourse to another judge; and, if this judge has been chosen by consent of both parties, they must abide by his award" (Sangermano, *Description of the Burmese Empire,* p. 224).

43. *SIP,* no. 21, pp. 43–44; *SMK,* nos. 112–113, pp. 184–185.

44. *SIP,* no. 41, p. 108; *EM,* no. 31, p. 66.

45. *SMK,* no. 83, pp. 128–129 (A.D. 1219).

46. *SMK,* no. 125, p. 204 (A.D. 1229).

47. *SMK,* no. 118, p. 190 (A.D. 1226).

48. *SMK,* no. 113, p. 185 (A.D. 1226), and no. 97, p. 157.

49. Forchhammer, *Wagaru Manu Dhammasattham,* chap. 4, no. 53, p. 10.

50. Sangermano, *Description of the Burmese Empire,* p. 242.

51. Ibid., p. 275; Forchhammer, *Wagaru Manu Dhammasattham,* chap. 18, nos. 183–184, pp. 67–68.

52. Forchhammer, *Wagaru Manu Dhammasattham,* chap. 17, no. 170, pp. 62–63.

53. U Gaung, *Digest,* 1: 25; Forchhammer, *Wagaru Manu Dhammasattham,* chap. 18, nos. 183–184, pp. 67–68.

54. Forchhammer, *Wagaru Manu Dhammasattham,* chap. 15, nos. 152–154, p. 57.

55. Sangermano, *Description of the Burmese Empire,* pp. 244–245.

56. Marc Bloch, *Feudal Society,* trans. L. A. Manyon, 1:118.

Chapter 7

1. C. C. Berg, "The Javanese Picture of the Past," in *An Introduction to Indonesian Historiography,* ed. Soedjatmoko et al. (Ithaca: Cornell Univ. Press, 1965), pp. 87–117. See also D. G. E. Hall, "Recent Tendencies in the Study of the Early History of Southeast Asia: Notes and Comment," *Pacific Affairs* 39 (1966–1967): 339–348.

2. Archaeological Survey of Burma, *SMK,* no. 209, p. 356 (A.D. 1192); *SMK,* no. 153, p. 256 (A.D. 1235); G. H. Luce and Pe Maung Tin, *SIP,* no. 40, p. 102 (A.D. 1271).

3. *SMK,* no. 153, p. 256.

4. *SMK,* no. 97, p. 152 (A.D. 1223).

5. See, for example, *SMK,* no. 214, p. 363, which stated: "King Cañsū, who owns and rules land and water."

6. No study has been conducted on the population of monks in precolonial Burma, but some information in the inscriptions gives us a clue as to their numbers during the Pagan period. One inscription of 1102, relatively early in the development of Pagan, mentions 4,108 monks (see G. H. Luce, *Old Burma–Early Pagán,* 1:69). This appears to be a low estimate and may have referred only to the particular sect who followed Shin Arahan, King Kalancacsā's primate, for another inscription only eighty-one years later stated that there were 2,008 monasteries (*tuik,* distinct from the administrative unit) in which the *sangha* lived (*SMK,* 2:204). If only twenty monks lived in each monastery—some had far more and others less—the population of monks would be around 40,000. It is estimated in some sources that there are today 800,000 monks (Hans Johannes Hoefer et al., comps., *Burma* [Hong Kong: Apa Productions, 1981], p. 100), while other unpublished estimates put the number of monks registered in the purification of 1980—which is usually thought of as a conservative estimate—to have been around 1,250,000. The latter estimate comes close to the percentage of monks in today's population, placed at around 3 percent by some (see Victor B. Lieberman, *Burmese Administrative Cycles: Anarchy and Conquest c. 1580–1760,* p. 20, n. 18). Turned around, if 40,000 monks equaled 3 percent of the population of Pagan, the population of Pagan must have been around 1,500,000. This figure (of 1,500,000) is extremely close to the figure calculated by others according to methodology and factors with no relation to the above mentioned inscription.

7. *The Glass Palace Chronicle,* trans. Pe Maung Tin and G. H. Luce, p. 155, stated that there were eight major monasteries in Pagan and quoted an inscription as its source as well as the eight monasteries. The inscription is apparently lost, but another one during Narapatisithu's reign mentioned a royal dedication, at whose ceremony were present eight senior monks, perhaps representing these monasteries. See n. 8, below.

8. For example, in the late eleventh century at Prince Rājakumār's dedication were present six religious dignitaries (Archaeological Survey of Burma, *EB,* 1:26) and in 1190, there were eight such personages present at one of Narapatisithu's dedications, "who recited *paritta*"; see *SIP,* no. 11, p. 19.

9. There were, however, "northern" and "southern" monasteries mentioned in Pagan; see *SMK,* no. 91, p. 138. Moreover, the "royal monastery" was at Mlacsā, *east* of the capital, and may have assumed that post; see Tun Nyein, trans., *Inscriptions of Pagan, Pinya, and Ava,* pp. 47–48. There were others on different sides of the capital, but to what extent they were deliberate one cannot be certain. See Archaeological Survey of Burma, *Pictorial Guide to Pagan,* ed. U Aung Thaw (map), for a plan of the city's religious buildings as well as Map 4. Tun Nyein, p. 132, *did* mention one Mahāthera Dhammasiri "of the west cave."

10. For example, see Than Tun, *Khit Haung Myanma Yazawin* [History of ancient Burma], p. 246, and ASB, *Pictorial Guide,* p. 15, for temples that were "four sided."

11. J. George Scott and J. P. Hardiman, *Gazetteer of Upper Burma and the Shan States,* 2:156.

12. E. Michael Mendelson, *Sangha and State in Burma,* ed. by John P. Ferguson (Ithaca: Cornell Univ. Press, 1975), pp. 57–58 and passim, gives a different, less centralized view of the *sangha.*

13. Tin Hla Thaw, "History of Burma: A.D. 1400–1500," *JBRS* 42, 2 (December 1959): 135–151.

14. *SIP,* no. 5, p. 11; Tun Nyein, *Inscriptions,* p. 64; *EM,* no. 61, p. 179; *EM,* no. 17, p. 35; *SIP,* no. 25, pp. 16–18; *SIP,* no. 41, p. 107; Tun Nyein, *Inscriptions,* p. 55, *SMK,* no. 154, p. 258; and *SIP,* no. 40, p. 106, and *EM,* no. 33, p. 93. These references document the following instances in order. In 1139, appropriately during King Aloncañsū's well-administered reign, we found him granting "royal permission" to a donor who had wanted to dedicate to the Tuin Khywat Pagoda. In 1144, another donor had twice to specify the lands he wished to dedicate before obtaining permission; even then it was only after the ownership of this land had been first carefully confirmed by the land registers under the care of the *mahāsaman.* In 1205, even the king's own preceptor needed permission to erect a *kū* (temple) west of the Dhammaram Temple. In 1212, permission was required to repair a *sīmā* that had been in ruins for a long time, originally erected by King Caw Rahan. In 1236, a donor stated the exact day that permission was requested, and even the queen mother needed the authority of the king to dedicate lands and people. At the end of the Pagan dynasty, a minister needed royal permission to dedicate land and people to the *sangha.* The *bona fides* of ownership was determined not only to confirm that the donation indeed belonged to the donor but also to make certain that the property being given was actually going to the *sangha.* For example, in 1235, a certain Sarabhun bought land with 20 gold pieces and 200 silver *pyañ* (flat pieces?) from another who had pawned the land, then proceeded to donate this acquisition to the *sangha.* But the judges, whose duty it was to check such transactions, did not believe that the former had actually donated the land, and so held an investigation. It was only when the *mahāsaman* found in the register that the dedication was indeed bona fide that it was consequently declared legally valid as a dedication. Similarly, in 1272, because "the judges did not believe that the property was actually donated to the Buddha, (an) investigation was opened to confirm [the allegation]." All tax-exempted lands, that is, religious dedications, were recorded in a register affixed with the owner's seal, then placed in a wooden box and locked. The box was then given to someone else, possibly a relative, to keep in case the donor died and the property became a source of contention. See *SMK,* no. 154, p. 258.

15. *SIP,* no. 10, p. 19; *SMK,* no. 211, p. 359.

16. *SIP,* no. 26, pp. 55–56; *SIP,* no. 27, p. 61.

17. *SIP,* no. 15, p. 27.

18. Burma Home Department, *BODAW,* 2:720–721.

19. *EM,* no. 16, p. 33.

20. *EM,* no. 24, p. 46.

21. *SIP,* no. 22, p. 47.

22. Burma Home Department, *PPA,* no. 16, p. 25.

23. Paul Ambrose Bigandet, *The Life, or Legend, of Gaudama, the Buddha of the Burmese, with Annotations: The Ways to Neibban and Notice of the Phongyis, or Burmese Monks,* p. 176.

24. Paññacāmi, *Sāsanavaṁsa,* trans. Bimala Churn Law, p. 106.

25. *EM,* no. 15, p. 29.

26. *EB,* 3:182.

27. Ibid., p. 185.

28. Ibid., no. 24, p. 46.

29. *SIP,* no. 22, p. 47.

30. *SIP,* no. 43, p. 114.

31. *SIP,* no. 45, p. 124, and Tun Nyein, *Inscriptions,* p. 55.

32. U Gaung, *A Digest of the Burmese Buddhist Law concerning Inheritance and Marriage; being a collection of texts from thirty-six Dhammathats, composed and arranged under the supervision of the Hon'ble U Gaung, C.S.I. ex-Kinwun Mingyi,* 2:467.

33. *EM,* no. 42, p. 115.

34. *EM,* no. 43, p. 116.

35. *SIP,* no. 49, p. 132.

36. *SIP,* no. 27, p. 60.

37. *SIP,* no. 30, pp. 71–72.

38. *SIP,* no. 49, pp. 135–136.

39. *EM,* no. 56, p. 153; J. S. Furnivall, "The Pagan Revenue Inquest of 1127 B.E. (1765 A.D.)," typescript. Another one was referred to as "my father's monastery."

40. *EM,* no. 61, p. 180.

41. See note 4 of the Conclusion. Moreover, the story of Chapada and the four Theras, sent to Śrī Laṅka for the purposes of reordination and purification is mentioned on p. 230, note 16. Dhammaceti's fifteenth-century example is also discussed. Thalun's edicts of the early seventeenth century contained laws that regulated the number of people entering the *saṅgha* and strictly defined glebe property from state lands, using purification as one of the methods; see Than Tun, "Administration Under King Thalun (1629–1648)," *JBRS* 51, 2 (1968): 187. The late eighteenth- and early nineteenth-century "Revenue Inquests" of King Bodawhpaya are also quite well known, the target of these inquests being the *saṅgha.* For example, see D. G. E. Hall, *A History of South-East Asia* (New York: St. Martin, 1968), p. 585, for a brief summary of the incidents. For a glimpse of the type of material recovered from these inquests, see Harry J. Benda and John A. Larkin, *The World of Southeast Asia* (New York: Harper and Row, 1967), pp. 62–67. Much unpublished material of the latter kind exists in palm-leaf and other manuscripts called *pe cā* and *parabuik,* some of which have been reproduced in early volumes of the *JBRS* under the auspices of J. S. Furnivall, entitled "Early Historical Documents (Revenue Inquests)," *JBRS* 8 (1918): 4–42, and 9 (1919): 33–36.

42. Bigandet, *Life, or Legend, of Gaudama,* p. 154.

43. *SIP,* no. 4, p. 4, *Glass Palace Chronicle,* p. 126; J. S. Furnivall, "Sittan of 1145 B.E. and 1164 B.E.," leaf 37 (A.D. 1783).

44. *BODAW,* 2: 719; *SIP,* no. 28, p. 65 (A.D. 1242), no. 37, p. 89 (A.D. 1261). *Judson's Burmese-English Dictionary,* rev. and enlarged by Robert C. Stevenson and F. H. Eveleth (Rangoon: Baptist Board of Publications, 1966), p. 538, stated that *dakkhinā* is "south" in Pali, and the person was in charge of the "Southern Division."

45. *SIP,* no. 37, p. 89 (A.D. 1261), which had "Śrī Tribhavanādityapavara-dhammarājā, the great king, whose son, the Lord of the Eastern Palace, Narasiṅkha Uccanā . . . ," who later became king. In 1364, another inscription declared him "the Great Royal Son, Lord of the Eastern (Front) Palace." See U Kyaw Dun, ed., *Myanma Sa Nyunbaung Kyan,* 1:111. *Maṅ hla* appears in *EM,* no. 18, p. 38; *SMK,* no. 63, p. 100 (A.D. 1211 and 1212); and *SIP,* no. 6, p. 12 (A.D. 1140).

46. *SMK,* no. 109, p. 179; no. 144, p. 243 (A.D. 1225).

47. Furnivall, "Sittan," leaf 37; *Glass Palace Chronicle,* p. 136, passim.

48. *BODAW,* 1:72; *SIP,* no. 4, pp. 4–5.

49. *SIP,* no. 30, p. 70.

50. *SMK,* no. 172, p. 297, (A.D. 1236).

51. Archaeological Survey of Burma, *Report of the Director,* 1916, passim.

52. *Glass Palace Chronicle,* pp. 126–127.

53. Atwinwun Maingkaing Myosa, *Pitakat Thamaing Sadan,* p. 185. According to this source, these hereditary titles originated with four families of hereditary *mriuw sūkrī* who governed the four quarters of the capital.

54. *SMK,* no. 47, p. 75; no. 133, p. 214; and no. 147, p. 248. G. E. Harvey, *A History of Burma,* p. 351, showed how the *cañsū* title became functionless when its earlier role of manpower control no longer became applicable. See also B. S. Carey, *Myingyan Settlement Report* (Rangoon: SGP, 1901), p. 2, and J. S. Furnivall, *Myingyan Settlement Report* (Rangoon: SGP, 1914), as well as his "Notes on the History of Hanthawaddy," *JBRS* 4 (1914), and "History of Syriam," *JBRS* 5 (1915). Even Dr. Ba Maw, head of state in Burma during World War II, claimed the title of *cañsū,* stating that he had descended from the nineteenth-century royal family.

55. *Glass Palace Chronicle,* p. 126.

56. *EB,* 3:51–52.

57. Scott and Hardiman, *Gazetteer of Upper Burma,* 2:542.

58. *SIP,* no. 35, p. 86.

59. U Kyaw Dun, *Myanma Sa Nyunbaung Kyan,* 1:42, in which the "Great Queen of Mingyi Swasawke" referred to herself as "the Southern Queen, Acaw. . . ." Moreover, one of King Klacwā's queens was Queen Toṅphlaṅ Sañ, that is, "of the South" or associated "with the South," while another was Mlac Plaṅ Sañ, "of the north"; see *SMK,* no. 58, p. 94, and Tun Nyein, *Inscriptions,* p. 113. Kyaw Dun, 1:331, refers to "Mlok Plaṅ Sañ," taken from an inscription without a date but whose spelling of *mlok* and *plaṅ* suggests a post-Pagan date. Nevertheless, it seems rather apparent that it is referring to the same title. *Judson's Burmese-English Dictionary,* pp. 665 and 581, mentions five places or posts of honor for being seated in the royal presence, one of which deals with the word *phlaṅ* (Old Burmese) or *plaṅ* (modern). Thus *toṅphlaṅ sañ* would be "the southern post" or "position" around the king; see also p. 497 of

Judson's for all the terms associated with the chief queen. See *SMK,* no. 153, p. 256, no. 52, p. 84; and *SIP,* no. 43, p. 111, no. 40, p. 102, for the queens and their residences situated in the directions of the cardinal points.

60. According to Scott and Hardiman, who may have been privy to the inner workings of the court at Mandalay, the king on his accession "had to take to wife the two princesses who were nearest of kin to the blood royal. Consequently, [King] Mindon's stepsister and his cousin became his consorts . . . ," *Gazetteer of Upper Burma,* 2:156. This implies that the previous chief queen gives up her position once a new king ascends the throne, unless he retains her to enhance his own (probably illegitimate) status.

61. *Judson's Burmese-English Dictionary,* p. 465; E. V. Foucar, *They Reigned in Mandalay* (London: D. Dobson, 1946), p. 21.

62. Shin Samantapāsādika Silāvaṁsa, *Jatatawbon Yazawin,* p. 41. Also *SIP,* no. 32, p. 75; *EB,* 1:5; *BODAW,* 2:779–780; *SIP,* no. 5, p. 8; *EM,* no. 57, p. 157; Tun Nyein, *Inscriptions,* p. 113, should be consulted for her Sanskrit title.

63. Robbins Burling, "Burmese Kingship Terminology," *American Anthropologist* 67 (October 1965): 108. See also Melford Spiro's work on the Burmese social system, *Kingship and Marriage in Burma: A Cultural and Psychodynamic Analysis* (Berkeley: Univ. of California Press, 1977).

64. *Glass Palace Chronicle,* pp. 45–46; see ASB, *Pictorial Guide,* p. 18, for the location of these images.

65. Sir Richard Temple, *The Thirty-Seven Nats: A Phase of Spirit-Worship Prevailing in Burma* (London: W. Griggs, 1906), p. 34.

66. Scott and Hardiman, *Gazetteer of Upper Burma,* 1:69; also U Tin, *Myanma Min Okchokpon Sadan,* (Rangoon: SGP, 1931–1933), 2:193, states that "the eldest son of the Chief Queen" succeeds, but as we shall see, the word "son" applied to a son-in-law as well.

67. *Judson's Burmese-English Dictionary,* p. 390; *SMK,* no. 82, p. 127.

68. *SIP,* no. 40, pp. 99–102; *EM,* no. 57, p. 159; Tun Nyein, *Inscriptions,* pp. 116, 119, 140.

69. G. H. Luce included Maṅ Yaṅ between Uccanā and Narathihapade in the chronological chart on the inside cover of *Old Burma–Early Pagán* vol. 2. There is no space here to discuss the reasons, except to say that it was based on Luce's theory concerning an alleged invasion of Pagan by Śrī Laṅka, which I have attempted to dispute elsewhere; see Michael Aung-Thwin, "The Problems of Ceylonese-Burmese Relations in the 12th Century and the Question of an Interregnum in Pagan: 1164–1174 A.D.," *JSS* 64, pt. 1 (January 1976): 53–74.

70. See Burling, "Burmese Kinship," p. 108, where "grandchild" is listed. Note that although "son-in-law" is not given, in Burmese to call one's son-in-law "son," as it is done in other societies, is certainly not unknown, as one would also say "mother" for one's "mother-in-law."

71. *SIP,* no. 40, pp. 99–102; *EM,* no. 57, p. 159; Tun Nyein, *Inscriptions,* pp. 116, 119, 140.

72. *SIP,* no. 22, p. 46.

73. *SMK,* no. 82, p. 127.

74. *Glass Palace Chronicle,* p. 141.

75. *SIP,* no. 30, p. 70.

76. *EM,* no. 52, pp. 146–147; *SMK,* no. 59, p. 94; no. 84, p. 130.

77. For the beginning of the Konbaung period, see Sangermano's account *A Description of the Burmese Empire,* pp. 61–63, which was firsthand. In this case, Alaunghpaya, on his deathbed, told his ministers that his seven sons were to succeed him in order of their age. But Alaunghpaya's second son, Hsinphyushin, a powerful king, instead decided to appoint his own eldest son as heir apparent, going against Alaunghpaya's wishes and instigating a revolt by Alaunghpaya's third son, younger brother of Hsinphyushin; thus the conflict was between king's son and the latter's uncle. Upon Hsinphyushin's death, the ministers raised his eldest son, rather than his brother to the throne, according to the former's wishes, disregarding Alaunghpaya's wishes at the same time. If asked to do so again for Hsinphyushin's son, the ministers would probably have done it again, the present king's demands being "more legal" than those of his predecessors. When the third son of Alaunghpaya, with the regnal title of Bodawhpaya, eventually took the throne he put to death all the queens and concubines, including babes, according to Sangermano, of his predecessors in order to eliminate the many claimants. He then had his son publicly recognized as legitimate heir, as "he was born of the second queen," and "in order to strengthen his claims still further, he was married to his own sister, and daughter of the first" queen (i.e., his "half-sister"). This pattern and type of conflict continued throughout the Konbaung dynasty and were probably no less applicable to the Pagan dynasty, whose succession rules were essentially the same.

78. Aniruddha, son of the northern queen (fourth) fought against Sokkate, son of the second queen, and it was Kalancacsā, son of the fourth queen or concubine versus Co Lu (Sawlu), heir apparent and son of the chief queen; Aloncañsū the *grandson* of the king by the daughter of his chief queen, against Rājakumār, apparently son of the chief queen; Narasū, either non-royal or far from the succession in any case, against Aloncañsū's son, Manrhancō (Minshinsaw), who was exiled by the king; Narasinkha, the heir, against Narapatisithu his brother; and Nātonmyā, son of a concubine, against his elder brothers. Klacwā, his successor, had no other claimants to deal with as far as we know, but his son Uccanā ruled for only five or six years and was probably deposed by Narathihapade, who was non-royal (in the sense that his genealogy went back to certain artisan families) and therefore married Uccanā's chief queen to enhance his own status.

79. See, for example, Silāvamsa, *Jatatawbon,* pp. 37–40.

80. This trend also occurred in the last succession struggle in Burmese history, between Thibaw's and Mindon's reigns, when princesses were maneuvered by their mothers to marry whom they thought would be appointed heir; thus the reverse would also apply, that is, if the chief queen had sons instead of daughters. For a detailed and excellent discussion of the inner politics of the Mandalay court, see the second of Paul Bennett's essays in *Conference Under the Tamarind Tree: Three Essays in Burmese History,* especially pp. 79–83.

81. *SMK,* no. 107, p. 175, has *"Tuiṅ chok sō amat Mantalapatiy."* The terms "four directions" or "four sides" were used often with regard to many things, such as temples and their "four sides," the kingdom and "its four sides," etc. See also *SMK,* no. 96, p. 143.

82. *SIP,* no. 41, p. 107; no. 49, p. 138.

83. *SIP,* no. 4, pp. 4–5.

84. *SIP,* no. 30, p. 70.

85. *SMK,* no. 201, p. 342 (a copy of an A.D. 1171 inscription), and no. 172, p. 297.

86. *SIP,* no. 35, p. 85; *EM,* no. 51, p. 144; *BODAW,* 1:72; *Glass Palace Chronicle,* pp. 140, 150.

87. *Glass Palace Chronicle,* p. 126; *EB,* 3:51–52.

88. Than Tun, "Administration Under King Thalun," p. 182.

89. I actually counted sixteen different *amat* during King Nātoṅmyā's reign.

90. *SIP,* no. 22, p. 45; no. 49, p. 134.

91. Sir Arthur Phayre, *History of Burma* (London: Susil Gupta, 1883; reprint ed., New York: Augustus M. Kelley, 1969), p. 9; *SIP,* no. 40, p. 102.

92. *Glass Palace Chronicle,* pp. 150–151; *SIP,* no. 4, pp. 4–5; *BODAW,* 1: 72; *SIP,* no. 30, p. 70.

93. *SMK,* no. 172, p. 297.

94. *PPA,* no. 16, p. 26, mentions "the scribe, *Mahāsaman*" in 1375. In 1783, the Pagan and Sale *sittans* showed this family still performing the type of tasks that the *mahāsaman* of Pagan once did.

95. *SMK,* no. 205, p. 347.

96. *SMK,* no. 125, p. 347.

97. *EM,* no. 33, p. 43; *SMK,* no. 154, p. 258.

98. *SIP,* no. 40, p. 102.

99. *Glass Palace Chronicle,* pp. 150–151; *SIP,* no. 4, pp. 4–5; *BODAW,* 1:72; *SIP,* no. 30, p. 70.

100. *SIP,* no. 45, p. 122.

101. *PPA,* no. 16, p. 26 (A.D. 1375).

102. Than Tun, *Khit Haung,* p. 163.

103. A. L. Basham, *The Wonder That Was India* (New York: Grove Press, 1959), p. 82. He notes the distinction between *mahāsammata* and *mahāsammanta.* Strictly speaking, the latter is known in Indian political ideology as "the great vassal" and is altogether different from the former.

104. The various components mentioned were taken from contemporary inscriptions, as subsequent notes will show. By also studying military structure from the eighteenth to the nineteenth centuries, we can see to what extent the ranks mentioned in Pagan inscriptions were found in this later period. Although they may not have been identical, the titles that distinguished one level of officers from another were probably the same. The breakdown of the troops at least followed general principles, that is, commander-in-chief, followed by commanders, then majors, captains, and sergeants. See also Silāvaṃsa, *Jata-tawbon,* p. 92, which covered the transitional period between Pagan and the Thalun era. Than Tun's "Administration Under King Thalun," moreover, mentions a structure for which there were Pagan equivalents:

10 men were under 1 leader called *khoṅ*
10 *khoṅ* – 1 *cac kay*
10 *cac kay* – 1 *buih mhū*

10 *buih mhū* – 1 *cac sū krī*
10 *cac sū krī* – 1 *King*

In Pagan, there were the *khoṅ* levels (as in *mraṅ khoṅ*); *cac kay* was not mentioned but there was an equivalent rank of *ciy,* at least in the cavalry *(mraṅ ciy);* followed by *mhū* (as in *mraṅ mhū); and* lastly there was *cac sūkrī,* but whether or not it fit the ideal of 10 *cac sūkrī* equaling one king is another question.

105. *EM,* no. 42, p. 115 (A.D. 1239).

106. *SMK,* no. 41, p. 66.

107. U Kyaw Dun, *Myanma Sa Nyunbaung Kyan,* 1:17, 125, printed an A.D. 1417 inscription that mentioned the elephantry, as did Silāvaṁsa, *Jatatawbon,* p. 92, which went a step further and gave the titles for officers (?) of that corps, called *chaṅ kay* and *chaṅ ū cī.* In Pagan, *SIP,* no. 28, p. 64 (line 14), noted a *chaṅ ū lay,* that is, lands given to the officers called *chaṅ ū.*

108. Luce, "The Early *Syāṁ* in Burma's History," *JSS* 46 (1958): 132.

109. Than Tun, "Administration Under King Thalun," p. 180; Sangermano, *Description of the Burmese Empire,* p. 97, n. 1, where he quotes Symes and Crawfurd's accounts. For the story in the *Hmannan* that dealt with war between Burma and Siam, translated into English in the *JSS,* see Luang Phraison Salarak (Thein Subindu), "Burmese Invasions of Siam, Translated from Hmanan Yazawin Dawgyi," *Selected Articles from the Siam Society Journal: Relationship with Burma—Parts 1 and 2,* (Bangkok: The Siam Society Society, 1959), 5:1–207, and 6:1–183.

110. *EM,* no. 11, p. 20.

111. *SIP,* no. 41, pp. 107–108 (A.D. 1276).

112. *SIP,* no. 40, p. 106.

113. *SIP,* no. 30, p. 71; *SMK,* no. 73, p. 117.

114. *SIP,* no. 31, p. 72; no. 30, p. 71.

115. *SMK,* no. 170, p. 289 (A.D. 1236), no. 65, p. 103 (A.D. 1213); *SIP,* no. 49, p. 134 *(sukhamiṅ),* and *Judson's Burmese-English Dictionary,* p. 1028.

116. *SMK,* no. 65, p. 103.

117. Ibid.

118. For his activities, see *SIP,* no. 47, pp. 126–130 (A.D. 1285).

119. Alton Becker, "A Linguistic Image of Nature: The Burmese Numerative Classifier System," *International Journal of the Sociology of Language* 5 (1975): 109–121.

Chapter 8

1. George Coedès, *Angkor: An Introduction* (New York, 1963), passim; L. P. Briggs, "The Ancient Khmer Empire," *Transactions of the American Philosophical Society,* n.s., 31 (February 1951): 1–295; and G. E. Harvey, *A History of Burma,* p. 63.

2. Melford E. Spiro, "Buddhism and Economic Action in Burma," *American Anthropologist* 68 (October 1966): 1171–1172.

3. Ibid., p. 1168.

3. Ibid., p. 1168.

4. Karl Polanyi, *Primitive, Archaic, and Modern Economies: Essays of Karl Polanyi,* ed. George Dalton; and Karl Polanyi, C. M. Arensberg, and H. W. Pearson, eds., *Trade and Market in the Early Empires.*

5. Marshall David Sahlins, *Stone Age Economics,* pp. 185–275.

6. Edmund R. Leach, *Political Systems of Highland Burma: A Study of Kachin Social Structure,* p. 149.

7. *EM,* no. 35, pp. 95–97 (A.D. 1236). As stated in the preface, I owe most of the correctness of these readings to John Okell of the School of Oriental and African Studies, London.

8. The majority of donations originated with the royalty and officialdom, with the artisans benefiting the most. The following table provides a sample from 220 inscriptions chosen during the period A.D. 1100 to 1250 when the greatest number of temples were built. From this, the role of the ruling "class" in economic redistribution is clear. Officialdom is used here simply as a category to distinguish between the royalty and commoners. The commoner "class" here refers to that sector below the royalty and officialdom (see Chapter 4).

Number of Donations

Date	Royalty	Officialdom	Commoners	Total
1100–1200	20	39	11	70
1200–1250	21	83	46	150
TOTAL	41	122	57	220
	Approximate Percentage			
	20	55	25	100

As can be observed, more than 55 percent of all these donations were made by the officialdom, and if donations from royalty are combined with them it is clear that a large majority (75 percent) of the donations originated with this elite segment of society. Numerically, commoners accounted for more donations than royalty in this sample, but not, by any means, in terms of value. Particularly by the latter half of the thirteenth century the distinctions between the officialdom and the "upper commoners" had blurred, as many of the latter became wealthy and, economically at least, were virtual equals to the former. If we combine the officialdom and this group in the thirteenth century and label it "the privileged class," their donations would amount to 65 or 70 percent of all the 220 donations presented in this sample. The majority of all recorded donations in Pagan on which we have information were inscribed between 1200 and 1300.

9. Personal communication: U Bokay, resident archaeologist and curator of the Pagan Museum.

10. For the best example, see *EM,* no. 35, pp. 95–97 (A.D. 1236), the translation of which was presented above.

11. G. H. Luce and Pe Maung Tin, *SIP,* no. 19, pp. 38–39; *EM,* no. 19, p. 40.

12. *EM,* no. 11, pp. 19–23; *SIP,* no. 15, p. 27.

13. Tun Nyein, trans., *Inscriptions of Pagan, Pinya, and Ava,* p. 40, 128; *EM,* no. 31, p. 60.

14. *SIP,* no. 29, p. 67.

15. Archaeological Survey of Burma, *SMK,* no. 54, p. 88; Tun Nyein, *Inscriptions,* p. 40; *EM,* no. 44, p. 120.

16. *SMK,* no. 41, pp. 65–69, 76, 104, 339; Tun Nyein, *Inscriptions,* pp. 40, 108; *EM,* no. 31, p. 61, no. 35, pp. 95–96, no. 47, p. 129, no. 48, p. 135, and no. 53, pp. 148–150; *SIP,* no. 4, p. 5, no. 18, p. 32, no. 19, p. 38, no. 43, p. 114; see also Than Tun, *Khit Haung Myanma Yazawin,* p. 240, for a diagram of a typical temple-monastery complex with adjacent waterworks.

17. *EM,* no. 51, p. 144; *SIP,* no. 25, p. 52, no. 26, p. 58.

18. Tun Nyein, *Inscriptions,* p. 87.

19. *SIP,* no. 25, pp. 53–54; Tun Nyein, *Inscriptions,* p. 91; *EM,* no. 33, p. 93.

20. *EM,* no. 57, p. 162.

21. *EM,* no. 19, p. 39.

22. *SIP,* no. 25, p. 52.

23. Aniruddha's dedication to Gavaṁpati in 1058 showed, for example, how work was provided for people in places distant from the temple. See *SIP,* no. 1, pp. 1–2. Tun Nyein, *Inscriptions,* p. 128 also shows how people from places as distant as Mraṅkhuntuiṅ, approximately 100 miles from the city of Pagan, were employed as a result of temple construction at the capital.

24. J. George Scott and J. P. Hardiman, eds., *Gazetteer of Upper Burma and the Shan States,* pt. 2, pp. 304, 536, 719–730; pt. 3, p. 36.

25. Ibid., pt. 2, p. 132.

26. *SMK,* no. 41, pp. 65–68.

27. Ibid.; see also G. H. Luce's "Old Kyaukse and the Coming of the Burmans," *JBRS* 42, 1 (1959): 85, in which he wrote that the first reference to Maṅbū and Toṅpluṅ as *kharuin* occurred in this inscription.

28. Marc Bloch, *Feudal Society,* trans. L. A. Manyon, 1:70.

29. Archaeological Survey of Burma, *Pictorial Guide to Pagan,* ed. U Aung Thaw, pp. 62–64.

30. *SMK,* no. 71, p. 115, mentions a *kulā phlū* or "white foreigner" though it might have meant a light-skinned Indian.

31. Mabel H. Bode, *The Pali Liberature of Burma,* pp. 14–30.

32. Paul Ambrose Bigandet, *The Life, or Legend, of Gaudama, the Buddha of the Burmese, with Annotations: The Ways to Neibban, and Notice of the Phongyis, or Burmese Monks,* p. 352. This work was known in Pali as the *Mālālaṅkāra-vatthu.*

33. *Mānāvulu Sandesa* [A message from Mānāvulu], ed. M. Nānānanda. Parts of this have been translated from the Pali into English by L. D. Barnett in *JRAS* 9 (April 1905): 279.

34. Archaeological Survey of Burma, *List of Monuments: Meitila Division* (Rangoon, n.d.), p. 17.

35. Archaeological Survey of Burma, *Report of the Director,* 1906–1907, p. 10.

36. Bode, *Pali Literature of Burma,* p. 45. For the best account to date of the Toungoo dynasty, see Victor B. Lieberman's *Burmese Administrative Cycles: Anarchy and Conquest, c. 1580–1760.*

Chapter 9

1. Edmund R. Leach, *Political Systems of Highland Burma: A Study of Kachin Social Structure,* pp. 6–14.

2. The third volume of *She Haung Myanma Kyauksa Mya* is yet to be published.

3. Than Tun, *Khit Haung Myanma Yazawin,* p. 181, gives a different estimate, approximately 62,441 productive acres. I am not certain of all the reasons for this discrepancy between his figures and mine, but part of it might have to do with the thirty or more incriptions found in 1962–1963 that he may not have counted, as his manuscript was in press at the time. Moreover, Than Tun, like Luce, was inclined to use only those inscriptions he considered to be original. This would reduce the number considerably. Two donations of the Pagan period by themselves totaled over 65,956 acres, already over Than Tun's entire estimate. See the inscriptions of King Nātoṅmyā and King Narapatisithu in Archaeological Survey of Burma, *SMK* 1:65–69, 83–86.

4. Even Than Tun's low figures in *Khit Haung* show that 95 percent were *lay* (or *padi*).

5. G. E. Harvey, *A History of Burma,* pp. 318–320.

6. The price of a full-grown male, for example, remained at thirty *klyap* of silver throughout the two hundred years of the Pagan period, to become legalized as "the price." The differences that did occur, on closer scrutiny, showed that factors such as age and sex were involved. In 1225, eleven male *kywan* were commended to a patron for 330 *klyap* of silver, exactly 30 *klyap* each. In another case, nineteen were "sold" for 570 *klyap,* and four for 120 *klyap;* again, exactly 30 *klyap* each. When females and children were included, however, the total cost was less. In 1301, almost a century later, a potter still commended himself for 30 *klyap* of silver. One thus bought and sold, commended and redeemed oneself, or paid the "death price" (a form of mortmain, I suppose) almost always for 30 *klyap* of silver. Like labor, land also was a commodity important enough to the state to be administered. Here, too, differences in price under closer scrutiny occurred between *types* of land—wild, cleared, irrigated—but rarely, if ever, for the same type over the two hundred years of the period we are studying. *Muryaṅ* land—regardless of what it came to mean later—was recognized as a particular type of land and retained its average price of 18 to 20 *klyap* of silver per *pay* (1.75 acres). Virgin land, on the other hand, sold for as little as one *klyap* per *pay,* while *kokkrī* land (suitable for a different crop), remained between 10 and 12 *klyap* of silver per *pay* during these same centuries. As a result, the price of rice also remained stable throughout this period, while differences were determined by the variety sold.

7. E. Michael Mendelson, "Observations on a Tour in the Region of Mount Popa, Central Burma," *France-Asie* 19 (January–June 1963): 785.

8. G. H. Luce and Pe Maung Tin, *SIP,* no. 47, pp. 126–130.

9. The ethnic background of these three brothers, who were most likely members of the royal family, is unclear. In most English-language histories of Burma, they have been referred to as Shan, for which there is neither contem-

porary (epigraphic) nor convincing subsequent (chronicle) evidence. In this particular book, their ethnicity is largely irrelevant, although it is an issue that needs to be addressed for Burmese history as a whole.

10. Tun Nyein, trans., *Inscriptions of Pagan, Pinya, and Ava,* p. 156.

11. Paul J. Bennett, "The 'Fall of Pagan': Continuity and Change in 14th-Century Burma," *Conference Under the Tamarind Tree: Three Essays in Burmese History,* pp. 4–11.

12. Michael Aung-Thwin, "The Role of *Sasana* Reform in Burmese History: Economic Dimensions of a Religious Purification," *JAS* 38, 4 (August 1979).

13. Ibid. See also my "A Reply to Lieberman," *JAS* 40, 1 (November 1980): 87–90, and n. 5, Conclusion.

Conclusion

1. Michael Aung-Thwin, "The British Pacification of Burma: Order Without Meaning," *JSEAS,* forthcoming.

2. Michael Aung-Thwin, "Jambudīpa: Classical Burma's Camelot," *Contributions to Asian Studies* 16 (1981): 38–61.

3. Michael Aung-Thwin, "Prophecies, Omens, and Dialogues: Tools of the Trade in Burmese Historiography," in *Moral Order and the Question of Change: Essays on Southeast Asian Thought,* ed. Alexander Woodside and David K. Wyatt, Yale University Southeast Asia Monograph Series, no. 24, pp. 78–103.

4. Michael Aung-Thwin, "The Role of *Sasana* Reform in Burmese History: Economic Dimensions of a Religious Purification," *JAS* 38, 4 (August 1979).

5. It has been argued by some that this trend—of land alienation to the *sangha* —was *reversed* in the Toungoo and Konbaung periods; that land once belonging to the *sangha* became crown (or at least non-religious) property. Thus William Koenig wrote that "there was . . . a definite tendency for glebe lands to become alienated to secular purposes over a period of time," reiterated by Victor Lieberman for the Toungoo period (see Koenig's statement in Frank Trager and William Koenig, *Burmese Sit-tàns 1764–1826; Records of Rural Life and Administration* [Tucson: Univ. of Arizona Press, 1979], p. 42, and Victor B. Lieberman, "The Political Significance of Religious Wealth in Burmese History: Some Further Thoughts," *JAS* 39, 4 [August 1980]: 753–769. For a rebuttal, see my "A Reply to Lieberman," *JAS* 40, 1 [November 1980]: 87–90). Both of them cited the *Upper Burma Gazetteer,* which had mentioned an 1802 *sittan* (land record) of a pagoda that was said to have stated in part that certain lands, once glebe, were now mostly secular. The pagoda in question was said to have been built by Aśoka (!) and repaired by Aniruddha of Pagan. Of the 1,236 *pay* of land originally dedicated, only 94 were said to remain glebe. This example was used as evidence par excellence to support that "definite tendency" of religious lands becoming secular.

Not to mention the authenticity of the record itself, questionable for its claim that the donation went back to Aśoka, the arguments are rather weak for several reasons: First, even if this pagoda's land in fact became secular, to derive a "definite tendency" from one (or even a few) example(s) misrepresents the evidence and in so doing, places Burmese society on its head, for exceptions are made to appear as rules. Consider the contrary: there are over 2,000 inscriptions and other forms of land records that show the "tendency" to go the other way, from secular to religious. Second, the point they make is only marginally relevant in terms of the consequences of land devolution from the state to the *saṅgha* in any case, for even if most of this land did go back to secular use, because it was obtained illegally, its records undoubtedly will continue to show its exempt status. Since fraud was the method of acquisition, the true status of the land would be disguised, and therefore its revenues would still be unusable by the government. Third, that donations to the *saṅgha* in later centuries continued at a relatively equal rate—relative to the total wealth of the state—can be well documented. As Paul Bennett has shown, for example, the immediate post-Pagan period, especially the fourteenth and fifteenth centuries, saw continued large-scale donations by royalty and elite to the *saṅgha,* as pretenders to the throne sought to establish their legitimacy according to the same criteria accepted by their predecessors: as patrons and defenders of the faith (Paul J. Bennett, "The 'Fall of Pagan': Continuity and Change in 14th-Century Burma," in *Conference Under the Tamarind Tree: Three Essays in Burmese History,* pp. 3–30). The pattern continued during the sixteenth- and seventeenth-century Toungoo dynasty, because the need to patronize the *saṅgha* as legitimating criteria of king and society clearly remained an essential part of the Burmese conceptual system. Even if the extent of *land* alienation is disputed, the continued sequestration of wealth at a comparable rate is indisputable. To mention only a few of many examples recorded on stone: In 1504, King Narapati built the Nikrodha Kula Monastery, endowed it with over 800 acres of land, gave several thousand bushels of *padi* to its permanent workers and 13,644 *kyat*s of silver in salaries for the artisans and other craftsmen who constructed it. Even King Thalun, the so-called reformer of his administration to correct precisely these problems was compelled to build in the first half of the seventeenth century his great Rājāmanicula Pagoda (the Kaungmhudaw) with its four major and forty supporting monasteries (*BODAW* 1:336). Similarly, King Bodawhpaya of the last (Konbaung) dynasty, noted for his strict scrutiny of religious property, nevertheless felt the need to patronize the *saṅgha* lavishly, particularly toward the end of his reign, a time when merit-making becomes extremely important to monarchs. His Mingun Pagoda, had it not been destroyed by earthquake prior to completion, would have been the largest and one of the most expensive pagodas in all of Burma, the costs alone commanding fifteen pages in the chronicle that recorded it (see, for instance, the *Konbaungset Mahayazawindaw Gyi* [The great royal chronicle of the Konbaung dynasty], vol. 2 [Rangoon, 1967], pp. 101–118). In 1785, the king rededicated a previous donation comprised of 6,000 *ta* (about twelve feet to the *ta*) of irrigated land, along with (among other things) twelve gardens, three lakes, three tanks, two weirs, and four canals (*BODAW* 1:56–57). Bodawhpaya also rededicated to the Shwezayan Pagoda in 1793 the 10,000 *ta* of land donated to it during the Pagan period, adding his own donation of fifty households of attendants in labor-scarce Burma (*BODAW* 1:49–50). All of (his successor) Bagyidaw's works of merit are too numerous to mention, many of which were begun and left unfinished by Bodawhpaya (Tun

Nyein, trans., *Inscriptions of Pagan, Pinya, and Ava,* pp. 173–181; U Aung Than, "Relations Between the Sangha and State and Laity," *JBRS* 48 [1965]: 1–7; *Konbaungset,* 2:247–256, 269–273, 292–308). Even the dedications of Bagyi-daw's general, Maha Bandula, were considerable: building, repairing, and regilding fourteen different pagodas (see R. R. Langham Carter, "Maha Bandula at Home," *JBRS* 26, 2 [1936]: 127). Henry Burney, who was the British Resident during that time, wrote that "the monasteries are numerous, and always full of men who desire to avoid public service . . ." (H. Burney, "On the Population of the Burman Empire," *JBRS* 31, 1 [1941]: 25). Although each king of the Konbaung dynasty built at least one work of merit—even Pagan Min who reigned only a few years built one—the greatest patronizer of them was Mindon (*BODAW* 1:3–11). In 1857, only a few years after the costly Second Anglo-Burman War and subsequent loss of revenue from Lower Burma, he built the Ahtumashi Monastery at a cost of approximately ten lakhs of *kyats* (*Burma Gazetteer, Mandalay District,* vol. A [Rangoon, 1928], p. 239). He then convened the 5th Great Buddhist Synod in the tradition of Aśoka, for which he constructed the Kuthodawgyi Pagoda, a *stupa* surrounded by 729 marble slabs on which were inscribed the entire Buddhist scriptures (the *Tipiṭakas*), each slab housed in an individual miniature temple. Although this work took several years to complete, the total costs were said to have amounted to 226 million *kyats* (Ludu Daw Ahmar, *The World's Biggest Book* [Mandalay, 1974], p. 20; *BODAW* 1:17–22, gives the inscription that records the occasion). Mindon also placed a new finial on the Shwedagon Pagoda at Rangoon, which cost 6,220,917 *kyats* ("The New Htee for the Shwe Dagon Pagoda [Official Memorandum], *JBRS* 14, 1 [1924]: 46–47). I have some doubts about this figure since the official Burmese chronicle's figures are more precise and far more modest. It records the total to be 1,400,479 *kyats* and some *pai* (see *Konbaungset,* 3:387). Mindon's Northern Queen, in 1862, spent approximately 535,350 *kyats* on various works of merit (*BODAW* 1:12–16). Each month, Mindon fed 15,000 monks and novices, made royal land available at no cost to anyone who could construct ordination halls on it, and vigorously supported monastic and lay Buddhist scholarship by material grants (John P. Ferguson, "The Symbolic Dimensions of the Burmese Sangha," Ph.D. diss., Cornell University, 1975, p. 236). King Thibaw, his successor and last king of the dynasty, even with the end of the kingdom drawing near—or perhaps precisely because that had become clear—spent 80,000 *kyats* for the redemption of debtor *kywan* (of whom 1,394 entered the monasteries); 18,360 *kyats* for rebuilding the Mahamuni Pagoda; and 30,000 *kyats* in 1884 on the eve of the Annexation for transferring the Mahāmuni Image from Amarapura to Mandalay (J. G. Scott and J. P. Hardiman, eds., *Gazetteer of Upper Burma and the Shan States,* vol. 1, no. 1, pp. 93–94).

Indeed, well into the twentieth century, the merit-path to salvation continued to have similar relationships to economic action. Melford Spiro's study of a small but typical village in Upper Burma showed that 30 to 40 percent of the village's annual disposable cash income went to religious giving, not to mention time and energy (Melford E. Spiro, *Buddhism and Society: A Great Tradition and Its Burmese Vicissitudes,* p. 459). There, "merit books" were kept of individual good deeds to help determine the number of "points" one had on the path to a better rebirth (ibid., p. 454. For a nineteenth-century example, see Tun Nyein, *Inscriptions,* pp. 161–163, which showed a minister who recorded in his "account book" the amount he had donated to the religion in his lifetime, between the age of seventeen and fifty, amounting to 55,445 *kyat*s). In 1953, when land was to be nationalized, many wealthy landowners, to insure their likelihood of a better rebirth, donated their property to the *sangha* rather than "give" it to the government, precisely the same type of reasoning that people in premodern Burma used when giving their wealth to the church. At present, Ne Win, now officially retired from office, in the tradition of Burmese kings nearing the end of their reigns, is in the process of building *his* work of merit in the shadows of the Shwedagon Pagoda. (Jon Wiant, in his forthcoming dissertation, "Lanzin: Ideology and Organization in Revolutionary Burma" [Cornell University] discusses the continuity of certain traditional legitimating ideologies that carried into even Socialist Burma; see also Michael Aung-Thwin "The British Pacification of Burma: Order Without Meaning," *JSEAS,* forthcoming).

To argue then, as Lieberman has done, that the short, last half of the Toungoo period caused a *reversal* of trends in subsequent Burmese history and society, or as Koenig has stated, that there was a "definite tendency" of religious property to become secular, is to ignore the evidence.

6. Aung-Thwin, "British Pacification of Burma."

7. Victor B. Lieberman, "The Political Significance of Religious Wealth in Burmese History: Some Further Thoughts," *JAS* 39, 4 (August 1980): 753–769. See also his recent book on the Toungoo dynasty entitled *Burmese Administrative Cycles: Anarchy and Conquest, c. 1580–1760.*

8. Hiram Cox, who visited Burma during this king's reign, mentioned the tremendous revenues Bodawhpaya had stored in his treasury by that time. See Captain Hiram Cox, *Journal of a Residence in the Burmhan Empire* (London, 1821).

9. George W. Spencer, "The Politics of Plunder: The Cholas in Eleventh-Century Ceylon," *JAS* 35, 3 (May 1976): 405–419.

10. Akin Rabibhadana, *The Organization of Thai Society in the Early Bangkok Period, 1782–1873,* Cornell University Southeast Asia Program Data Paper no. 74 (Ithaca, 1970).

11. W. P. Buell, 8 September 1842, reel 181, no. 19, The Collection of the Presbyterian Historical Society, Philadelphia, Pennsylvania.

12. Aung-Thwin, "Role of *Sasana* Reform."

13. I owe all of the information on the Ne Win government and its ideologies to Jon Wiant. See his "Tradition in the Service of Revolution: The Political Symbolism of *Taw Hlan Ye Khit,*" in *Military Rule in Burma Since 1962: A Kaleidoscope of Views* (Singapore, Maruzen Asia, 1981), as well as his forthcoming dissertation, "Lanzin: Ideology and Organization in Revolutionary Burma." See also Aung-Thwin, "British Pacification of Burma."

Glossary

This short glossary contains mainly Old Burmese words, arranged alphabetically, and follows John Okell, *A Guide to the Romanization of Burmese*. Each is followed in brackets by a more modern spelling and a short definition of the term as it is thought to have been used in Pagan. Those terms that appear only once in the book are clarified in the text and are not included here.

amat or *amatayā* [*amat, amataya*]: minister.
amhudan [*ahmudan*]: crown service people.
ami purā [*ami hpaya*]: queen; consort of the king.
arap [*ayup*]: a ward or section of a city or town.
asañ [*athi*]: people not legally bonded to anyone.
asañ sūkrī [*athi thugyi*]: headman of *asañ*.
buih pā [*boh pa*]: troops, troopers, officers.
cactam [*sittan*]: register, record.
cā khī [*sa khi*]: scribe.
dhammasat [*dhammathat*]: civil code.
kamma [*kamma*]: karma, the moral law of cause and effect.
kharuin [*khayaing*]: core, nucleus, "heartwood"; later "district."
khwan [*khwin*]: circle, province.
kī tō [*ki daw*]: royal granary.
klyap [*kyat*]: unit of money equivalent to one *tical* or approximately a half ounce of silver.
kok krī [*kaukkyi*]: type of rice, usually cultivated only at certain times of the year.
kū [*gu*]: cave-temple; a pagoda with an interior space.
kywan [*kyun*]: subject; a person obligated to someone; later, slave.
kywan sañ [*kyun thi*]: one who deals in the business of *kywan* or indentured labor.
kywan sūkrī [*kyun thugyi*]: headman of *kywan*.
kywan-tō [*kyun daw*]: same as *ahmudan* (above); people in crown service.
lhwat [*hlut*]: release, as in releasing a person from legal obligation.
mahādan [*mahadan*]: "great gift"; royal grant, secular or religious.

mahāsaman [*mahathaman*]: minister in charge of land records.

mahāsenāpati [*mahathenapati*]: commander-in-chief.

Metteyya [Metteyya]: the future Buddha; last of this kappa or age.

maṅ nhama tō [*min hnama daw*]: king's "royal younger sister" or queen.

maṅ krī [*min gyi*]: "great king."

maṅ mliy [*min myi*]: grandchild of the king.

maṅ ṅai [*min nge*]: lesser king.

maṅ ñi [*min nyi*]: younger brother of king.

maṅ sā [*min tha*]: prince; son of king.

maṅ samī [*min thami*]: princess; daughter of the king.

mle tō [*mye daw*]: royal land.

moṅ ma [*maung ma*]: concubine.

mraṅ ciy [*myin si*]: cavalry officer.

mraṅ khoṅ [*myin gaung*]: head of cavalry soldiers.

mraṅ mhū [*myin hmu*]: cavalry officer of a high rank.

mriuw [*myo*]: town or stockade.

mriuw sūkrī [*myo thugyi*]: headman of town or stockade.

muryaṅ [*mayin*]: type of rice grown in certain areas.

nat [*nat*]: spirit, supernatural being.

nuiṅṅaṁ [*naing ngan*]: conquered territory; later nation or state.

pay [*pe*]: unit of land equivalent to approximately 1.75 acres.

prañ [*pyi*]: "country," capital.

prañ cuiw [*pyi so*]: governor of a *prañ;* administrator of capital.

purā [*hpaya*]: Buddha, lord, monk, temple.

purā kywan [*hpaya kyun*]: a glebe subject.

rhok [*shauk*]: small village.

rwā [*ywa*]: village.

rwā sūkrī [*ywa thugyi*]: village headman.

Sakka [Thagya]: Buddhist equivalent of Indra or Sakra.

saṁbeṅ-kalan [*thanbyin-kalan*]: crown administrators.

saṅ [*thin*]: suffix with status implications.

sañ [*thi*]: suffix which describes one's occupation.

saṅ pha ma [*thin pha ma*]: judge.

sūkrī [*thugyi*]: headman.

sūkrway [*thuhtay*]: rich person.

swe sok [*thwe thauk*]: literally "blood drinker"; officer of troops to whom loyalty is given by a blood ritual.

taryā sūkrī [*taya thugyi*]: judge.

Tāvatiṁsa [Tawatheintha]: abode of Sakka.

samuiṅ [*thamaing*]: record.

tuik [*taik*]: hamlet; building; outpost; monastery.

tuik sūkrī [*taik thugyi*]: headman of tuik.

tuiṅ [*taing*]: province, division.

Selected Bibliography

Primary Sources

Inscriptions

Archaeological Survey of Burma. *Epigraphia Birmanica: Being Lithic and Other Inscriptions of Burma.* Rangoon: SGP, 1919–. Mostly translated from the Mon inscriptions of King Kalancacsā.

———. *A List of Inscriptions Found in Burma.* Compiled by Chas. Duroiselle. Rangoon: SGP, 1921–. A valuable though incomplete list and details of all inscriptions compiled at the time.

———. *Report of the Director.* Rangoon: SGP, 1921–.

———. *She Haung Mon Kyauksa Paung Chok* [Collection of ancient Mon inscriptions]. Edited and translated (into Burmese) by U Chit Thein. Rangoon, Ministry of Union Culture, 1965. All known Mon inscriptions of Burma, (106 altogether) comprise the first part of this book, while the second half is the translation into Burmese.

———. *She Haung Myanma Kyauksa Mya* [Ancient Burmese inscriptions]. II vols. Rangoon, Ministry of Union Culture, 1972, 1982. The first volume is edited by the Director of the Archaeological Survey of Burma, U Aung Thaw, and compiled by U Bokay and Associates. The 225 Old Burmese inscriptions are arranged chronologically into two sections (*Ka* and *Kha*). The first section comprises all the "original" inscriptions found from A.D. 1112 to 1238, while the second consists of good copies of originals. Only those inscriptions dating to 1238 are included, the extent of volume 1. Volume 2, comprised of 145 inscriptions, was edited by U Nyein Maung and begins with 1238 and ends with 1250. New inscriptions found since the first volume was published are placed in a separate section of volume 2. Subsequently, all inscriptions of Burma will be arranged chronologically in forthcoming volumes. This particular work is perhaps the most useful of all such volumes so far published, not only for its hand-copied and mimeographed format (eliminating printer's errors) but for its organization into dated and undated inscriptions, its readability, and its currency.

Archaeological Survey of India. *Report of the Director.* Delhi/Calcutta: SGP, 1902–1937.

Ba Shin. *Pagan Minsasu Thuteithana Lokngan.* Rangoon: Burma Historical Commission, 1964. A collection of ink inscriptions of the Pagan period extremely difficult to read, edited by the late Col. Ba Shin, a well-known scholar and member of the Burma Historical Commission.

British Library. London. Oriental MS. OR. 6,452 B. Three black *parabuik* containing five inscriptions copied in the nineteenth century. Some are of stones now lost.

———. OR. 6,452 B. (1) A palm-leaf book containing a large number of inscriptions copied from stones that were available around the 1700s. This source is important for another reason: it represents a tradition of record keeping whereby stones in situ were duplicated on palm leaf and kept in government archives, exactly as described in Pagan records.

Burma Home Department. *Inscriptions Collected in Upper Burma.* 2 vols. Rangoon: SGP, 1900, 1903. A printed reproduction in modern Burmese of all the inscriptions found in Upper Burma at the time.

———. *Inscriptions Copied from the Stones collected by King Bodawpaya and placed near the Arakan Pagoda, Mandalay.* 2 vols. Rangoon: SGP, 1897. Bodawhpaya had these inscriptions collected, ostensibly for writing a royal history of the kings of Burma. They were collected also for keeping an accurate record of *sangha* holdings. The volumes contain only copies of original stones, written in the Burmese of Bodawhpaya's time. They are still a valuable source.

———. *Inscriptions of Pagan, Pinya, and Ava (in the Burmese text as) deciphered from the ink impressions found among the papers of the late Dr. E. Forchhammer (and edited by Taw Sein Ko).* 2 vols. Rangoon: SGP, 1892, 1899. A more valuable collection than Bodawhpaya's collection, for these were reproduced without any editing, retaining their original state. They are arranged according to where they were found, not chronologically. Most of them belong to the Pagan period, although some are of later periods, including the Konbaung dynasty. The published text retained the Old Burmese spelling in those that were original, but there are duplicates (later copies) of originals, both found in the collection, about which the compilers seemed unaware. Like its translation (see Tun Nyein below), it needs to be carefully edited.

———. *Original Inscriptions collected by King Bodawpaya in Upper Burma and now placed near the Patodawgyi Pagoda, Amarapura.* Rangoon: SGP, 1913. This volume is more useful than the others collected by the king, for the inscriptions were in their original state. However, modern spelling in some of them suggest some copying occurred. But unlike the others that were collected by King Bodawhpaya and copied, these were collected to be copied, but it was never done.

E. Maung, U. *Pagan Kyauksa Let Ywei Sin* [Selected Pagan inscriptions]. 2 vols. Rangoon: n.p., 1958. This is another invaluable collection of inscriptions, chosen from originals and carefully edited and reproduced in their original format. Volume 1 contains sixty-four inscriptions arranged chronologically from A.D. 1081 to 1255.

Luce, G. H. and Pe Maung Tin. *Inscriptions of Burma.* 5 vols. Rangoon: Rangoon University Press, 1933–1956. Perhaps the ultimate primary source short of the stones themselves, for these are photographs of the original stones or their rubbings, arranged chronologically from the (then) earliest-known inscription of Pagan (A.D. 1053) to 1364, when a new dynasty was founded. Since 1956 several hundred more inscriptions have been found but remain in situ and uncatalogued, although some have been properly housed by the Archaeological Department. These volumes need to be supplemented by more recent collections, like *She Haung Myanma Kyauksa Mya,* mentioned above, but nevertheless represent the bulk of the primary material for the study of Pagan.

———. *Selections from the Inscriptions of Pagan.* Rangoon, British Burma Press, 1928. Although much like E. Maung's work, this however represents a pioneering effort on the part of the two scholars. The inscriptions are arranged according to an edited chronology and like E. Maung's are reproduced in Old Burmese. Many are duplicated in E. Maung's work, though several inscriptions after 1255 (where the former stopped) and some ink inscriptions are included in this volume.

Tun Nyein. *Inscriptions of Pagan, Pinya, and Ava: Translations, With Notes.* Rangoon: SGP, 1899. An English translation of Forchhammer's collection mentioned above. In general, the translations give the gist of the contents and are fairly accurate, but in several places, there are mistakes in reading as well as in translation. It also needs careful editing, for copies and original inscriptions are sometimes confused. However, it is the only translated volume of Burmese inscriptions that has been published.

Dhammathats

British Library. London. Oriental MSS. Add. 12,249; Add. 12,250. Called the *Dhammathat Kyaw,* it is an abridged version of the original *Manu Dhammathat* brought to Pagan by Dhammavilāsa. Although the original is dated to A.D. 1025, this is a copy, perhaps seventeenth century, as the spelling of some of the words suggests.

———. OR. 3,447 Add. This *Dhammathat* is in two parts and entitled the "Manu Mano Dhammavilāsa Shwe Myañ Dhammathat," which is discussed in chapter 6. It may be the basis of all law codes in Burma.

E. Maung, U. *Expansion of Burmese Law.* Rangoon: n.p., 1951.

Forchhammer, Emil, ed. and trans. *King Wagaru's Manu Dhammasattham. Text, Translation, and Notes.* Rangoon: SGP (?), 1885 (?). Another very valuable and out-of-print work. It was thought to have been compiled by King Wagaru's scholars in Lower Burma in the thirteenth century, who based their work on another (perhaps the *Dhammavilāsa Dhammathat*), mentioned in chapter 6. The Burmese and English translations have corresponding paragraph numbers to aid one in searching for original Burmese terms.

Gaung, U. *A Digest of the Burmese Buddhist Law concerning Inheritance and Marriage; being a collection of texts from thirty-six Dhammathats, composed and arranged under the supervision of the Hon'ble U Gaung, C.S.I. ex-Kinwun Mingyi.* 2 vols. Rangoon: SGP, 1899. Although the Table of Contents and the title are in English, the text is in Burmese. As the title states, U Gaung used thirty-six different *dhammathat* to compile these volumes on civil law. A useful feature of this work is U Gaung's insertion, in the side columns of the text, of the sources that contributed to a particular law.

Jardine, John, Sir. *Notes on Buddhist Law.* 8 vols. Rangoon: SGP, 1886. Because this contains translations of various Burmese law codes in toto, I believe it belongs in this section of primary sources. Very old, worn, and long out of print, it is an invaluable book, parts of which can be obtained only from the British Library.

Sittan*s*

British Library. London. OR. MSS. 3,450. Record of the Ananda Temple as well as a copy of the Dhammāraṁ Pagoda Inscription, it includes a list of Pagan kings with their works of merit. A good source to use as a basis of comparison with the extant inscriptions it describes.

―――. OR. 3,421. This record is called the "Shwe Sandaw Thamaing," that is, the "history" of the Shwe Sandaw Pagoda, built by Aniruddha.

Furnivall, J. S. "The Pagan Revenue Inquest of 1127 B.E. (1765 A.D.)." Typescript.

―――. "Sittan of 1145 and 1164 B.E." Typescript.

Furnivall, J. S., and Pe Maung Tin, eds. *Zambudīpa Okhsaung Kyan.* Rangoon: Burma Research Society, 1960. A valuable collection of land records, mostly *sittan, thamaing,* and a few royal edicts. It includes sources from virtually all periods in Burmese history beginning with the 10th century, although most are of the post-Pagan period.

Chronicles

British Museum. London. OR. MSS. 1,021. This palm-leaf manuscript entitled "History of Pagan" differs little from the standard histories which incorporated the many and regionally diverse accounts written by individuals on their own initiative.

Hmannan Yazawindaw Gyi. 3 vols. Meiktila, Ma E Tin Press, 1936. A compilation conducted at the order of King Bagyidaw in 1821 by the ablest scholars of his court. But essentially it followed the *Mahayazawindaw Gyi,* produced a century earlier by U Kala (below), and was in part a reaction to the *Yazawin Thit,* compiled by another scholar also under King Bodawhpaya, who had challenged some of the dates and myths in Burmese history.

Kala, U. *Mahayazawindaw Gyi* [The great royal chronicle]. 3 vols. Edited by Pe Maung Tin, Saya Pwa, and Saya U Khin Soe. Rangoon: Hanthawaddy Press, 1960–1961. The published version was derived from the manuscript written by U Kala in the early to mid-eighteenth century. In the tradition of Burmese chroniclers who went before him, he apparently wrote this "Great Chronicle of Kings" on his own initiative.

Paññacāmi. *Sāsanavaṁsa.* Translated by Bimala Churn Law. London, Pali Text Society, 1952. A history of the Buddha's religion, most of it deals with the Burma chapter written by a monk in the mid-nineteenth century under King Mindon, who used an earlier work.

[Pe] Maung Tin and Luce, G. H. "The Chronicle of the City of Tagaung." *JBRS* 9 (1921): 29–54. The article is essentially a translation of the Chronicle.

Silāvaṁsa, Shin Samantapasadika. *Jatatawbon Yazawin* [History of royal horoscopes]. Edited by U Hla Tin. Rangoon: n.p., 1961. A very valuable chronicle, which helped to confirm most of the chronological data on Pagan kings that appeared in the inscriptions. It is thought to have been a work first written in the sixteenth century (though it may have been based on an earlier work) and contains a variety of types of data. As the name suggests, the horoscopes of kings was its primary purpose. It includes a variety of statistical material mostly of the Ava kingdom, which succeeded Pagan, including a list of towns liable for military service, the numbers required, and so on. It includes extracts of some *sittan,* the locations of cavalry units, some geographical information, and some details on court punctilio. Portions apparently have been added to it by subsequent writers.

―――. *Yazawin Gyaw.* Edited by Pe Maung Tin. Rangoon: Burma Research Society, n.d. Another chronicle probably by the same author of the *Jatatawbon,* compiled in 1520. Its existence is important as a testimony to the earlier chronicle tradition in Burma, although its usefulness as a source for the Pagan kingdom is limited.

"*Slapat Rājawaṅ Datow Smin Roṅ.*" Translated by R. Halliday, *JBRS* 13, 1 (1923):5–67. A history of Mon kings beginning with Wagaru in the mid-thirteenth century.

The Glass Palace Chronicle. Translated by Pe Maung Tin and G. H. Luce. Rangoon: Rangoon University Press, 1960. Reprint of Oxford University Press edition, 1923. The translation is Pe Maung Tin's, with Luce's help on English style. It is a translation of parts 3, 4, and 5 (the section on Pagan) of the *Hmannan Yazawindaw Gyi* noted above.

Twinthintaikwun Mahasithu. *Twinthin Myanma Yazawin Thit* [Thwinthin's new royal chronicle of Burma]. Rangoon: Mingala Ponhneik Press, 1968. Although written in 1798, it was only recently published and is considered the most "scientific" of the chronicles, in the sense that it began to challenge accepted traditional dating and information. However, for the most part, it too, like the others, was a reproduction of U Kala's work. The author was in charge of the collection of inscriptions under Bodawhpaya and therefore had access to those epigraphic records that explained in part his skepticism of certain dates and facts. But he did not challenge the traditional Burmese concept of history nor its methodology.

Miscellaneous

Kyaw Dun, U, ed. and comp. *Myanma Sa Nyunbaung Kyan.* 2 vols. Rangoon: SGP, 1961. A short "anthology" of Burmese literature from the earliest (Pagan) period to the nineteenth century. The few works from the

Pagan period are of dubious value, since literature, strictly defined, did not appear in Burma until about the fifteenth century.

Manavulu Sandesa. Edited by M. Nānānanda. Colombo: n.p., 1925. This is a letter from a monk in Śrī Laṅka to a colleague in Pagan written in Pali during the thirteenth century, describing the splendors of Pagan. L. D. Barnett, in an article on the subject entitled "The Manavulu-Sandesaya." *JRAS* 9 (April 1905): 265–283, translated portions of it.

Secondary Sources

Conceptual Works

Dumont, Louis. *Homo Hierarchicus: The Caste System and Its Implications.* Translated by Mark Sainsbury, Louis Dumont, and Basia Gulati. Chicago: University of Chicago Press, 1980.

Geertz, Clifford. *Negara: The Theatre State in Nineteenth-Century Bali.* Princeton: Princeton University Press, 1980.

Leach, Edmund R. *Political Systems of Highland Burma: A Study of Kachin Social Structure.* Boston: Beacon Press, 1970.

———. "Hydraulic Society in Ceylon." *Past and Present* 15 (1959): 2–25.

Polanyi, Karl. *Primitive, Archaic, and Modern Economies: Essays of Karl Polanyi.* Edited by George Dalton. Boston: Beacon Press, 1968.

Polanyi, Karl, C. M. Arensberg, and H. W. Pearson. *Trade and Market in the Early Empires.* Glencoe, Ill.: The Free Press, 1957.

Rustow, Dankwart A., ed. *Philosophers and Kings: Studies in Leadership.* New York: George Braziller, 1970.

Sahlins, Marshall David. *Stone Age Economics.* Chicago: Aldine-Atherton, 1972.

Schmidt, Steffen W. et al., eds. *Friends, Followers, and Factions: A Reader in Political Clientelism.* Berkeley: University of California Press, 1977.

Spiro, Melford E. *Buddhism and Society: A Great Tradition and Its Burmese Vicissitudes.* New York: Harper & Row, 1972.

Tambiah, Stanley J. *World Conqueror and World Renouncer.* London: Cambridge University Press, 1977.

Special Reference Works

Bigandet, Paul Ambrose. *The Life, or Legend, of Gaudama, the Buddha of the Burmese, with Annotations: The Ways to Neibban, and Notice of the Phongyis, or Burmese Monks.* Rangoon: American Mission Press, 1866.

Bloch, Marc. *Feudal Society.* Translated by L. A. Manyon. 2 vols. Chicago: University of Chicago Press, 1970.

Bode, Mabel Haynes. *The Pali Literature of Burma.* London: Royal Asiatic Society of Britain and Ireland, 1909. Reprint, London, 1966.

Buddhadatta, A. P. Mahathera. *Concise Pali-English Dictionary.* Colombo: The Colombo Apothecaries' Co., 1968.

Hall, D. G. E. *Burma.* London: Hutchinson, 1960. 3rd edition.

Harvey, G. E. *A History of Burma: From the earliest times to 10 March 1824: the beginning of the English Conquest.* London: Frank Cass and Co., 1925. Reprint, New York: Octagon Books, 1967.

Lieberman, Victor B. *Burmese Administrative Cycles: Anarchy and Conquest, c. 1580–1760.* Princeton: Princeton University Press, 1984.

Maingkaing Myosa, Atwinwun. *Piṭakat Thamaing Sadan* [A history of literature]. Rangoon: n.p., 1906.

Okell, John. *A Guide to the Romanization of Burmese.* London: Royal Asiatic Society, 1971.

Rhys Davids, Thomas William. *The Pali Text Society's Pali-English Dictionary.* London: Pali Text Society, 1966.

Sangermano, Vincentius (Father). *A Description of the Burmese Empire: compiled chiefly from Burmese documents.* Translated by William Tandy. London: Susil Gupta, 1893. Reprint, New York: Augustus M. Kelley, 1969.

Scott, J. G., and J. P. Hardiman, eds. *Gazetteer of Upper Burma and the Shan States.* 5 vols. Rangoon: SGP, 1900–1901.

Wheatley, Paul. *Nāgara and Commandery: Origins of the Southeast Asian Urban Traditions.* University of Chicago Department of Geography Research Papers 207–208. Chicago: University of Chicago Press, 1983.

Studies of Pagan

Archaeological Survey of Burma. *Pictorial Guide to Pagan.* Edited by U Aung Thaw. Rangoon: The Universities' Press, 1971.

Aung-Thwin, Michael. "The Nature of State and Society in Pagan: An Institutional History of 12th and 13th Century Burma." Ph.D. diss., University of Michigan, 1976.

Bennett, Paul J. "The 'Fall of Pagan': Continuity and Change in 14th-Century Burma." *Conference Under the Tamarind Tree: Three Essays in Burmese History.* Yale University Southeast Asia Monograph Series, no. 15. New Haven: Yale University Press, 1971.

Bokay, U. *Pugam Sutesana Lam Hnwan* [Research guide to Pagan]. Rangoon: Sapebeikman, 1981.

Luce, G. H. *Old Burma–Early Pagán.* 3 vols. Locust Valley, N.Y.: J. J. Augustin, 1969–1970.

Than Tun. *Khit Haung Myanma Yazawin* [History of ancient Burma]. Rangoon: Maha Dagon Press, 1964.

Selected Articles

Aung-Thwin, Michael. "Kingship, the *Sangha,* and Society in Pagan." In *Explorations in Early Southeast Asian History: The Origins of Southeast Asian Statecraft.* Edited by Kenneth R. Hall and John K. Whitmore. Michigan Papers on South and Southeast Asia, no. 11. Ann Arbor, 1976.

———. "The Problem of Ceylonese-Burmese Relations in the 12th Century and the Question of an Interregnum in Pagan: 1165–1174 A.D." *JSS* 64, 1 (January 1976): 53–74.

————. "The Role of *Sasana* Reform in Burmese History: Economic Dimensions of a Religious Purification." *JAS* 38, 4 (August 1979): 671–688.

————. "A Reply to Lieberman." *JAS* 40, 1 (November 1980): 87–90.

————. "Prophecies, Omens, and Dialogue: Tools of the Trade in Burmese Historiography." In *Moral Order and the Question of Change: Essays on Southeast Asian Thought.* Edited by Alexander Woodside and David K. Wyatt. Yale University Southeast Asia Monograph Series, no. 24, New Haven: Yale University Press, 1983.

————. "Jambudīpa: Classical Burma's Camelot." *Contributions to Asian Studies* 16 (1981): 38–61.

————. "Divinity, Spirit, and Human: Conceptions of Classical Burmese Kingship." In *Centers, Symbols, and Hierarchies: Essays on the Classical States of Southeast Asia.* Edited by Lorraine Gesick. Yale University Southeast Asia Monograph Series, no. 26. New Haven: Yale University Press, 1983.

————. "Hierarchy and Order in Pre-Colonial Burma." *JSEAS* 15, 2 (September 1984): 224–232.

Blagden, C. O. "A Further Note on the Inscriptions of the Myazedi Pagoda, Pagan, and other Inscriptions throwing light on them." *JRAS* (1910): 797–812.

————. "A Preliminary Study of the Fourth Text of the Myazedi Inscriptions." *JRAS* (1911): 365–388.

————. "Mon and Ramannadesa." *JBRS* 4 (1914): 59–60.

————. "Mon, Rmen, Ramanna." *JBRS* 5 (1915): 27.

Brown, G. "The Origin of the Burmese." *JBRS* 2, 1 (1911): 1–8.

————. "The Kadus of Burma." *BSOAS* 1 (1912): 1–7.

Duroiselle, Chas. "The Art of Burma and Tantric Buddhism." *ASI Annual Report* (1915–1916): 82.

Furnivall, J. S. "The Foundation of Pagan." *JBRS* 1 (1911): 6–9.

Godakumbura, C. E. "Relations Between Burma and Ceylon." *JBRS* 49 (1966): 145–162.

Grant-Brown, W. F. "The Pre-Buddhist Religion of the Burmese." *Folklore* 32 (1921): 77–100.

Hla Aung, U. "The Burmese Concept of Law." *JBRS* 53, 2 (1969): 27–41.

Huber, Edouard. "La Fin de la dynastie Pagan." *BEFEO* 9 (1909): 633–680.

Kan Hla, U [pseud. Sergey S. Ozhegov]. "Pagan: Development and Town Planning." *Journal of the Society of Architectural Historians* 36, 1 (March 1977): 15–29.

Lehman, F. K. "On the Vocabulary and Semantics of 'Field' in Theravāda Buddhist Society." *Contributions to Asian Studies* 16 (1981): 101–111.

Lieberman, Victor B. "The Political Significance of Religious Wealth in Burmese History: Some Further Thoughts." *JAS* 39, 4 (August 1980): 753–769.

Luce, G. H. "A Cambodian (?) Invasion of Lower Burma—A Comparison of Burmese and Talaing Chronicles." *JBRS* 12 (1922): 39–45.

————. "Burma's Debt to Pagan." *JBRS* 22 (1932): 120–127.

————. "The Ancient Pyu." *JBRS* 27 (1937): 239–253.

———. "Economic Life of the Early Burman." *JBRS* 30 (1940): 283–335. Reprinted in *JBRS Fiftieth Anniversary Publications* 2 (1960): 323–374.

———. "Mons of the Pagan Dynasty." *JBRS* 36, 1 (1953): 1–19.

———. "The Early *Syām* in Burma's History." *JSS* 46 (1958): 123–214.

———. "The Geography of Burma Under the Pagan Dynasty." *JBRS* 42 (1959): 32–59.

———. "Note on the Peoples of Burma in the 12th-13th Century A.D." *JBRS* 42 (1959): 52–74.

———. "Old Kyaukse and the Coming of the Burmans." *JBRS* 42, 1 (1959): 75–109.

———. "Dvāravatī and Old Burma." *JSS* 53 (1965): 9–25.

———. "Rice and Religion: A Study of Old Mon-Khmer Evolution and Culture." *JSS* 53 (1965): 139–152.

———. "The Career of Htilaing Min (Kyanzittha)." *JRAS,* 1–2 (April 1966): 53–68.

Pe Maung Tin. "Women in the Inscriptions of Pagan." *JBRS* 25 (1935): 149–159. Reprinted in *JBRS Fiftieth Anniversary Publications* 2 (1960): 411–421.

———. "Buddhism in the Inscriptions of Pagan." *JBRS* 26, 1 (1936): 52–70. Reprinted in *JBRS Fiftieth Anniversary Publications* 2 (1960): 423–441.

Smith, Bardwell L. "The Pagān Period (1044–1287): A Bibliographic Note." *Contributions to Asian Studies* 16 (1981): 112–130.

Stewart, J. A. "Kyaukse Irrigation—A Side-light on Burmese History." *JBRS* 11 (1921): 1–4.

Than Tun. "History of Burma, A.D. 1300–1400." *JBRS* 42 (1959): 119–134.

———. "Social Life in Burma, A.D. 1044–1287." *JBRS* 41 (1958): 37–47.

———. "Mahākassapa and His Tradition." *JBRS* 42 (1959): 99–118.

———. "Religion in Burma, A.D. 1000–1300." *JBRS* 42 (1959): 47–69.

———. "History of Burma: A.D. 1000–1300. *Bulletin of the Burma Historical Commission* 1 (1960): 39–57.

———. "Administration Under King Thalun (1629–1648)." *JBRS* 51, 2 (1968): 173–188.

Wickremasingh, S. "Ceylon's Relations with South-east Asia, with Special Reference to Burma." *Ceylon Journal of Historical and Social Studies* 3 (1960): 38–58.

Index

About the Author

Michael Aung-Thwin received an M.A. in Chinese and Japanese history from the University of Illinois in 1970 and a Ph.D. in South and Southeast Asian history from the University of Michigan in 1976. His dissertation research in England at the British Library and the School of Oriental and African Studies, as well as in Sri Lanka and Thailand, was supported by a JDR 3rd grant. He received a postdoctoral grant from the Social Science Research Council/American Council of Learned Societies to study Burmese kingship, spending some time in Burma in 1978. Thereafter a National Endowment for the Humanities Translations grant allowed him to translate one volume of Old Burmese inscriptions, at present in manuscript form. He currently teaches Asian history at Elmira College in New York and is spending the 1985–1986 academic year as visiting professor of Asian history at the Center for Southeast Asian Studies at the University of Kyoto.

Production Notes

This book was designed by Roger Eggers. Composition and paging were done on the Quadex Composing System and typesetting on the Compugraphic 8400 by the design and production staff of University of Hawaii Press.

The text and display typeface is Baskerville.

Offset presswork and binding were done by Vail-Ballou Press, Inc. Text paper is Writers RR Offset, basis 50.